NONCOMPLIANT

CARMEN SEGARRA

NONCOMPLIANT

A Lone Whistleblower
Exposes the Giants
of Wall Street

NATION
BOOKS
New York

The names of some of the actors in this story have been changed, because this book is not about their individual actions, but about an institutional culture at the New York Federal Reserve Bank that has subverted its regulatory mission.

Nation Books
116 East 16th Street, 8th Floor, New York, NY 10003
www.nationbooks.org
@NationBooks

Printed in the United States of America
First Edition: October 2018

Published by Nation Books, an imprint of Perseus Books, LLC, a subsidiary of Hachette Book Group, Inc. Nation Books is a co-publishing venture of the Nation Institute and Perseus Books.

The Hachette Speakers Bureau provides a wide range of authors for speaking events. To find out more, go to www.hachettespeakersbureau.com or call (866) 376-6591.

The publisher is not responsible for websites (or their content) that are not owned by the publisher.

Editorial production by Christine Marra, *Marra*thon Production Services. www.marrathoneditorial.org

Book design by Jane Raese
Set in 12 point Whitman

Library of Congress Cataloging-in-Publication Data has been applied for.

ISBN 978-1-56858-845-2 (hardcover), ISBN 978-1-56858-851-3 (ebook)

LSC-C

10   9   8   7   6   5   4   3   2   1

For my husband, my guardian angel,
the Allies, and St. Jude—a promise kept

CONTENTS

All we have to decide is what to do
with the time that is given us.
—J.R.R. TOLKIEN, *Fellowship of the Ring*

Children say that people are hung sometimes
for speaking the truth.
—JOAN OF ARC

November 21, 2014

"But, given the long list of supervisory failures at the New York Fed, both before and during your tenure as president, would you say that the New York Fed has its own cultural problems?"[1] asked Senator Elizabeth Warren, facing the audience from her seat behind the raised semicircular podium.

"Well, first, I would not accept the premise that there has been a long list of failures by the New York Fed since my tenure," replied New York Fed president Bill Dudley, clearly ruffled by the question. A few feet in front of him a TV camera, encased in a wooden box, captured his sweating face.

"I have to stop you there, Mr. Dudley. That is part of why we called this hearing, is the evidence of the failures at the Fed. So are you saying that these are not true? I mean, are you denying the facts that have already been reported and established about this?" Warren retorted.

"Well, first of all, I am not clear that there are facts." Dudley answered.

I gripped the pen as tightly as I could, struggling to keep my composure.

Earlier that morning I had been the first to line up outside the door of Room SD-538 at the Dirksen Senate Office Building in Washington, DC. Nothing, I had promised myself, was going to prevent me from sitting in that room and witnessing Dudley's testimony.

As soon as he had taken his seat, photographers had moved into the empty space between the testimony table and the Senate podium. The clicking of their cameras quickly drowned out all other noise in the room. Dudley's sizeable entourage occupied most of the reserved seats directly behind him, then open seating began in the third row.[2] I had carefully chosen a seat there, with a clear view of Dudley's back and the right side of his face.

As the hearing began, Senator Sherrod Brown had wasted no time laying down the stakes in his opening statement: "With all of its resources and its new authority, is the Federal Reserve up to the task of regulating financial institutions that are so large and complex? That is the question. Or, are these Wall Street banks simply too big to regulate?"

I watched Dudley's trembling hand reach for a glass of water. *Good*, I thought. I bit back a smile and did my best to keep a straight face. I have never been good at keeping a poker face—but on this day I did my best to give nothing away. I must admit I was happy. *He deserves to be nervous*. Not a noble sentiment but, after all I had been through the past three years, a human one.

"We are here today because of issues raised by Carmen Segarra. She has done—" Brown stopped reading from his prepared statement, lifted his head, and looked briefly in my direction, "and she is here today, welcome—and she has done a public service in bringing them to light."

At the sound of my name my heart skipped a beat. Time slowed down, and I felt all eyes in the room turn toward me. I was not nervous—quite the contrary. I had deliberately worn a red jacket, the better to stand out in that sea of men wearing dark suits. I sat just a little bit straighter and kept my eyes glued on Dudley. He shifted uncomfortably in his seat.

"The Federal Reserve is tasked with supervising the nation's largest banks and is our first line of defense against another financial crisis. Yet we have seen time and again the Fed has failed to strike the proper balance when regulating these large firms. The most obvious example is the 2008 financial crisis, from which we are still recovering. Their inability to properly regulate the banks led to an economic catastrophe," intoned Senator Joe Manchin.

Coughing and the clicking of cameras occasionally interrupted Senator Manchin's words. Dudley sat silently at the witness table, hands crossed. To his left and right two wooden tables were packed with journalists, furiously tapping away on their laptops.

"As Senator Warren and I have said, the stakes could not be higher. With the proper supervision," Manchin's voice rose slightly and his right hand gestured in the air, "we might have averted the 2008 crisis that cost so many people on Main Street in America their jobs and wiped out over a decade of economic success."

Then, as Senator Warren began her opening statement, Dudley again shifted uncomfortably and, this time, clenched his hands. "We need bank regulators who work to protect the American people, not the profits of giant banks, and that is what this hearing is about today," she said.

As Dudley began his prepared testimony, I wondered how he would respond to New York Fed officials' allegations of misconduct. A small part of me still could not believe what I had witnessed, recorded, and brought to light. It all felt like a lifetime ago.

THREE YEARS BEFORE this hearing the New York Fed had hired me as an expert in legal and compliance to help supervise some of the nation's largest banks. I took the job thinking I would be protecting the safety and soundness of the financial system on behalf of the taxpayers who paid my salary.

Before joining the New York Fed I had been a lawyer deep in the trenches of some of the world's biggest banks: MBNA America Bank (now part of Bank of America), Citigroup, Société Générale. Many other large banks—JPMorgan Chase, UBS, Barclays, Morgan Stanley, Merrill Lynch, Goldman Sachs—have interviewed and courted me countless times. I had been sent to many places around the globe, responsible for implementing regulations whose impact went far beyond American shores. I worked with many different kinds of people—competent, high strung, difficult, lazy, friendly, passive-aggressive, clueless, arrogant, forgetful, and too smart for their own good—discouraging many from engaging in foolish and risky behavior and even managing to stop a few from breaking the law.

But nothing I had seen during my decade of legal work had prepared me for what I witnessed in just a few short months at the New York Fed.

In those months I discovered a disorienting world full of hidden clues, where people said one thing but meant another. Beneath the public face of the Fed laid a web of incompetence, corruption, rampant mismanagement, secrets, and lies. In the "fake work" culture of the Fed, where supervision was a job title, not a job, the most important thing was to control the process to serve the ultimate master. The New York Fed was not simply failing to stop the banks; it was actually enabling their bad behavior.

CHAPTER 1

Special Team.
Different Training

New York City was busy cleaning up from a nor'easter that claimed countless trees and threatened to derail Halloween as I zigzagged my way through downtown Manhattan. Dodging fallen trees and harried commuters as best I could, I hurried to my first day on the new job with a sense of positive expectation. On the corner of Broadway and Liberty Street, while waiting for the light to turn, I looked over at the World Trade Center area construction site and Zuccotti Park. Occupy Wall Street protesters who had braved the storm huddled in the rectangular enclosure, their signs and tents poking out of the ground. Some drank coffee; others chatted—the roughness of the night etched on their faces. I held back a smile as I pondered how incongruous it was.

I was headed to the New York Fed to help fix the bank supervision problems that motivated the protests in the first place.

After filling out some paperwork, I headed to Marylou's office, one of my new supervisors. Marylou was tall, blond, blue-eyed, and polite almost to a fault. Her slender frame neatly tucked into her chair, she pivoted ever so slightly to the left as she welcomed us into her office. The new hires crowded in between the stacks of papers scattered about, like mushrooms sprouting out of a forest floor.

After some introductions, Marylou started the meeting by announcing that the New York Fed had changed its supervisory structure that summer. Indeed, she and Connor O'Sullivan, our boss, had mentioned this new supervision structure during my interview. Now that Marylou brought it up, it seemed like we were finally getting into the basics.

She explained that she and Riley Murphy were co–team leaders of the legal and compliance risk team. Their job would be to guide me and the other new legal and compliance risk examiners through the onboarding process and to be our boss for day-to-day administrative matters. They both reported to Connor, and Connor in turn reported to Sarah Dahlgren, who was in charge of the entire New York Fed supervision team. Sarah in turn reported to Bill Dudley, the president of the New York Fed. We would each be assigned to supervise one of the too-big-to-fail banks.

She did not tell us which one each of us would be assigned to supervise.

Instead, she jumped straight into describing one of the features of the new supervision structure—the creation of a new group known as "relationship managers." These relationship management teams were in charge of managing the relationship between the New York Fed and an assigned supervised bank. The relationship managers were, according to Marylou, no longer in charge of *examining* the supervised bank; rather, their new job was to better understand the division or function they had been assigned to in order to assist us, the risk specialists, in our examination work—should we need their help. Thus, actual supervision and examination work now fell to us, the risk specialists, experts who were recruited and assigned to different areas—market risk, credit risk, audit risk, operational risk, and legal and compliance risk. A few of these experts were prior bank examiners, but most were new to the New York Fed.

Just like the risk specialists, the relationship managers were divided into teams—one for each of the too-big-to-fail banks. Technically, the relationship managers assigned to cover a specific bank division were also referred to as business line specialists, and the relationship managers assigned to cover a function, such as corporate functions, were referred to as corporate functions specialists. Each relationship management team was led by a senior supervisory officer (SSO) and his or her deputy. The New York Fed had chosen to staff the new relationship management teams with "old bank examiners"—employees who had been working at the New York Fed for a long time, most since well before the 2008 financial crisis.

As I listened, I thought back to my interviews, where Connor, Marylou, and Riley had explained they were looking to upgrade the New York Fed's personnel. They had alluded to the phasing out of old bank examiners but had not explained how it would be done. This convoluted and confusing structure had more to do with giving the old bank examiners the appearance of a job so as to improve their prospects of getting hired out of the New York Fed and less to do with how supervision would work moving forward under the new structure.

This all sounded more political than practical to me, and it promised an extra layer of challenges: we were tasked with working alongside the people who used to do our jobs. And they did not yet seem to have a specific and well-defined role to play. Implementing a new supervisory structure while keeping the previous supervisors in a hastily defined relationship was one of the signs of the labyrinthine qualities of my new environment. *Oh well*, I thought. *No one said the job would be easy.* It seemed I would have to do some in-the-field detective work to figure out the nuances and realities of the balance of power.

You see, when it comes to the New York Fed, you have to be there to truly begin to understand the redundancies, the ambiguities, the meaningful looks, the silences.

As Marylou ended the meeting, many things were still up in the air. First and foremost: no word yet about which bank I would be assigned to supervise.

As I thought this through, Marylou walked us to Connor's office, the big boss. As I walked out of her office I saw the third person who had interviewed me and another of our team members: Riley. I flashed a smile. With pursed lips and an expressionless face he looked back and nodded. For some reason Riley's poker face seemed slightly out of place. I archived it: it was time to meet Connor and hopefully learn the rest of the details about my new job.

Connor O'Sullivan was the new head of the legal and compliance risk supervision team within the Financial Institutions Supervision Group (FISG). This blue-eyed Harvard Law School lawyer had joined the New York Fed in 2005 as an attorney in the legal department, focused on bank regulatory and supervision matters. Prior to leaving the New York Fed's legal division and assuming the leadership of the legal and compliance risk supervision team, he had been providing legal support to the supervision team assigned to cover Goldman Sachs.

Connor's portly frame stood stick straight as he greeted us. Because he was busy, this meeting was just a quick meet-and-greet: no more information forthcoming. I patiently made my way back to the secretary's desk to get the details on my cubicle location and computer.

Suddenly Riley appeared out of nowhere and stopped me. "Do you know which bank you have been assigned to?" he asked.

"No," I replied, excited to finally find out.

His blue eyes widened, his attention fixed on me so intently that my guard instinctively went up. "You are going to Goldman," he said.

Uh-oh, I thought, feeling the hairs standing on the back of my neck. I did the best I could to not react. Easier said than done, though. I'm one of those people who finds it hard to put up—and keep—a poker face.

Goldman Sachs. The Ted Cruz of the banking world—if you are into politics.

Goldman had a reputation in the industry of having weak legal and compliance departments, among many other issues. I had spent a lot of time in my career cleaning up bad, complicated messes at bigger, more complex, and better diversified banks than Goldman, so I guess they thought it would be a good fit.

But from the start there was something amiss. Goldman is about as high profile a bank as it got. My position would be the type of plum job typically reserved for more connected alpha males. If this was a plum job that led to promotions, no one at the New York Fed would give it to a woman, much less a minority like me. Another mystery to be solved.

"You are going to be replacing Johnathon Kim. His office is down the hall—you should talk to him," Riley continued, his cold eyes never once leaving my face. Then he added, "You are very lucky. That is our very best supervisory team."

As I approached his office, I could see Johnathon sitting on his desk, looking at some documents. In those few seconds as I approached, it wasn't clear whether he was reading the documents or just looking at the paper in a way that made him seem like someone carrying a burden. Or was it a sense of regret? The second he saw me, though, he immediately looked up and smiled, a tinge of relief on his face. I was there to replace him, and from his vantage point, that was a good thing.

His office was very similar to all other offices on that floor, with a navy-blue carpet contrasting the dark-brown wall-unit wood office furniture so commonplace in American banks. The only object in his office that truly distinguished it from anybody else's was the picture of his wife and children.

Conspicuously placing photos of your smiling family members for all to see is a cultural imperative in an American banking office. What was remarkable about this photo was the impeccable traditional Korean clothes they wore. This was not just unusual; it was completely unexpected in what is arguably the US government's most important banking branch. It is an unspoken cultural rule among minorities that you show your allegiance to the United States by having photos of your family members decked out in all-American attire or even stars and stripes. But not this picture. *See*, his photo seemed to say, *my family is Korean*.

We exchanged pleasantries, and he invited me to take a seat in one of the two chairs opposite his desk. The obligatory small talk was made easier by the beckoning family photograph. "Oh, is that your family?" I remember asking. His face lit up. Like a proud father, he gave me the family tour and concluded by saying that his wife homeschooled the kids. We then moved on to the obligatory beat about ourselves, whereupon we bonded over both being minority lawyers. He then explained how he came to be at the New York Fed.

He had been at Citi prior to the financial crisis, where he had been working for collateralized debt obligation compliance, and had joined the New York Fed about three years prior. Collateralized debt obligations (CDOs) are better known as one of the toxic financial instruments that played an important and lethal role in the 2008 financial crisis. And Johnathon was the first one to mention that. "I was one of those guys," he said, his mood darkening. Shortly after Dudley and

Dahlgren had rolled out the new supervision structure in January of 2011, he was assigned to the New York Fed onsite team responsible for supervising Goldman.

The New York Fed had implemented "onsite teams" during the 2008 financial crisis. These were groups of employees expected to do their daily supervision work primarily from the offices of the bank they were assigned to supervise as opposed to sitting at their assigned office space within the New York Fed. Traditionally, these teams consisted of three to four people, which doesn't sound like a lot of people to supervise the comings and goings of a bank like Citi (with over 150,000 employees worldwide) or Goldman (with over 30,000 employees worldwide). Thus, post–financial crisis and as part of reforming its supervision structure, the New York Fed had been told, in so many words, to "staff up."

So it was that Johnathon had joined the onsite team assigned to supervise Goldman sometime in the summer of 2011. I was now to take his place.

Johnathon eagerly moved on to supervision matters. He began by going over the topics he was currently working on, starting with an overall review of Goldman's compliance and legal departments. On its face this made perfect sense and is a great starting point for a new regulator to get to know and understand the supervised bank in question. I remember asking myself why such an overview didn't already exist for Goldman. I did not have to ask the question—Johnathon volunteered an explanation: the New York Fed had been too busy with the 2008 financial crisis and had not gotten around to doing an overview of Goldman until 2011.

He followed this by mentioning consumer compliance and anti–money laundering. Then he quickly glanced at me. "And conflicts of interest," he concluded.

That quick glance was telling. Even then I knew conflicts of interest were a particularly sensitive issue at Goldman.

"Conflicts of interest" is an old, well-known issue in banking. If you have a vested interest in the outcome of something, you have a conflict. US banks have divisions dedicated to performing conflicts checks and monitoring both banking divisions and bank employees.

Investigations into the 2008 financial crisis had laid bare widespread malfeasance by both Goldman divisions and employees. Widely covered congressional hearings had been held, the US Senate had issued a published report in April 2011,[1] and a former member of Goldman's board of directors, Rajat Gupta, had been charged in October 2011 with one of the most commonly understood conflicts of interest violations, insider trading.[2] Gupta was scheduled to go on trial in April 2012.

There was pressure from both Congress and the press for governmental agencies to do something about it. Within the New York Fed word had come down from the top that the team assigned to Goldman had to investigate this. In practical terms, I assumed that meant Connor had told Johnathon to look into it. Because I was to replace him, it would be my task to carry that hot potato.

Johnathon made it clear that these issues were ongoing priorities to be handled in the context of the new examination procedures the New York Fed was implementing as a result of the change in supervision structure. I casually mentioned that I presumed this would all be made clearer during the New York Fed official training sessions, or "FISG 100" and "FISG 200," in Fed-speak. The new-employee protocol called for two distinct training courses separated by a few weeks.

These two courses were critically important. Taught by respected senior employees through team-building exercises, new employees were shown how to perform and document "supervision examinations"— Fed-speak for how the New York Fed expected supervision employees to carry out and document their job. The training was where I would learn how to perform bank examinations, interrogate bank employees, prepare letters to request information from banks, inform bank employees of the results of examinations, and store the examination documents and results in the New York Fed databases. Without this training, the new supervisor was not allowed to use the New York Fed electronic database that stores the official bank examination records. In a nutshell, until a new employee took the training, one couldn't do any real work.

Johnathon paused when I mentioned the supervisory training. This was very strange, as I hadn't asked a question. "The Goldman supervision team is special," he then said. "Your training will be different from everyone else's."

Though I tried not to show it, this took me by surprise. According to Johnathon, the New York Fed had staffed the Goldman supervision team with its very best people. As a result, my training would be different from the typical training given to my colleagues charged with supervising the other big banks. I would not be attending those training sessions with my new colleagues; instead, I was to follow him for the first month or so and imitate exactly what he did. Only after my training period with him ended and I was integrated into my new job would I be enrolled in the FISG 100 and 200 courses.

In practical terms, my official training would be delayed a few months.

Numerous red flags went up as he spoke. Without the training, I wouldn't be able to do my job—particularly as you can only check the "track record" for the supervised bank when you have access to the electronic database. A consistent track record of misbehavior could serve as the foundation and justification for enhanced penalties or even suspension of the supervised bank's operational license.

"Why am I getting different training?" I asked. I thought there must be a clear answer, as this deviation from my peers was so marked. Johnathon did not reply to my question—at all. After another pause, he smiled and assured me that although my training would be different, the "special" training was no big deal. I would still have the opportunity to participate in the additional weekly training meetings with the other bank examiners led by our mutual boss, Connor, and his team leaders, Marylou and Brian.

While listening to Johnathon I wondered where this special training he was speaking of fell under the new supervision structure Connor had alluded to during my interview. This special training was clearly outside the norm—not just internally within the New York Fed but also externally. In the private sector it is imperative to immediately integrate new employees into the culture—the bank's profitability is at stake. Critical introductory and systems training is not delayed for months.

This course of action eliminated my exposure to the New York Fed way of conceptualizing supervision over banks in general. Following Johnathon around at Goldman instead of spending the first few weeks with my peers at the New York Fed would add another layer of isolation. And attending the additional weekly training meetings meant that my job performance would be monitored equally despite this unequal training.

As a female minority lawyer, I was acutely aware of the need to relentlessly "punch above your weight" just to keep your job. This suppression of critical knowledge was a direct threat to my ability to hold on to my job. I made a mental note to circle back with Connor and Marylou as soon as possible.

In the months to come, my apprehension proved to be right on the money. Regardless of whether Johnathon was a party to this, it became clear that delaying my official training was but one of the many strategies in an unspoken but well-thought-out plan among some New York Fed employees to improve the New York Fed's rating of Goldman Sachs.

CHAPTER 2

The Regulator Floor

"Don't say anything. Just watch I how do it."

Johnathon paused but kept walking down the hallway to Michael Silva's office on the regulator floor of the Goldman Sachs building. I followed.

"And take notes," he added.

Only a few hours into the first day of my special training, and it was already clear that mine was not an ordinary situation. I had been bombarded by dozens of introductions, most of them perfunctory, all of them confusing. It seemed that confusing the new employee was part of the strategy—or was this just the way they worked? Yet another reason to dig deeper and figure out the real hierarchy, not the theoretical one.

Now we were rushing to meet the two New York Fed relationship management team leaders to discuss Johnathon's next assignment—which would be my first. The SSO and head of the team was Michael Silva, a tall, dark-haired, light-skinned, blue-eyed man who carried himself like a military officer. He occupied the surprisingly paper-sparse inner office at the apex of the L-shaped floor. His deputy was Michael Koh, a slim Korean American man of average height with a slicked-back haircut frozen in place by wet-look gel in the style of Michael Douglas in the movie *Wall Street*. His office was located immediately to the left of Michael Silva's.

Interestingly enough, the meeting was to discuss a new set of issues that had arisen at Goldman regarding conflicts of interest. And Johnathon instructed me to observe and take notes.

The day had started on a different note, as I followed Johnathon from the New York Fed offices to Goldman Sachs and got my first impression of the bank from the outside. I am certain that if this had been my first job in the industry, I would have found it to be an impressive building. But I had spent the better part of the previous ten years working in impressive offices all over the world and had written my Harvard college thesis on how Emperor Charles the V used architecture to express his idea of empire and culture. So it was that my mind immediately focused on the subtleties—the first one being the building's deliberately dated, unimpressive, anonymous, and antiseptic architecture. Drop it into London's Canary Wharf, Hong Kong, or the Singapore business districts circa 2005, and it would fail to stand out.

The second most remarkable thing about the building is its location—right in front of the noisy, car-filled, and pedestrian-unfriendly West Side Highway, the only office building in the entire block. There is no retail bank branch to welcome customers, no big, blaring Goldman Sachs sign proclaiming its presence. Instead, the glass-encased lobby is full of guards and turnstiles, seemingly designed to facilitate the entrance and exit of those who belonged and impress and repel those who have no business there. A few pieces of artwork can easily be seen through the enormous glass windows covering the walls. The building's ground-floor lobby acts as the transparent moat of a modern-day fortress.

The third noteworthy aspect was just how easily one could quickly sort out who was a Goldman employee and who was not, even from the other side of the street. The employees had a Goldman look about them—top-of-the-line suits for the men, top-of-the-line shoes for the women. As they approached the building during the morning rush hour, they consciously presorted themselves into an orderly line designed to maximize building entry speed and efficiency, like so many cans on a conveyor belt. They walked purposefully into the building, entry badges within easy reach, nary a stumble or a sideways glance at the guards, as they continued their march toward the back of the lobby.

As Johnathon and I walked up to the building and into this lobby on that chilly November morning, we deviated from the flow of Goldman employees pouring into the building and headed straight for the guards to inquire about my entrance badge. A bank-entry badge is no trivial matter; it gives the bearer access to areas full of confidential information. Any bank worth its salt will carefully follow identification protocols when issuing such a pass. Johnathon informed me on my way there that prior to our visit he had provided Goldman with the required paperwork. He expected the badge to be ready for pickup when we arrived. But it wasn't, so we had to wait for the lobby personnel to prepare it.

Johnathon was annoyed and spent the time voicing his displeasure. He had already spent quite a few months supervising Goldman and saw the firm's failure to have the badge ready on time as a deliberate delay tactic. He made it clear to me that he had no patience for their insincere excuses and incompetence. I listened to him silently: his seemed a half-hearted show for one, more sound than fury.

I followed Johnathon toward the back of the lobby and into one of the elevators, watching and mimicking the behavior of those in front of me. Each elevator in turn filled up back to front, side to side, with military precision. Employees were spaced the precise minimum number of inches necessary to avoid touching each other—a veritable human canning operation. Once the elevator was full, it automatically closed and ushered everyone up to the real Goldman lobby—the one deliberately hidden from view.

The Goldman sky lobby had at its center a takeout coffee shop with espresso machines and displays full of breakfast pastries and other snack items. About fifteen people stood patiently in line waiting to order. To one side was the entrance to the large cafeteria. To the other side a series of stairs led to conference rooms. We hurriedly walked past the cafeteria and headed to the end of the center hallway and into the second elevator bank. Johnathon selected our floor number on a separate panel located in front of this elevator bank. The panel screen flashed, assigning us to an elevator. We proceeded to make our way into the designated elevator and on to the New York Fed's office inside the Goldman building—our "home away from home."

The L-shaped office layout of the regulator floor mimicked the typical trading floor set-up in vogue at that time. The two outer walls—one facing the Hudson River and midtown, the other Lower Manhattan—were floor-to-ceiling glass. Automatically programmed curtains would rise or fall following the sun's trajectory, working together with the air conditioning system to regulate the office temperature. Uninterrupted rows of brown tables began next to the windows and worked their way toward the middle of the office. An open hallway lay between the rows of tables and the offices and conference rooms. Kitted out with brown furniture matching the desks lined up outside, each office was separated from the other by an interior floor-to-ceiling white partition wall. The biggest conference room was situated at the apex of the L, a rectangular fishbowl encased in glass walls and windows.

Upon arrival Johnathon began casually introducing me to everyone who crossed our path, rattling out their names and roles, rarely taking a moment to help me connect the dots or make the necessary associations. I remember politely shaking many hands and politely nodding in recognition several times as the names, titles, departments, and institutions flew by—business line specialists, credit risk, asset management relationship managers, FDIC (Federal Deposit Insurance Corporation), NYSDFS (New York State Department of Financial Services) . . . the list went on and on.

"Come," Johnathon said, and without offering much background information, he led me down the hall to meet the head of the relationship management team and his deputy. The one thing I already knew about Michael Silva and Michael Koh was that Johnathon and I did not report directly to either of these men. In fact, according to Connor and Marylou, that was the whole point of the new supervisory structure: from now on I would be the one regulating Goldman, and Silva's team was supposed to provide me with their institutional knowledge of the bank to help me along the way.

So I was a bit confused when, as we were about to go into the meeting, Johnathon told me that Michael Silva had requested Johnathon do something, so Johnathon had set up this meeting to confirm what the marching orders were. "This isn't necessary," Johnathon tried to clarify. "But it's culturally expected and political prudent."

After the obligatory lengthy introductions, we sat down in Michael Silva's office. Johnathon carefully placed the printed emails he had received from Silva earlier in the week on the table. I found that to be a strange tactic at the time: Was he intimating that this was evidence? Or maybe he was trying to make the meeting seem about something else? Johnathon finally got to the point: he had received Silva's request to look into three Goldman deals that were written up in the press recently. He wanted to confirm that Silva was asking him to set up a meeting with the Goldman legal team to investigate these transactions.

Silva didn't miss a beat. He immediately rattled off the names of the transactions Goldman had recently worked on that had been adversely reported in the newspapers as allegedly being riddled with conflicts issues: Solyndra, El Paso, and Capmark. Because the press had made such a stink, Silva continued, Johnathon should set up a meeting with the Goldman legal and regulatory counsel to ask about these transactions and possible conflicts issues. He should also find out more about their conflicts-of-interest program: check if they have a policy, who runs the program, and so on.

I kept taking notes but was stunned: Wasn't that what our work was about? Why was Silva ordering Johnathon to do his job? Why was Johnathon confirming that this is what Silva wanted? I made a mental note to read up on the transactions as soon as I could. I immediately knew I needed to prioritize figuring out more about this strange dynamic between the relationship management leader and us. After all, in a month's time Johnathon wouldn't be there—it would be just me.

Neither Silva nor Koh committed to attending the meeting with Goldman; instead, they asked Johnathon to invite some of the other relationship managers who reported to them. A few names were tossed out. Names of people I did not yet know. Johnathon acquiesced. He thanked them both for their time, and we headed to my future desk.

Located right by the window, the desk faced out to the West Side Highway. The Lower Manhattan skyscrapers could be seen through the window on the left-hand side. The desk had a landline, a laptop docking station, and a large desktop computer, the back of which almost kissed a nearly identical screen facing the desk directly on the other side of mine. Johnathon glanced at that empty desk on the other side and looked around, as if trying to locate the person it belonged to. Not finding who he was looking for, he turned to me and walked me through the desk equipment. He explained the laptop docking station was for the New York Fed–issued laptop I would be receiving. He pointed out that the internet line dedicated to the laptop was supposed to be encrypted: Goldman could not monitor any work done through the laptop.

Goldman owned the phone and the desktop computer. Johnathon smiled as he explained how they worked. The phones were configured to function just as they did for all other Goldman employees. A unique number was assigned, with external and internal shortcut dialing capabilities. It even received the voicemails periodically left by Goldman senior management to all its employees. The desktop was likewise configured as if for a Goldman employee. Regulators had a Goldman email and access to certain sections of the Goldman intranet. It was even possible to surf the web. I smiled back, signaling I understood.

As an experienced attorney, I was well aware of the extensive surveillance systems big banks had in place. Such measures had increased exponentially over the years as technology advanced. By 2011 the big, complex banks I had worked for were not just keeping logs of every telephone number you dialed on their phones; they were also recording every single computer keystroke, email, voicemail, telephone conversation, and swipe of your entry badge. The ones who took surveillance most seriously had cameras everywhere.

Special teams of ex-CIA and -FBI agents worked in dedicated units performing surveillance and monitoring tasks as needed. An ordinary day might be filled with background checks and fingerprint scans of incoming employees. Occasionally they would perform special investigations and enhanced surveillance of suspicious or potentially troublesome customers and employees, sharing the results with the legal department or law enforcement as needed. Given the trillions of dollars at stake and the ease with which a rogue employee could deploy numerous tactics against the bank and its customers from within, these measures made good business sense. As I thought back to some of my past experiences at other banks, I wondered where Goldman's surveillance fell on that spectrum.

Johnathon focused next on the desk drawers. One by one he opened them, walking me through his filing system and various work products.

I listened and occasionally glanced around. Silva's relationship managers went from discreetly glancing our way to exchanging glances with
each other while going about their business. It was clear they could
hear every word we were saying and were closely following our conversation. Johnathon inevitably noticed too—it was impossible not to.
The open space functioned like a stage. He wrapped up the desk tour.
Come, he signaled. We made our way a couple of rows down toward the
relationship managers.

He nodded to a few people as we walked by and stopped in front
of a woman with shoulder-length black hair parted to one side and
a ponytail way too tight to be either comfortable or fashionable. Her
light olive skin contrasted with her brown eyes, which were framed by
dense, dark eyebrows.

Johnathon stole a quick glance at me and addressed her by name,
Donna (I would later learn her full name is Donna Bianca). Turning
his attention to her, he inquired about the status of some remediation
issue having to do with Litton. Though I hadn't been introduced to the
details of the Litton situation, the name rung a bell. I made a note and
noticed that Donna chose not to answer Johnathon. I thought that was
bizarre.

Instead, Donna turned her back on us and focused on filing something in a desk drawer. I looked at Johnathon, who stood there, neither
defeated nor enraged. Just ... stood there. Perhaps this was one of the
reasons he was relieved I was replacing him.

When she finally answered—still without looking at us—Johnathon glanced at me again, arching his eyebrows as an unspoken warning: *Watch out for this one.* He then reminded her that as the legal and
compliance supervisor, he had an obligation to follow up with her on
the matter. She was no longer in charge of supervising Goldman from
a legal and compliance risk angle; she was now a New York Fed relationship manager. Donna refused to continue the conversation. If it
hadn't been clear by then, it was obvious now: the way the new supervisory structure had been implemented had driven a wedge between
relationship managers and risk specialists. It was also causing tensions
between the old guard and the new employees. Lines were blurry, it
seemed. And the old guard was not going anywhere anytime soon.

As if in response to this interaction, Johnathon took me to meet Donna's boss, Mila Mirka. That made sense. Because Donna was not forthcoming with the information he needed, Johnathon was going to ask her supervisor. When we reached Mila's office it seemed like she was not expecting us. We walked in and she looked at us in silence. *What was it about that look?* I wondered. *Was it exasperation? Or was it fear?*

Johnathon quickly introduced me to Mila. She was the New York Fed relationship manager and business line specialist focused on Goldman's Investment Management and Asset Management divisions. As Donna's superior, she reported to Michael Silva and Michael Koh. As a way of saying hello, she looked at me and attempted a smile. Johnathon then lobbed the same question he had asked Donna, and her smile disappeared. She looked away from me and straight at him. She responded with the same hostility and dismissiveness as Donna had.

And then she told Johnathon that he should discuss the matter with Donna—not with her. *But you're the boss!* I thought, hoping my face didn't betray my surprise. However, it seemed that was that: Johnathon withdrew and signaled for me to follow him back to our desk. Once we were out of Mila's sight he looked at me and said, "We will discuss those two later."

My intuition signaled this wasn't going to be a matter of one or two individuals; the problem could be more spread out, even systemic.

We headed back to my future desk. Upon arrival we found a woman in her early thirties right in front of her desktop computer, located immediately opposite my future desk, pretending to shuffle some documents. Was this her desk? Was she waiting for us? She stopped fiddling with the papers and looked straight at Johnathon, as if to say, "Are you going to introduce me?" He obliged, introducing Lily Rose as a New York Fed relationship manager and corporate functions specialist— and part of Silva's team. She had joined the New York Fed in 2006. That was, indeed, her desk. She threw her head back and cocked it to one side, fixing her lightly freckled face and brown eyes on mine. "Hi!" she exclaimed in that high-pitched, insincere way a "cool" high school girl greets someone she'd rather not be seen dead with. Her body language made it clear that shaking hands would not be welcomed.

Lily turned to Johnathon and casually asked about our meeting with "the two Mikes"—Silva and Koh. He filled her in on what had transpired. She politely listened, looking like she already knew. She ended the conversation abruptly by signaling she was expecting an invite from Johnathon to the conflicts-of-interest meeting her boss had asked us to set up with Goldman. It was clear she did not like him. Johnathon sat down, and after making sure she was not looking our way, he said, "We'll talk about her later."

THE FOLLOWING DAY Johnathon did provide some background information on these women—though not nearly enough. According to him, Lily, Mila, and Donna were holdovers from the New York Fed team assigned to supervise Goldman during the 2008 financial crisis. None of them were attorneys. They shared the responsibilities for consumer, legal, and compliance supervision just before Johnathon took over the job in mid-2011.

That meant they used to do the job I was hired to do now.

In the reshuffle they had remained assigned to Goldman as relationship managers. Lily had become a corporate functions specialist reporting to the two Mikes; Donna and Mila became business line specialists, with Donna reporting to Mila and both in turn reporting to the two Mikes. They had, for reasons Johnathon did not elaborate, failed to get around to transitioning certain issues they had been working on to him, including key findings related to the Litton situation. Even though they had been told to. He did not elaborate on specifics but made it clear this made it difficult for him to do his job.

He closed by pointing out that he disliked their "sharp elbows." I had never heard that expression and asked him what it meant. He smiled and did not answer.

Johnathon then turned his attention to introducing me to the other New York Fed risk specialists also assigned to work from the regulator floor. He explained how risk supervision had been split into five components: legal and compliance risk, market risk, financial risk, operational risk, and audit risk. I was to take his place as the legal and compliance risk supervision specialist.

He signaled that from a supervision standpoint, these other risk-supervision individuals were not relationship managers. They each shouldered similar responsibilities to mine, albeit in their respective areas. Like me, they had their respective risk function bosses they reported to at the New York Fed. Johnathon kept glancing around the regulator's floor. Whenever he noticed that one of the risk individuals seemed open, we would get up and walk over for introductions.

The man in charge of market risk sat in a desk relatively close to the door. Levi Geller's portly figure was camouflaged by his deliberately oversized, ill-fitting suit. His round open face sat beneath a mop of curly, reddish-brown hair. Sitting on the other side of the L-shaped office was Evan Brown. He was in charge of audit risk. His perfectly cut and combed-straight mousy-brown hair, parted to one side, complemented his well-fitting office attire. He welcomed me with impeccable manners. The woman in charge of operational risk was my desk neighbor, Elizabeth Alfonsina, who had a rail-thin frame and bright blue eyes framed by abundant, long, frizzy hair. Johnathon did not motion for me to watch out for any of them.

Back at my future desk I looked around the open floor, wondering why the risk specialist functions were not sitting together; instead, they were mostly spread out—with the exception of Elizabeth and me. We sat next to each other, in direct line of sight of the two Mikes. Like all the other risk specialists, we were surrounded by relationship managers and corporate functions specialists. Suddenly the constant watching I had noticed from seemingly random people since the moment I arrived made sense: the relationship managers were watching every move the risk specialists made. Sitting us apart meant it would be harder for us to "team up" or "gang up" against the relationship managers without them noticing. The risk specialists were like lab rats under really bright lights, being studied, poked at, pushed, and prodded.

Back at the New York Fed Johnathon and I met with our bosses Marylou and Connor to debrief them on what had transpired during our meeting with the two Mikes. This wasn't just politically prudent;

whether we would go ahead with scheduling the meeting with Goldman to discuss conflicts really was up to those two. Both agreed and gave us the green light to proceed.

As Johnathon and I parted ways, I almost discussed with him what I thought was an interesting moment with my New York Fed peers, but I thought it prudent not to share my personal insights this early in my tenure. As is customary in the industry, I was on probation for the first six months. It was very important that I, as a new employee, keep my mouth shut as much as possible until I had the opportunity to figure out who was who and what was really going on. Still, it was a telling scene.

Earlier that day I was on the Goldman regulator floor when the Occupy Wall Street protesters' chants started coming through the windows. At first the regulators kept working at their desks, silently looking at each other, not knowing how to react. The protests continued. Slowly a chill emerged in the air. Fear began to creep into their faces. Still, no one dared move closer to the windows. As the noise grew louder and a bullhorn started blaring, I stood up from my desk. One of the other risk regulators sitting close to the exit door stood up as well and drew closer to the window. As if on cue, one by one the rest quickly followed.

I looked out the window and down at the protesters. The glare of the sun made it a bit of a challenge, but you could see and hear them below. They were surrounded by police officers.

A low murmur spread across the floor. While looking out I could hear snippets of conversations around me. One of the regulators on my right asked, "What are they saying?" I looked to see who it was. I saw smiling faces—some wry, some condescending. None remorseful or sympathetic.

Their reactions surprised and shocked me. The protesters were part of the taxpayer base paying for our work. They had been protesting in downtown Manhattan since September 17 against, among other grievances, New York Fed employees' failure to properly police big banks like Goldman. They were there now to protest Goldman's behavior—the behavior the New York Fed employees standing next to me arguably should have been policing and addressing before the

2008 financial crisis. I knew I was standing next to a number of people whose failure to do their job contributed to the crisis—in fact, I had been brought in to address just that issue. I hadn't been there long, but I had gleaned enough to know that the protesters had a point. I expected to see shame, silence—maybe even remorse.

Suddenly, on my left I heard a laugh. I turned. Lily and a couple of others were looking down and laughing at the protesters. She looked my way, and I looked sharply back at her. I was not laughing. Her face froze.

Michael Koh's arrival put an end to all conversation and window gazing. In the most condescending tone he could muster he made it clear there was no need for us to concern ourselves with the protesters. Management did not care what they thought. They would be gone soon enough. Everyone made their way back to their desks.

Occupy Wall Street continued to protest throughout my tenure at the New York Fed. Sometimes in front of the New York Fed, sometimes in front of Goldman, oftentimes elsewhere in Manhattan. Yet at the Goldman regulator floor not another word was said about the protesters or their grievances. It was as if they did not exist.

CHAPTER 3

We Want Them to Feel Pain, but Not Too Much

"How do you like your new job?"

His piercing blue eyes not leaving the screen, Hendrik quietly listened as his family asked me this question. Hendrik and I had settled into our couch to chat with them in the Netherlands. I expected the question, but given what I had already experienced at the New York Fed, it was not one I wanted to answer. I wanted to know how the family was doing. And Hendrik was home.

Hendrik and I had met in 2009, at the New York Philharmonic's summer concert in Central Park. Over the following two years we moved into a tiny rental apartment together and built the anonymous, quiet life we had both dreamed about. Although we hadn't yet made specific plans, "When is the wedding?" was the most common question we got from everyone. But now that I had this new job, a wedding was the furthest thing from my mind. From the beginning Hendrik had advised me not to take the job, even though he fully supported the decision once I made it. And I was beginning to think he was right.

As if on cue, Hendrik wrapped his arm around me and repeated the question, this time adding a mischievous "or is it too early to tell?" He smiled. I laughed. Thousands of miles away—and oh, in such a different world—Hendrik's family patiently allowed us our moment. They knew, as I knew, as my friends knew, that we loved each other fiercely and for all the right reasons. We had already been through much, and we would go through much more, but we had and would continue to go through it together.

I turned to look at the screen again and addressed his family. "Yes, it's too early to tell. And a bit complicated."

"Interesting. How so?"

Not only was I a lawyer but, in late mornings like these, at home chatting with Hendrik's family, I was surrounded by them too. Hendrik, a Dutch lawyer fluent in four languages, was blessed with an elegant legal mind worthy of envy. This, I came to discover, was no accident. Prominent lawyers, judges, and legal scholars populated both sides of the family tree going back over five centuries. His grandfather had founded what became the Netherlands' largest and most prestigious law firm. His portrait prominently hangs on the walls in one of their oldest law schools, where for years he had taught law with such brilliance that he was still, to this day, reverently referred to by those familiar with his work as the Great One.

They had always impressed me as a serious family with a strong moral compass and a profound awareness of the bigger picture. The Great One hadn't let such minor inconveniences as starvation and a weak heart get in the way of habitually hiding a Jewish child from the Nazis inside his home during World War II. The other side of the family had spent the war starving in concentration camps. Both sides of the family were deeply grateful to the United States and their soldiers for their sacrifices in World War II. When Hendrik's legal career had provided him with the opportunity to work in the United States, the family encouraged him to take it. When he had introduced me to his family, they welcomed me with open arms.

They were delighted to find out I was an avid history buff. One of the first things we did with his family was walk around the vicinity of the town they lived in to see the German installations and the beach where the Allies arrived to free them from starvation.

When any topic of conversation came up, especially one as legally interesting and important as the New York Fed, it was unlikely to be casually dismissed. This was a family who was well aware of the role the US Federal Reserve played in the global financial system. Living in Europe gave them a perspective that factored in the US financial system's impact on European banks, the Euro, their savings, their pensions, their jobs, and their ability to pay their bills.

Of course they were going to ask. And of course they were genuinely interested. But where to begin? And at that time, what exactly did I know for sure? A few days earlier, for instance, in what should have been a standard lunch to welcome the new hires, yet another alarming situation had arisen. As Hendrik continued to chat with his father, my mind returned to that lunch.

In most banks the welcome lunch is usually an opportunity for management to communicate priorities, grease the wheels, and establish the foundations for a pleasant working relationship with the new hires. For a new employee the smart thing to do is to display good manners and an open, receptive disposition to the information being conveyed to you. And keep your mouth shut.

Who sits where is the first part of the dance. As other people angled for position in the sumptuously decorated formal New York Fed dining room, I somehow ended up sitting in between Connor and Michael Silva.

As we ate, senior management dictated the flow of conversation. They relayed gossip about the leadership at all the big banks and carefully scrutinized our reactions, which was par for the course. Surprisingly, they did not mention Goldman. Not even once.

I filed that mental note away and focused my attention on the gossip at hand. And then it happened. Connor turned to me and casually asked a direct and charged question: "Are you surprised by how much we don't know about what's going on inside these big banks?"

Are you kidding me? I thought to myself, knowing there was no good answer I could give him. I had been at the New York Fed just a few days—not nearly enough time to conclude whether they knew enough about what was going on at the big banks. If I were to assert the opposite—that I was surprised by how much more they knew than appeared to be the case from the outside—that would also be premature.

"I don't know yet," I said and took a sip of the coffee the uniformed staff had just brought to the table. It was bitter—low on taste, high on caffeine—but it bought me some time. It seemed to me that the Fed may not be great at regulating banks, but they were certainly good at examining their employees. This was an opportunity to step up or let it go. In that half-second I thought of Hendrik and his sage lawyerly advice, how he would suggest I let this one go. I heard him and felt him, and I missed him a little. But then I decided to go against his advice, step up, and answer Connor's question with a question of my own: "To your point, how do you expect us to supervise Goldman?"

Connor pushed back his chair, leaned toward me, and looked me straight in the eye.

"We want them to feel pain, but not too much," he answered.

That night I lay awake in bed, long after Hendrik had a good laugh mocking Connor's take on supervising Goldman. I pondered how a Harvard Law School–trained lawyer who received a rather generous taxpayer-paid salary to ostensibly advocate for compliance with the rule of law came to conceptualize legal and compliance supervision over Goldman Sachs as a matter of inflicting "pain" on the bank. This was not an insignificant matter; it was, after all, my job to translate his instructions into action.

I was quite familiar with how different banks approached the topic of legal and compliance practices. Some banks took a "pay one fine, then comply" attitude. This translated into zero compliance with the law until a regulator fined the bank. At that point the bank went all-out with compliance—that is, they would implement all required compliance programs and jump through any and all hoops in order to never pay another fine. Others took the opposite approach—"comply, pay no fine." In practical terms, they went all-out with compliance upfront, deeming payment of any regulatory fine as an embarrassment to management and a waste of shareholder money.

Most big banks I had worked for fell somewhere in between. Their bread-and-butter products were backed by pretty solid legal and compliance programs. Newer products were often plagued by growing pains, which included incomplete or leaky legal and compliance programs. Stretch products and products that came into the bank through acquisitions were the most likely to be in suspect shape. The older the bank and the greater the range of products, the likelier it was that their legal and compliance programs were sophisticated and developed enough and their management and sales people sufficiently well trained to fill any gaps created by either stretch or new products relatively quickly.

Irrespective of the philosophical approach, establishing the procedures employees needed to follow to comply with the rule of law so that, for example, a check or a stock trade would be cleared according to a clear set of rules had nothing to do with inflicting pain. Instead, it had everything to do with upholding the credibility of the US dollar and the US banking system as legitimate, reliable vehicles for the payment of debts and the settlement of trades.

Long before I arrived at the New York Fed, Goldman's reputation in legal and compliance circles was not good. Their approach to legal and compliance practices was unlike most other banks. This was partly because Goldman was a private company for many decades and, as such, was not subject to the same standards that apply to a publicly traded bank holding company. In fact, Goldman only became a traditional bank holding company during the 2008 financial crisis. If the word on the street was right, my job would be incredibly easy. Finding issues with their legal and compliance programs would be like shooting fish in a barrel.

The real question was: How was I to process all this while applying US rule-of-law principles? Pain was, at best, a rather suspect guiding principle. But that was Connor's answer. Besides figuring out how to best address the tension in the new business model between the new risk specialists and the veteran relationship managers, it now seemed I would also need to work hard to extract clarity from management.

———

THE NEXT DAY, when I arrived at the New York Fed, the office was abuzz. I made my way through the floor, found Johnathon, and asked him what was happening. It turned out that our direct boss, Marylou, had just announced her retirement, effective in a few weeks. As we gathered in her office she first assured us that this was happening a year ahead of schedule. She recounted—a little too joyfully—a story about how she had unexpectedly received an offer for her New York apartment that was "just too good to refuse." She then decided to put in for retirement as soon as possible and call it a day.

It was clear that Connor did not want her to leave in this way or this soon. His serious and disappointed face spoke for itself. A replacement would be named soon, he assured us. Our work as risk examiners was to continue as scheduled. I remember spending quite a bit of time discussing with Johnathon and others who exactly would be replacing Marylou. He tried to tell me not to worry. It did not help.

In truth, nothing but knowing exactly who would replace her would have helped. But Johnathon had no way of knowing.

Back at the Goldman regulator floor I learned that the New York Fed regulators shared our busy office space with two other regulatory agencies, also charged with supervising Goldman: the New York State Department of Financial Services (NYSDFS)[1] and the Federal Deposit Insurance Corporation (FDIC).[2]

Physically, there was no clear separation between the employees of the three agencies on the Goldman regulator floor. The open layout, glass walls, and rows of tables with work stations in close proximity to each other ensured a complete lack of privacy. As we made our way through the floor Johnathon pointed out that the employees of the three agencies were more or less contiguously located. The New York Fed occupied the side of the floor facing Lower Manhattan. The NYSDFS faced the Hudson and midtown Manhattan. The FDIC occupied the space in between.

Johnathon introduced me to various FDIC and NYSDFS employees, mostly men. All were uniformly affable. Only one person stood out—a young woman by the name of Analisa Rodríguez. Although her medium-length, curly brown hair and office suit were unremarkable, how she carried herself was not. *This*, I remember thinking, *was a woman who knew who she was.* Her brown eyes radiated both intelligence and a deep sense of peace. She smiled openly and comfortably as Johnathon introduced her. He made it clear that she had my equivalent job at the NYSDFS, supervising and examining Goldman for compliance with New York State banking laws, rules, and regulations. She was an experienced examiner—over ten years of experience—and I was to work with her on all matters.

As we walked back to his desk, Johnathon continued to outline the dynamics between the regulatory agencies. Although Analisa shared my scope of responsibility for New York State, to his knowledge no one did at the FDIC. Although all three agencies were supposed to work together as much as possible on all subjects, this was by no means the case for all matters. There would be times when the New York Fed would work on a matter and not bring in the other agencies. There were no clear rules dictating when and why that would occur.

Having said that, he saw no reason—and great benefit—in me working all matters together with Analisa. He did not say the words "for your protection" as such, but his insistence made his meaning clear.

Johnathon then directed me into one of the conference rooms. As he dialed us into a meeting, Johnathon explained he wanted me to have a better perspective on the challenges we were facing. He wanted me to have a direct connection with the Federal Reserve Board in Washington, DC. I was taken aback: I had no idea I was to have direct contact with the Board. Johnathon explained that our direct line to the Board was Bob Sarvis. He did not expand on where Bob fell within the Federal Reserve Board organizational structure but did make it clear that I was to meet at least once a month with him and assist him as required. Before I could ask any questions, Bob was on the line.

Bob—or Telephone Bob, as I came to think of him, for we never met in person—wasted little time with pleasantries. Unlike everyone else I had met so far at the New York Fed, who somehow managed to make a meeting out of an introduction, Bob jumped straight into the call, the way a veteran executive at a big bank with too much work and not enough time would.

He started by explaining he was there to ensure consumer compliance was "properly integrated and monitored in the context of the onsite teams." What he meant, in other words, was that his job at the Board was to make sure the New York Fed employees supervising Goldman's compliance with consumer banking laws were not forgetting to check if Goldman was complying with the laws that applied to consumer banking products. If Goldman was not complying, his job was to track our progress in making sure we pushed Goldman to fix the issues we found.

Encouraged by Johnathon, Bob provided some context to his portfolio. He was in charge not just of Goldman but also of twelve or so other banks. These included the biggest too-big-to-fail banks in the country (New York Fed employees used the Fed-speak sanitizing term "systemically important financial institutions"—SIFI for short—to refer to these banks).

He insisted, however, that he intended to "focus on Goldman" during the coming year.

Bob skipped ahead to his next point: what the division of work would look like once Johnathon had transitioned out. Johnathon answered that easily: Terry Stewart (whom I had yet to meet) and I were to cover all topics. This seemed to suffice.

One final thing remained on Bob's list—following up on the status of the consent order. For my benefit, Bob helpfully added that, for Goldman, that meant Litton. Goldman had acquired Litton, a mortgage servicing company, in 2007, allegedly in the hopes of getting its hands on subprime mortgage market information that would give its traders an edge. In May 2011 the New York Fed had received a whistleblower letter from the *Financial Times* written by a Litton employee claiming Litton used various internal procedures—which came to be known as "robosigning"—to wrongfully deny mortgage modifications to distressed homeowners.[3]

With the media hot on the story, the New York Fed conducted an investigation, during which it found a lot of issues at Litton.

In September of 2011, less than two months before our call with Telephone Bob, the New York Fed and Goldman had agreed to a consent order,[4] as a result of which Goldman would hire a consultant to fix the issues as well as agreed to reimburse injured customers and pay regulatory fines in exchange for avoiding further legal action against them. Goldman also reached a separate agreement with the NYSDFS over the same issues, which allowed Goldman to still sell the unit, even if they remained on the hook for fixing the issues as per the consent order. Goldman's shares had tumbled 3.5 percent when the agreement with the New York Fed was announced.[5]

Bob wanted an update on Goldman's progress. Johnathon's expression darkened as he let Bob know he had no additional information.

Was this the information he was trying to get from Donna and Mila? If so, why were they obstructing his work? And just as importantly: Were these relationship managers keeping the Federal Reserve Board in the dark on purpose?

As my head was spinning with these kinds of questions, Bob closed the meeting by agreeing on a monthly meeting schedule and suggesting that the next meeting include Donna, Mila, Lily, and Terry. The stated purpose was to transition Donna, Mila, and Lily out of covering consumer-related matters currently overseen by Bob, thereby leaving Terry and me to cover them going forward.

I listened silently, trying to work out why Johnathon had not been covering them so far. Or had he? Again, I couldn't tell.

After we signed off the call, I intended to pepper Johnathon with questions. Time was short, though, as he had other matters to attend to before our next meetings. I made a judgment call and asked only about the consent order.

"Who knows what was going on with Litton's consent order?" I asked. Johnathon's face darkened further. Sitting back, he fixed his eyes on me.

"Mila and Donna," he answered.

CHAPTER 4

The Shadow

As a regulator at the New York Fed, I expected to engage in conversations about the current international financial climate. In the fall of 2011 the category-three hurricane known as the European debt crisis was already blowing with sustained winds. In Spain the 15-M[1] anti-austerity protests had begun in May, laying the groundwork for protests elsewhere and inspiring the Occupy movement[2] that had spread to Wall Street by September. In Greece there was ongoing anxiety about a potential Eurozone-financed bailout.[3]

Freed from the constraints of Glass-Steagall, America's biggest banks had spent the better part of the early 2000s expanding their presence abroad. Some of the biggest foreign banks—many of which had the advantage of not having ever had to deal with such legal constraints—had in turn made significant inroads into the American banking market. I had spent a good portion of my career working at some of these big American and foreign banks, mostly covering banking and securities products typically sold to US and international retail customers as well as quite a few international cross-border legal projects.

In practical terms, this meant I was well aware that a financial crisis outside the United States was likely to have a significant impact on the biggest American banks, especially those that had expanded by taking on risky customers or risky deals. I did not know how many risky customers or risky deals Goldman had in their portfolio, but I knew they did have significant exposure to Europe—$23.8 billion in exposure to France, $24.4 billion in exposure to Germany, and $7.6 billion in exposure to Ireland.[4] Those figures did not account for Goldman's additional exposure to Greece, Italy, Portugal, and Spain.[5]

It was against this backdrop of developing chaos that I shadowed Johnathon into the weekly New York Fed relationship manager's team meeting led by Michael Silva and Michael Koh. On this Tuesday afternoon the team held the meeting in the main conference room of the Goldman regulator floor. All risk examiners assigned to Goldman were expected to attend. I expected we'd hear something from one of the two Mikes about the European financial crisis, perhaps receive some guidance or expectations as to how we were to look into Goldman's international portfolio, or, at the very minimum, receive an offer of help that, as Johnathon pointed out, would have made sense under the Fed's redesigned supervision model. After all, according to Connor, Marylou, Johnathon, and others, under this new supervision configuration it was the work of risk examiners that mattered—the relationship managers were simply there to assist us if and when we needed them.

But none of that came to pass. First, Koh introduced me and another new member to the team, Esther Abramson. Esther, who joined the New York Fed in 2005, had followed Timothy Geithner from the New York Fed to the Treasury Department, gone on maternity leave, and would now be joining the Goldman relationship management team as the leader of corporate functions. She would report to Michael Silva, and Lily was to report to her.

Because Esther was a new relationship manager but veteran New York Fed employee, I wondered where she would fall in the scheme of things. Would she help us do our work, or would she align herself with the group of relationship managers with different agendas? That question would be answered clearly in a few weeks, in a most dramatic fashion.

And then, almost three years later, Esther would go on to work for Goldman Sachs.

But on this day I did not know any of that. All I could do was learn, process, and try to find ways of doing the job I was hired to do. Koh continued. His next point: discussing the 2012 supervision plans, for which he used the Fed-speak shorthand, "sup plans." He claimed he wanted to know the team's feelings about this. Few voiced any feelings. And then he asked the risk specialists, "As teams are figuring out dual roles and responsibilities, how do we work together?" This was very telling. The new supervision model had been rolled out in January, eleven months ago. The relationship managers were supposed to assist the risk specialists in their job, mostly by providing institutional knowledge that could be beneficial. And yet here was Koh asking us that question as if none of that was clear.

It seemed to me that he wanted to keep it that way.

Fueling my suspicion, he continued by asking what he defined as a "pending question": "Is it okay that the rating will be based on continuous monitoring versus exams?"

Insofar as I had been told, this was not a pending question at all. An important part of the new supervision plan was the concept of using continuous monitoring, as opposed to exams, to rate a bank's performance. The difference between the two methods was that exams were defined. The exam method went something like an audit would: we picked a specific period of time—a week, a few months, or even a day—and a set of data from that period, such as a sample of records created by the bank around that specific period of time. We then looked at that sample to determine what issues, if any, we found. A report was then prepared to inform the bank of the "findings"—Fed-speak for a breach of the procedures the bank was supposedly using so as to ensure it was complying with the law.

Exams and reports would then accumulate through the year. The idea, as I understood it, is that the annual report (the "roll-up" in Fed-speak) would be based on the results of these examinations and reports. This was, prior to the new supervision plan, the traditional way of rating a bank.

The new way would be based on one continuous exam—that is, the examination period would cover the entire year, and all topics being examined. In theory, this meant that an examiner could issue findings more quickly and with less cumbersome paperwork. At the end of the year a bank's rating would be determined based largely on the findings reported through the year and whether the bank had done anything to address them properly.

But why was Koh wondering if it was okay that Goldman's rating be based on the new—and more efficient—continuous monitoring method? Was it because the new employees were the ones who would be in charge of it? Or because the relationship managers knew how to work the old method of exams and did not want to adapt to the new method? Or was it something else?

Changing topics, Koh talked about following up on remediation of MRAs. "Find out what your MRAs are," he declared, "the ones on your plate for next year." He then informed everyone that we were to have individual meetings with him to discuss them.

Remediation of MRAs—was this what Donna and Mila did not want to discuss with Johnathon? As I later found out, MRA remediation was a part of my job (and Johnathon's). MRA stood for "matter requiring attention" and was a finding that a regulator would issue the bank when the regulator encountered a problem that amounted to a violation of a law, rule, or regulation during an examination. Think of it as the parking ticket a cop issues when a car is illegally parked. If the regulator conducting the bank examination found a severe or critical violation, then the finding became an MRIA—a matter requiring *immediate* attention. This came with the added constraints that the bank had to correct the issue as quickly as possible, with ninety days functioning as a marker.

The New York Fed kept track of these MRA and MRIA findings in several computer systems, none of which I would have access to until I completed my training. Once the bank was issued an MRA, it would need to take steps to address those specific issues—in Fed-speak, remediate the MRA—or risk the New York Fed further punishing the bank. If the New York Fed wanted to punish a bank, it had a range of tools at its disposal. It could lower the bank's rating and restrict its ability to borrow money and do new business, shut down a bank division until the problems were fixed, or, if the problems were especially severe, work with prosecutors and other agencies to shut down the bank.

If the bank fixed the problems that had been flagged, then we would go ahead and, in Fed-speak, "close the issues."

I wondered why Koh was ordering us to find out what our MRAs were and to discuss them with him individually. I thought we were supposed to discuss them with our team and our direct supervisors. Coupled with Donna and Mila refusing to transition the MRAs to Johnathon, this request was troubling.

Koh moved on, mentioning the name "Erin," which caused an indescribable ripple to go through the room. Michael relayed that Erin had said the Consumer Financial Protection Bureau (CFPB) had reached out to Goldman. Koh then announced that the CFPB's "anticipated relationship with the Fed was being discussed." Apparently, the CFPB had Goldman rated as "high risk" and said that "they own the consumer compliance rating." Michael indicated that Johnathon and I were to join him in a meeting with the CFPB the following day. *Good,* I thought. Dodd-Frank had created the CFPB in response to the 2008 financial crisis and tasked it with protecting consumers from financial-sector abuses. It was designed as an independent unit located inside and funded by the Federal Reserve. The law required the CFPB to coordinate its supervision and examination activities with the Federal Reserve and made the Fed the backup enforcer.[6] I was looking forward to that meeting.

The meeting then segued into legal and compliance topics. I perked up involuntarily and felt my stomach tighten as I heard Koh direct Johnathon and me to "work with Lily to provide a copy of consumer regs on our portfolio for possible handover to the CFPB." I remembered Johnathon had told me to watch out for Lily. Curious how he would react to this request, I quickly turned and saw him nod slightly in acknowledgment. *Why was Johnathon being deferential to Koh?* I wondered. We did not work for him, and besides, the CFPB did not need such a list from us, as the law made clear what they were supposed to cover. When Johnathon warned me about the relationship managers I had to look out for, he hadn't mentioned Koh. I was now wondering why not.

We were also to follow up on the risk and control self-assessment (RCSA) meeting to review Goldman's RCSA "for methodology from a legal and compliance perspective." This I thought I understood. Banks use RCSAs to identify, assess, and report on various operational risks, and many regulators require big banks to conduct this assessment annually. This made sense. What didn't make any sense—again—was that Koh was asking us to do it: I thought Connor was our boss.

Johnathon then told everyone about our upcoming meeting with Goldman to discuss conflicts. To my surprise—but seemingly nobody else's—Koh concluded that discussion by casually commenting that "conflict is inherent in [Goldman's] business model."

I walked back to my desk after the meeting with puzzle pieces neatly written in my black notebook and a hundred questions fighting for attention inside my head: Why had not one word been spoken about what was going on outside the New York Fed and its potential impact on Goldman? Why, eleven months after rolling out the new supervision structure, was senior New York Fed leadership still debating how the relationship management and risk teams should work together? Why was the use of continuous monitoring instead of examinations to rate a bank still a pending question?

I was determined to find the answers ... at the same time as I did my job.

THE FOLLOWING DAY Donna, Lily, and Mila joined Johnathon, Koh, and me in the conference room for the CFPB meeting. The mysterious Chuck, whom I had yet to meet, together with Katrina and Nancy from the CFPB, joined via telephone conference call.

Katrina kicked off the call by letting everyone know that Aaron Katz was now with the CFPB and had been assigned to Goldman. He had expressed to them and they in turn were relaying to us Aaron's interest in looking at Goldman's "consumer ops with respect to mortgage servicing, fair lending, and items identified in an old 2008 MOU [memorandum of understanding]."

I looked at the others in the room. Lily smiled. Mila nodded. In general, everyone's reactions made it clear they knew who Aaron Katz was. I did not. Another puzzle to solve.

"The CFPB should do a baseline review of Goldman's operations to determine if high risks continue given the sale of Litton," Koh suggested, taking the lead for the New York Fed team. I looked up quickly from my meeting minutes, first at Johnathon, whom I was expecting to take the lead, then at Koh. I was taken aback when I noticed that

Johnathon seemed fine with Koh leading the meeting. But what surprised me most was Koh's suggestion.

I was new and had no idea in what state the rest of Goldman's operations were. But I did know that, in regulatory terms, the ink was barely dry on Goldman's agreement with the New York Fed to defer further legal action against the bank, provided they clean up Litton's messy mortgage servicing operations.

I highly doubted Goldman had made much progress in the two months or so since the agreement had been signed. The agreements with the New York Fed and the NYSDFS made it clear that Goldman remained on the hook for cleaning up the Litton mess *even after* selling the unit. Assuming—based on Koh's statement—that Goldman's operations had been classified as high risk and that Litton had something to do with that, it made sense that they would remain high risk until the mess had been cleaned up. I had worked in situations in which the bank had signed an agreement similar to the one Goldman signed for Litton; in my experience the regulators waited until *after* the mess had been cleaned up before lowering the risk level.

Why would Koh, a relationship manager for the New York Fed tasked with assisting the regulation of Goldman Sachs, suggest that the CFPB do a baseline review to determine whether the bank was no longer high risk when the process of addressing the high-risk issues was only just beginning? No one reacted to the suggestion. All I saw were serious, slightly bored looks—which was just as worrisome.

But the CFPB did not address Koh's suggestion; instead, one of the CFPB employees on the line responded by saying the CFPB now owned the consumer rating. From their perspective, the issue on the table was clarifying the coordination between the New York Fed and the CFPB. The conversation then turned to the feasibility of both agencies doing a joint exam or whether it was best to go on separately. No solid conclusion was reached. Koh did not seem satisfied. I could sense that this would not be the end of it for him.

After the participants wondered out loud who would take over monitoring the memorandums of understanding (MOUs) against Goldman—which, for our purposes, were akin to a consent order— Koh insisted again that the CFPB come in and do that baseline exam he had spoken about earlier. Katrina refused to commit; instead, she proposed another call at a later time to discuss that possibility. Koh calmly agreed, but the frown on his face made it clear he had hoped for a different answer. In my meeting minutes I noted his insistence.

As part of the wrap-up the participants discussed the agenda for the following meeting, which apparently was tomorrow, and Koh added to the agenda the CFPB coming in and doing that baseline rating review. Again. After having insisted on this for a third time, Michael pressed the telephone button and ended the call.

The postmeeting among those remaining in the room (Lily and Mila excused themselves and left shortly after the call ended) centered around Litton and the MOUs, of which, apparently, there were several. That little detail was another data point that worked in favor of continuing to view Goldman's operations as high risk, even without knowing what they were about. I knew from experience that these types of agreements came only after long fights with a whole bunch of lawyers and often came about after the bank had made a cost-benefit analysis, deciding that the risk to the bank of exposing additional details of its misdoings was not worth it.

Apparently, the other MOUs pertained to other subsidiaries Goldman had acquired and, as a result, inherited their MOUs. As for Litton, Goldman was indeed obliged to clean up the mess—which, in Fed-speak, was referred to as a "commitment"—despite the sale. Donna pointed out during the postmeeting that Goldman was trying to hire a vendor to do the clean-up, but there was "a vendor management" issue. This confirmed my suspicions that Goldman had not made much progress since signing the agreements with the New York Fed and NYSDFS. Fixing this was going to take a while.

I remember asking about the other MOUs. But instead of an answer, Koh told me to follow up with Lily and ask her to provide me a copy of the enterprise-wide consumer compliance presentation. I wondered just how helpful Lily would be. At some point before the postmeeting ended, someone mentioned that Aaron Katz's previous job was at the New York Fed and that his duties included covering Goldman. *What an interesting coincidence*, I thought.

In our follow-up call with the CFPB, I got to "meet" Aaron over the phone. He surprised Koh by announcing that he and the CFPB would "get a baseline understanding of how Goldman operates" by "relying on what other agencies have done." Koh shifted uncomfortably in his seat—this was clearly not what he wanted. The CFPB reacted somewhat evasively to the renewed suggestion that they come in and set a baseline. Koh's voice remained calm, but he looked a bit annoyed.

I was curious why Koh did not want the CFPB to rely on what other agencies had done. Doing so made sense from Aaron's perspective, particularly if he had been involved while he worked at the New York Fed in determining that Goldman's operations were to be rated as high risk. Why reinvent the wheel? Why was Koh insisting on a new review? Was he intimating that this new review should not take into consideration the past findings that led the New York Fed to rate Goldman as high risk? I felt like something was up.

In that largely repetitive follow-up meeting with the CFPB, the Goldman representatives kept wondering how the regulations and supervision activities were going to be divided between the New York Fed and CFPB. But the law was very clear on this point, setting July 21 as the deadline and the specific responsibilities for each agency. Still, I watched and heard employees from the two agencies waste time throwing the hot potato back and forth. Goldman's question should have been dismissed outright as a diversion and a waste of time. Only later would I realize the significance of this back and forth.

After the first CFPB meeting Johnathon and I left the room and had a few minutes before we were to head over to meet with the Goldman lawyers to discuss the conflict-of-interest issues.

I seized the opportunity to ask him about the mysterious Chuck mentioned by Koh in previous meetings. He explained that Chuck White was the attorney from the New York Fed legal department assigned to assist the New York Fed employees covering Goldman. "What does that mean?" I asked.

"If you need attorney-client privilege," Johnathon said, "you need to invite him in." He then reminded me that the New York Fed had deliberately not hired me as an attorney, so my job and all meetings connected to it were not covered under the attorney-client privilege. He pointed out that many New York Fed employees had side jobs, and this went all the way to the top levels. One of the benefits of our non-legal job, he remarked, was that we were free to set up our own legal practice on the side and make money practicing law while working full time at the New York Fed if we so wished.

It also meant that if I ever found myself in a situation in which I needed an attorney present or to explain how the law worked, Chuck White would be doing the honors. Johnathon ended by pointing out that he expected this to be not at all necessary in my case. I was, after all, a trained attorney, just like him. Understanding the law was not an issue for us. It was also unlikely, given my extensive experience, that I would put myself in a compromising situation that would require Chuck's legal assistance. Hiring a trained attorney into my position effectively lessened Chuck's workload—and allowed the New York Fed to pay less for what was, in practical terms, an individual with a higher skill set.

A few days later Johnathon introduced me to Chuck in a conference call and—as anticipated—it ended up being an extremely short meeting. Chuck mentioned that his focus was on regulatory actions, including, for example, the Litton enforcement action against Goldman. He indicated that he got regulatory updates from Michael Silva. Johnathon brought the conversation to my role, and Chuck intimated that he viewed my role as monitoring the legal and compliance systems within Goldman so as to ensure they were in compliance with the rule of law. This made complete sense to me. To end the call, he reminded me that if I was ever in doubt about whether he could be of assistance, I was free to reach out to him.

Johnathon then looked at the time and noted that we needed to head to the conflict-of-interest meeting. This would be my first opportunity to observe how Goldman employees interacted with the regulators. Johnathon quickly went over the mock questions I had prepared for Goldman to see what I had chosen to ask and how I had phrased them. After a quick review, he deemed them fine.

"Watch me during the meeting" I remember him telling me. "See how I go about asking my questions, okay?" I nodded. "Take notes" he reminded me.

Those orders, once more.

CHAPTER 5

The Goldman Lawyers

"It's probably more than one document. There is no one policy per se."

Bruce Acton II, Goldman Sachs's legal counsel, looked at us regulators, hoping this would sell it. It didn't. Not at all.

We had gathered around the table in one of Goldman's many conference rooms. The three Goldman employees sat on one side—James Muller in the middle, with Bruce on his left and Jack Dalton on his right—facing the regulators. James and Bruce were wearing light-colored shirts and no jackets. James had rolled up the sleeves of his light-blue shirt. His tie sat a bit askew and a little loose. His straight salt-and-pepper hair sat unkempt, parted to one side, on top of his rather prominent and bushy darker eyebrows. Bruce's shirt was white. Unlike James, Bruce's appearance was not unkempt. It was not impeccable either, but he came across as a man who bothered to look at himself in the mirror before walking out the door. Unlike James. Jack wore a suit and—more importantly—the face of a man who clearly did not want to be in that room.

I was sitting opposite James and next to Johnathon, who was slightly hunched, leaning sideways, his left elbow resting on one of the armchair handles, his right hand on top of his notebook. Lily, closed notebook in front of her, sat playing with her pen. Matthew, another relationship manager, made himself so inconspicuous that you could hardly tell he was there.

Analisa, curly hair tumbling down her shoulders, sat with an open notebook in front of her, pen at the ready, inquisitive look on her face.

Sitting across the table, all three Goldman employees looked at us. Were they hoping that was enough to close the issue? I quickly glanced at Johnathon and Analisa. Disbelief was all over their faces too. Lily, however, looked on impassively.

"Some of the information is automated," James jumped in, adding cynically, "I seriously doubt they have policies and procedures that are detailed."

This was unbelievable. A big global bank without a conflicts-of-interest policy was, simply put, not acceptable.

Johnathon and Analisa's jaws were slightly ajar. Both had been regulators at Goldman long enough to not be confused or fooled by what I would come to think of as Goldman's "tell": talking out of both sides of their mouth. Whether James understood the implications of what he had just said, I will never know. I glanced back at Bruce and Jack. Their faces quickly absorbed the regulators' reaction to James's statement. It struck me that this was it: after more than thirty minutes of trying to talk around the issue in circles, they finally admitted that Goldman did not have a firm-wide conflicts-of-interest policy.

Going into the meeting, I was well aware of what conflicts of interest are. But I did not have a clear idea of exactly how Goldman went about handling their conflicts. What I did know was that, with respect to handling conflicts, Goldman had a bad reputation. The three transactions that Michael Silva had referred to as raising red flags— Solyndra, Kinder Morgan–El Paso, and Capmark—were not unusual. Historically Goldman had a long and well-documented history of conflicts issues that were well covered in the media; indeed, the aftermath of the 2008 crisis had seen the CEO of Goldman testifying before Congress about it. Congress reacted with evident fury.

After the 2008 financial crisis Goldman figured out it had to do something to appease Congress, the media, and the masses. Goldman's "cost of doing business" calculation took almost two years to make. Announced on May 7, 2010, by the CEO during Goldman's annual meeting, the Business Standards Committee (BSC) was tasked with examining "possible conflicts of interest and other issues" at the firm.[1] The BSC finally issued its Business Standards Committee report in January 2011.[2]

In the report the committee made thirty-nine recommendations and a commitment to work to implement them throughout 2011.

One of these recommendations had to do with conflicts of interest, which the committee, unsurprisingly, found was an area Goldman needed to improve upon.

The newspaper articles about the three transactions I had read in preparation for this meeting painted a picture that seemed consistent with their pre-BSC reputation. Which is to say that four years after becoming a bank, Goldman seemed to not have done much beyond promising to change.

Solyndra was a startup company looking to make solar panels when it hired Goldman Sachs in 2008 as its exclusive financial adviser. The problem was that by September 2011 Solyndra had gone bankrupt, at which point the FBI raided the company's offices, and both the press and Congress started asking questions.[3] Our task was to figure out whether there were any conflicts issues involved.

Although the Solyndra conflicts issues may not have been immediately apparent from a casual read of the news articles, this was certainly not the case with the Kinder Morgan acquisition of El Paso. Kinder Morgan was one of the largest operators of natural gas pipelines in the United States. Its rival in that market space was El Paso, also one of North America's largest natural gas producers and owner of North America's largest natural gas pipeline system.[4]

When Kinder Morgan announced its intention to acquire El Paso for $21.1 billion on October 16, 2011—provided that regulators approved the deal—the transaction was set to make history as one of the biggest natural gas pipeline mergers ever in the United States. Kinder Morgan would emerge as the dominant player in that market.[5]

The New York Times quickly pointed out that El Paso had hired Goldman Sachs to advise it on its initial plan to spin off a couple of its businesses—before the deal with Kinder Morgan was announced. More importantly, they stressed that Goldman Sachs had a large investment in Kinder Morgan dating back to 2006 and that two Goldman managing directors sat on Kinder Morgan's board of directors. The article also indicated that Morgan Stanley had served as the main adviser to El Paso on the Kinder Morgan deal.[6]

What the article did not say—but we suspected—was that Goldman was the secondary adviser to El Paso on the Kinder Morgan deal.

Naturally, like any buyer, Kinder Morgan wanted to pay as little as possible for El Paso. Like any seller, El Paso wanted to be bought for as much money as possible. The question for us was to figure out if in fact Goldman was on both sides of this deal—with an incentive to ensure El Paso sold itself to Kinder Morgan for as little money as possible.

The Louisiana Municipal Employees' Retirement System that sued Goldman about a week after the deal was announced certainly thought so.[7] Their lawsuit, one of several filed against Goldman, alleged that Goldman had advised El Paso to accept a "low premium" deal from Kinder Morgan and abandon a previously announced plan to sell two of its business units, pointing out that Goldman's ownership stake in Kinder Morgan amounted to nearly 20 percent. Goldman would make more money from advising El Paso to sell itself than it would make from advising it on the spin-off—not to mention that, on the other side of the transaction Goldman stood to benefit if Kinder Morgan bought El Paso.

Conflicts of interest were just as apparent in the news articles about Capmark. In 2006 Goldman and other private equity investors had bought a 75 percent stake in Capmark Financial Group Inc., a large commercial real estate lender. Goldman eventually installed one of its managing directors in Capmark's board of directors. In October 2011 Capmark, which had just emerged from bankruptcy, sued Goldman to recover $147 million it alleged the bank had obtained in preferential transfers during the bankruptcy proceedings by taking advantage of conflicts of interest.[8]

Our job would be to ferret out these conflicts issues during our meeting with the Goldman lawyers.

———————

BEFORE THAT DAY'S MEETING with the Goldman lawyers, I was aware of their reputation. Word on the street was they were on the average side of the bell curve technically, regularly producing shoddy paperwork. They also tended to lean toward the more disagreeable, arrogant, and condescending side of the personality spectrum. Prior to joining the New York Fed I had worked on a handful of transactions in which Goldman was a party. In those transactions conflicts had not been an issue. I had been but one tiny lawyer in a very big group working through documents. The end result over the years was consistently the same: their paperwork was shoddy, and the attorneys were disagreeable.

The meeting had started at 3 p.m. in one of the smaller, brightly lit Goldman conference rooms. From the New York Fed Johnathon and I were joined by Lily and Matthew, another of the relationship managers. The NYSDFS sent Analisa. Goldman sent James Muller, Bruce Acton II, and Jack Dalton.

Johnathon adjusted his glasses and began the meeting by asking Goldman, in a friendly but neutral tone, "We know that reputational risk is VIP for Goldman. We are trying to understand the rationale for conflicts-of-interest determinations, who are the decision makers, etcetera." His voice trailed off—the cue for Goldman to jump in.

James went for it with the determination of a linebacker, football firmly in both hands and a clear path to the goal. He inhaled, straightened up, tilted his head back, and held it there for just about a second, plenty of time to firmly twist his face into the most condescending expression he could muster—and what an expression it was! He looked down at us and swept his eyes across the room. With a patronizing tone of voice and hand gestures to match, he launched into his monologue.

Now, I am an expert on condescending expressions and pronouncements. I developed this expertise by fate. I am, you see, a perfectly proportioned but very small woman. Four-feet-seven and three-quarters inches tall, to be precise. A "vertically challenged person" in baby boomer politically correct parlance. Not being a baby boomer myself, I prefer the term "travel sized." Membership in this tiny club does come with privileges, one of which is a lifetime of being on the receiving end of condescending, patronizing behavior. After four decades on this planet I can count with one hand the number of people who have not spoken to me in a condescending manner—and I don't need all fingers. More importantly, I have amassed an impressive collection of memorable experiences. It takes something truly special to crack my top fifteen.

So when I am describing James's performance at this meeting as firmly planted on the lower end of my top-fifteen list, I am not exaggerating. I am trying to do justice to this man's unique ability.

Having made sure all eyes in the room were on him, he put his hands up, brought his palms together, and began thus:[9]

"We are just lawyers ..."

At which point I immediately put my head down, bit my lip to stifle a laugh, and started writing. I already knew this was going to be *good*. With one eye on my meeting minutes and the other occasionally looking up, sometimes at James, other times at the other regulators, I kept on writing down his words: "We advise from time to time on conflicts-of-interest issues. We have a group that manages conflicts on a daily basis. It's a worldwide group that reports to the executive office. Rachel Epstein heads it and has been leading it since [I] joined [Goldman] in 1992."

He paused as if to let that sink in, just long enough for me to steal a glance around the table. Lily sat as if entranced, eyes wide and mouth slightly ajar. Johnathon called on his years of experience to keep his face neutral. Analisa was busy writing. *If this was so, I thought, why were we talking to them and not Rachel's group?*

James continued, occasionally gesticulating for emphasis: "Everything that we are going to be talking about flows through that group. That group will analyze the situation and, if necessary, say no or set parameters, which can range from such things as consenting-adult letters from clients to setting up teams [such as red and blue teams] to institutional internal walls. The group has evolved as the firm has evolved. In 1992 it was a simple set-up, no buy-side worries, only US law issues."

He paused for another second. I looked up at him. He had the face of a man remembering the good old days.

"... Now it is much more evolved. It covers buy-and-sell side, US and other foreign jurisdictions."

As interesting as his performance had been so far, the twist he gave to the words "foreign jurisdictions" took it to another level. It went beyond your run-of-the-mill patronizing contempt. He threw in a dash of cold disdain and made sure to top it up with just the right amount of disgust on his face, driving his point home by looking at Johnathon,

Analisa, and me—the one Asian man and two Latina women in the room.

Lily and Matthew looked at us, expectation written all over their faces. A slight smile played upon James's lips. Silence hung in the room. The unique stench of implied racism filled the air. What he was basically saying seemed to be: *We have a system. It works just fine and is frankly too complicated for your stupid little minority brains, so go run along and be grateful for your affirmative action job.*

Bruce, looking like a man who did not want to be outdone or left behind, broke the silence. Trying to compete with James as to who could sound more patronizing, he added, "We must differentiate between actual versus perceived conflicts."

I was taken aback—and not for the first or last time in that meeting. The law is the law, and a conflict of interest is a conflict of interest. Still, I followed Johnathon's orders: I wrote it all down and did not say a word.

James wasn't done. He took it upon himself to address the Kinder Morgan issue: "We have longstanding simultaneous relationships with El Paso and Kinder Morgan. After the IPO, [Goldman] still had a 19 percent interest in [Kinder Morgan] but also had a team working with El Paso discussing possible spin-offs. When Rich Kinder approached [Goldman] as part of the transaction to purchase El Paso, it was obvious to everyone that we could not advise El Paso."

James paused for a second. I glanced up at him. He shifted slightly in his seat, making himself as tall as he could. He went on: "The question was: Do we abandon the client, despite the longstanding relationship and vast institutional knowledge?"

After writing down his question I stole another glance at him. He had delivered the official Goldman party line with just the right amount of sincerity in his voice and managed to retain masterful control of his facial expression. *Nice!* I remember thinking.

James continued, "It was decided that Morgan Stanley would come in as senior adviser. We had a very narrow, circumscribed role that kept us out of the boardroom and all negotiations. In addition, [Goldman] did not offer a fairness opinion on the offer either." And there was the answer: they did not "abandon the client"; instead, they kept advising El Paso.

James felt he had to clarify further: "All that process of what the roles would be and where the line would be drawn was made by Rachel." *There we go*, I thought. Intimating again that this was all the responsibility of Rachel and her team. Why weren't they here, then? Why was I listening to James and not Rachel or her team members?

James continued, "No one has come to top the offer made, which is the ultimate barometer of fairness. Shareholder litigation caught on [that Goldman] maintains an interest in [Kinder Morgan] and was named as an adviser to El Paso in the disclosure documents. The complaints filed, however, do not highlight the fact that our role was extremely circumscribed."

Well, I thought to myself, *how about we let the court decide that?*

James made sure he finished his spiel by mentioning Rachel once again: "The ethical and reputational risk analysis was done by Rachel at the right time."

Finally, Johnathon waded in: "Who were the decision makers? Would legal have been involved?"

James answered, "I was the principal adviser at [Goldman] for conflicts for ten years. I still do it from time to time, but Sam Goldstein now does the day to day as the [Investment Management division] lawyer."

A second passed. Then two. Johnathon's face was perfectly still.

James went on, "Anyone relevant would have been brought on board and would have been present to make the decision."

Another second passed. Johnathon's face began to shift, betraying his thoughts.

Bruce spoke up, "Rachel's group contains former lawyers."

Johnathon asked, "Is Rachel an attorney?"

Bruce, swallowing hard, said, "No."

Bruce was not good with the poker face. He knew where this was going.

James interrupted with aplomb: "When items are presented before the conflicts group there are several layers of analysis done." Using his fingers to emphasize the point, he continued, "First, business selection: Who would you rather work for—buyer [or] seller? Then, reputational risk: which elements, the *Wall Street Journal* test. Third: legal obstacles: What are the issues involved? Sensitivity to market perception is . . ."—he paused for emphasis—"the hurdle for number [two] is so high that rarely is a decision made on the third factor."

As I continued to write down James's words, I thought about what that actually meant. James seemed to be saying that Goldman purportedly considered not working for both sides because they cared so much about their reputation. Even then that seemed debatable, but what really struck me was his conclusion: because those two things were so important to Goldman, the law was just never a factor in making a decision.

It looked like Johnathon was struck by this statement as well. After considering for about two seconds what James had just said, Johnathon continued tightening the noose: "Business selection and conflicts . . ."—he paused slightly for effect and, in an inquisitive tone tinged with a dash of cynicism, added—"are those two separate groups?"

Bruce, with the look of a child caught with his hand in the cookie jar, answered this one: "No, they are the same group." He quickly added, with a slightly pleading voice, "They have very varied and sophisticated backgrounds."

James, without missing a beat, kept dancing to his tune: "As business gets more complex, more factors go into the decision making. The conflicts group has access to the CLYDE database, but they have their own sophisticated system they use to make their determinations."

What exactly the CLYDE database was, I of course did not know. Neither, I suspected, did the other regulators at the meeting. It was yet another acronym, deliberately boring and mysterious, designed to exclude and confuse people. I had a strong suspicion I would be asked to find out after the meeting what it was, so I made sure to note it.

Johnathon pressed on, with the same serious, inquisitive, and slightly cynical tone: "Can we get a copy of the group's policy document?"

Silence enveloped the room. The three Goldman employees looked straight at Johnathon, stunned. I was stunned as well, for different reasons: this was an obvious request.

Johnathon continued: "Charter?"

Seconds ticked by. Slowly the three Goldman employees' faces morphed into looks of panic.

Analisa jumped in. With a "hello, earth calling Goldman" tone of voice, she added, "Checklist?" One of her eyebrows shot up in the air. Her head moved ever so slightly from side to side, as she looked directly at the three Goldman employees. Everyone's eyes focused on her. Her perfectly serious expression made it clear she, too, wanted an answer and was not going to let them off the hook.

James, Bruce, and Jack exchanged quick uneasy glances with each other. Bruce waded in, uncertainly: "Yes."

"It's probably more than one document," Bruce jumped in, as his gaze swept over the regulators. "There is no one policy per se."

I looked up in disbelief. All three Goldman employees looked at the regulators. I quickly looked at Johnathon and Analisa—disbelief was etched all over their faces too. Lily looked on impassively. My eyes moved from James to Jack, looking for their reactions.

James, adding to his patronizing tone of voice a "know-it-all" angle, punctuated by a dismissive side-eye aimed at Bruce, went on, "Some of the information is automated." Cynicism oozing in his voice, he added, "I seriously doubt they have policies and procedures that are detailed."

Again I glanced at the other regulators. At this point even Lily joined Team Disbelief. And for good reason: a big global bank without a conflicts-of-interest policy was, simply put, not acceptable. Johnathon and Analisa's jaws were slightly ajar. I glanced back at Bruce and Jack. Their faces quickly absorbed the regulators' reaction to James's statement.

Bruce recovered first. He put on his poker face and, with a composed look and neutral voice, added, "They do have policies and procedures [that lay down the basic parameters]. My suspicion is there is more than one."

Silence reigned. I quickly looked around. The regulators stared at the Goldman employees with *Really?* written all over their faces. James held his composure like a champ. Incredibly, Jack's head failed to explode.

After a few seconds Johnathon changed the subject to Solyndra and Capmark. Goldman denied having conflicts in Solyndra but readily admitted to having them with respect to Capmark.

Johnathon decided to close the meeting by asking the Goldman lawyers, "Who does Rachel report to in the Executive office?"

With an elegant, patronizing tone, James began his answer with: "Lloyd or Gary, not sure." He was referring to Lloyd Blankfein, at the time CEO of Goldman, and Gary Cohn, at the time Blankfein's number two.

After a brief pause to ensure his facial expression conveyed the importance of what he was about to say, he went on: "She also sits on the Business Standards Committee." And after another pause for emphasis, he ended with a wave of his right hand and a cynical "or whatever that is called," telegraphing disdain for the committee, its work, and its head.

To the regulators in the room it was a clear signal that Goldman's lawyers were not going to push the company to get its act together with respect to conflicts. The BSC was a smoke screen to appease the public.

This was a lot to digest: situations like this seemed to be the reason Connor had brought in new people like me. We would look into all of this, for sure. Johnathon, Analisa, Lily, and I silently walked out of the meeting and headed back to the Goldman regulator floor.

Upon arrival we stood close to the back entrance and had an impromptu—but essential—meeting.

We all agreed that Goldman's lack of a firm-wide conflicts policy was a big problem.

Analisa agreed to discuss it with her management. Johnathon made it clear that he and I would be following up with our legal and compliance team as well as the two Mikes.

But Lily just listened. She did not say anything. She did not offer to *do* anything.

CHAPTER 6

You Should Not Have Come

The following day I was seated at my desk, still processing all the information we gathered during the conflicts-of-interest meeting the day before. Johnathon came over, and I asked him about next steps. He told me that we would talk to Connor and the rest of the team about that soon. However, we first had to prepare for the meeting with Erin O'Brien, the Goldman person in charge of spearheading all interactions with the regulators.

He began by explaining Erin's role as Goldman's point person for all things regulatory. Any information or meeting requests with Goldman personnel were to go through her. Erin, he added, had come to Goldman by way of JPMorgan Chase. More importantly, prior to JP, she had spent a long time at the New York Fed. She, Sara Dahlgren, Esther Abramson, and Michael Silva had all known each other for a long time.

"How long?" I remember asking. He answered they went back to the nineties, though exactly how far back he could not say. Johnathon said Erin was one of the people I had to watch out for: she, too, was a woman "with sharp elbows." He informed me that, unlike the Goldman lawyers the previous day, she was likely to be curious about me and that I should keep my introductory remarks to a minimum. "Watch and take notes" he said. Again. He also told me to pay close attention to the newspaper articles she had pinned on her office wall, facing outward, for everyone to read and enjoy.

With respect to the meeting itself, Johnathon indicated he was going to press Goldman on their risk-assessment methodology and

57

framework. Risk assessments are the method and documents by which a bank catalogues all the laws and regulations they need to comply with, broken down by area and product, together with the steps they take to comply with them and the risks associated with each. The bank will periodically select samples of transactions and check to see whether the employees are complying with the prescribed steps. Johnathon and I had both come from banks that sold just as many, if not more, products than Goldman. When it is printed out, the typical big-bank risk assessment fills several binders.

Johnathon handed me a copy of Goldman's risk assessment framework—a few pages stapled together.

I remember stifling a laugh. Johnathon smiled knowingly. "Are you kidding?" I said.

"No" he answered. He wanted to make it a priority and, as such, had requested a follow-up meeting to take an in-depth look. We were to discuss scheduling it with Erin.

With that, we headed over to the meeting.

Erin politely welcomed us as we arrived. She was thin, on the taller side, and had light eyes. She pulled her chair up to the table with her notebook and stared intently at Johnathon, waiting for him to begin. Sitting next to her was her assistant, Sue—a shorter version of Erin. She also sat with her notebook open, pen at the ready.

The meeting proceeded as Johnathon had anticipated. He asked a few questions about the risk assessment and quickly moved on to his request that Erin and Sue set up the meeting with the Goldman personnel in charge of this particular compliance program. They agreed. Having taken care of business, Erin and Sue's eyes turned to me.

Johnathon proceeded to introduce me as his replacement. Erin asked about my professional background, with the normal condescending tone people meeting me for the first time consistently use. As usual, I went on to provide a brief summary of my educational background and work credentials, in my usual matter-of-fact-mixed-with-cheeriness-topped-with-just-a-dash-of-show-offyshness tone. Now, I admit it: I have a natural tendency to show off. The fact that such a quality is rewarded in banking helps keep it alive.

I then patiently waited for the customary "Really? I don't believe you" response—which everyone invariably gives, the only difference being the words used. Erin quickly obliged, picking on one of my work credentials. It was at this point that the meeting went from perfectly forgettable to utterly memorable.

For whatever reason, she decided to "pull out her New York Fed résumé card" and proceeded to claim it was not possible that I held such a position at a particular bank because if it existed, she would have known about it. Wrong move, Erin.

I looked at her for a couple of seconds, considering my options. This was, I quickly concluded, some sort of test. I quickly gamed out where each potential response was likely to lead. None of my options were good. I decided that, with Johnathon right there, I might as well give a go at my best impersonation of him. I took a deep breath and put on what I hoped was a pleasant half-smile. In the most appeasing tone I could muster, I casually pointed out that I was far from the only person working in that group—hoping she would move on.

She reacted by crossing her arms, titling her head slightly to the right, and sharpening the condescending look in her eyes with a slight squint. *Oh well,* I remember thinking, *so much for that.* I took another deep breath and steeled myself for what I was about to say, which went something like this: "I do remember while working there going to lunch with one of your Fed colleagues," then, calmly adding, after a pause, "a friend of mine. Just after he had finished an exam." She looked into my eyes, searching to see if it was a lie. I held her gaze. Slowly her face froze as she figured out it was not a lie. I pressed on: "I don't recall him mentioning you," implying she was either lying or had not properly familiarized herself with the bank the New York Fed had assigned her to supervise.

Her face shifted from frozen to embarrassment. Or was it anger? This was exactly what I had hoped to avoid in the first place. Oh well. I continued, "He's a math geek. He did mention there were other people with him. Maybe you worked in a different area?"

As I spoke she looked down at her notebook, shifted in her seat, and played with her papers a bit. She was not just clearly uncomfortable; I had utterly failed to live up to her expectations. Again I tried to give her an out, this time along the lines of "I am sure you did not know about it because you were very busy." This time, mercifully, she took my olive branch.

Johnathon seized this opportunity and changed the topic to administrative logistics, as if to signal to Erin and her assistant that our time was up. The message was received: after a few polite closing words, we made our way out.

As we walked through the Goldman regulator floor to our desk, Johnathon gave me a smile coupled with a knowing look, as if to say, *Now you know why we must look out for her.* I responded with a smile and the name of the Fed regulator I had gone to lunch with. Johnathon knew him—and knew he had been at that bank doing an exam. The New York Fed is not that big.

That day at lunch I finally saw a friendly face. Just as I was about to grab a tray and head over to the salad bar, I spied an old friend across the room. I called out his name and quickly made my way over with a big, excited smile on my face. Paul Lin turned around at the sound of his name, looked over, and, when he saw me, smiled and, delighted, called out my name in return.

"How are you?" I asked.

"I am okay."

"I wrote to you before I started here! Did you get my email?"

"I did, I did . . ." he paused. He seemed different somehow. Distant. "What do they have you doing?" Paul continued.

"I am supervising legal and compliance at Goldman."

"I see," he answered and started to move. Where was he going? It was all a bit awkward.

He stepped closer and said, "Listen, I have to go, but how about we do lunch next week?"

We made plans for lunch, and he quickly walked away. It was great to see him at first. And now I was very intrigued to have a conversation.

BACK AT NEW YORK FED HEADQUARTERS the next Monday morning I said hi to María, the New York Fed secretary, and made my way to my desk. There I found my colleagues gathered, still speculating about who Marylou's replacement would be. I greeted everyone, grabbed a writing pad and pen, and hurried over to grab coffee from the break room.

Our first meeting that day, which usually began at nine, was our legal and compliance group's weekly meeting with Connor O'Sullivan, our boss. Not everyone in the room was a lawyer, and unlike the others, this meeting was not plagued by obscure jargon or confusing statements. During the second half of the meeting Connor would encourage risk specialists to report on the main legal and compliance issues they encountered the previous week.

It was then that Johnathon walked the group through what had transpired during our conflicts meeting with Goldman. He outlined the matter in a few sentences, closing with something like: "We were surprised to learn that it seems the bank does not have a conflicts-of-interest policy."

Everyone looked surprised, even shocked. This was a group of people who understood the implications of Goldman not having a policy. A few people uttered "What?" Someone asked, "Are you sure?" To which Johnathon responded along the lines of, "It certainly seemed so, based on the statements made by their lawyers. Carmen took down meeting minutes, which she is currently transcribing. The New York State Department of Financial Services was present and concurred after the meeting with our assessment. Should we follow up?" Everyone nodded in agreement.

We were to schedule a follow up meeting, this time with Rachel Epstein, the head of the Goldman conflicts-clearing group.

This wasn't the only highlight of that meeting. In fact, most of the time was spent devoted to Connor's main agenda item: the Supervision and Regulation Letter (SR) 08-8. He announced that he wanted it to be the basis of our group's annual supervision plan.

There are literally hundreds of federal, state, and international laws that banks need to comply with—especially big banks doing business across the US states and around the world. Regulators cannot look at how a bank is complying with every single one of them every year. In practice, management selects a big-picture set of rules that the regulatory team will be focusing on for the year, and they become the team's annual supervision plan. Using the annual plan like a checklist, the team gathers data through daily supervision and examination work—think continuous monitoring and exams. In our case, this was to be SR 08-8.

The Federal Reserve Board had issued SR 08-8 in 2008 as part of the US government's response to the 2008 financial crisis.[1] Its purpose is to ensure that competent management run large complex banks like Goldman Sachs in compliance with the law. It calls, among other things, for these large banks doing business in many different US states and countries to establish firm-wide compliance programs, documented with policies and procedures and enforced through training, testing, and tracking (in Fed-speak, "monitoring"). The banks need to implement these programs in different areas of the law that are highly regulated but have much in common. The point is to force banks to standardize these areas, the way McDonald's standardizes its Big Mac menu in the United States and the rest of the world.

Connor also discussed how he expected us to go about implementing the new supervision structure as we went about examining our respective banks. By the end of the meeting it was clear that the requirements we would be looking at could be divided into four main areas:

1. We had to make sure that Goldman had firm-wide compliance programs establishing policies and procedures for areas like conflicts of interest, anti–money laundering, privacy, fair lending, structured products, and affiliate attractions. Due to the complexity of Goldman's operations, there should be a firm-wide policy, and each division should have policies and procedures tailored to the products and services they offer.

2. We had to ensure that Goldman's compliance staff was appropriately independent from the business lines from which they had compliance responsibilities. This meant that Rachel Epstein and her group, for instance, needed to be independent from the business. In practical terms, for example, their compensation needed to be determined by someone other than the

business—someone, for example, from the corporate compliance function. The performance of the compliance staff also needed to be independent from the performance of the business to make sure monetary considerations did not guide compliance determinations.

3. Goldman needed to implement firm-wide compliance monitoring and testing of, for example, the conflicts-of-interest policies and procedures. How a bank determines which rules to test when and how often to test them is written down in a document called a "risk assessment." The bigger the bank, the bigger and more complex this document typically is. The flimsy risk-assessment framework Johnathon had shared with me was not a promising start. SR 08-8 expects the bank to have a strong and active testing and monitoring team.

4. And finally, it was imperative that Goldman's board of directors, senior management, and corporate compliance function established and implemented a comprehensive compliance risk-management program and oversight framework for each of these SR 08-8 types of compliance programs. Starting from the top, members of the board of directors are responsible for setting a culture of compliance with the law, leading by example with words and deeds.

From a legal standpoint SR 08-8 dated back to 2008, but in practice all it did was put on paper a lot of what the big, complex banks being supervised by my other colleagues had already been doing for a number of years. I was familiar with SR 08-8, as I had worked on many projects throughout my career that were tied to it. I knew old big banks like Citi and JPMorgan were far along in implementing these types of programs.

Goldman and Morgan Stanley had only become bank holding companies in 2008. Which is not to say that Goldman had not had enough time to get their act together. In my experience it took a much bigger bank than Goldman about a year—maybe a year and a half—to put a big SR 08-8 firm-wide compliance program together. We were in November of 2011.

As I listened to Connor, I wondered how far along Goldman would turn out to be.

Our second meeting of the day was a more specialized affair meant for the new members of the legal and compliance risk supervision group. Its purpose was to provide additional training, support, and guidance as the new people figured out and navigated the new environment. It was often led by Riley, with Connor occasionally joining in.

Because my formal training had been delayed until January, I jumped at the opportunity to ask questions so I could start piecing together what seemed to be important basic things to know.

Connor and Riley's explanation went something like this: the job of a risk specialist was to collect information (i.e., data points) from different areas of the bank. The information was collected through three types of examinations. Two had been in use prior to the new supervision program: bank exams and continuous monitoring. Bank exams was the original method. Think of it as a polite cross between an audit and an FBI raid.

Full-blown exams are premeditated affairs executed over a longer but fully dedicated period of time. A week would be used to plan the exam. A very formal, introductory letter would be sent to the institution thirty days prior to the examination team coming onsite for the exam. Bank examiners would spend anywhere from two weeks to a month onsite examining the bank, followed by one to two weeks offsite, drafting the closing documentation. A formal closeout meeting and a formal closeout letter were then sent to the institution.

In the years before the 2008 financial crisis this bank examination process had grown into a bloated, contested, obstacle course. A less formal, more flexible way to examine a bank had been developed after the crisis to achieve the same results in less time—continuous monitoring. In practice, continuous monitoring was an open-ended exam, with no official end. Instead of coming and going, New York Fed employees would be permanently stationed at the bank. Risk specialists would gather data points daily. We would then spend our time rifling through different types of bank records, questioning bank employees on various supervision matters and identified issues as directed by management.

The open-ended nature ostensibly stopped banks and examiners from using the minor procedural issues of formal bank exams, such as official starts and ends, as delay tactics.

In response to the 2008 financial crisis, Dahlgren and Dudley had rolled out their new supervision structure with a new way of gathering information, which they called "enhanced continuous monitoring." This was an abbreviated exam performed in the middle of continuous monitoring. It kicked in when inquiries regarding a certain topic became sufficiently in-depth—when, for example, Johnathon and I asked Goldman for additional documentation on conflicts of interest or specific meetings with Goldman personnel to discuss conflicts. At that point we had begun an abbreviated exam.

The short-term purpose of collecting information was to determine whether the particular area being examined was in good or bad shape. If it was in bad shape, the bank would be given specific feedback about what needed to be fixed and how quickly they needed to fix it—these were the MRAs (matters requiring attention) and MRIAs (matters requiring immediate attention). Once we had the list of issues, we had to prepare a "summary memo"—a report explaining each issue and including supporting evidence.

If an issue was uncovered that was particularly bad, the New York Fed legal department was supposed to get involved. Their job was, for example, to represent the New York Fed in enforcement actions against the banks, such as consent orders. Consent orders allowed the bank to avoid prosecution or further legal action against it—provided they fixed the problems. Once issued, sometimes bank examiners such as myself might be requested to be involved in monitoring the bank's efforts in fixing the problems.

The long-term purpose of these exams was to collect all the evidence that would, in turn, be used to prepare the bank's annual report. The annual report itself consisted of different sections. There was a section at the beginning with an overview of the institution—the institutional overview, or IO. Later I would discover that this section was a simple copy-and-paste job from the bank's public disclosures that would take a regulator about half a day to put together.

I was responsible for producing the legal and compliance risk ratings for Goldman. These were based on standards outlined in SR letters. The bank was measured and rated against *those* standards—not compared to how other banks did. The results of the annual report were communicated to the institution annually through a formal letter that also contained the bank ratings and any pertinent MRIAs and MRAs that had not previously been sent to the institution.

I left the meeting feeling a bit more grounded, thinking I had a better grasp of how things were supposed to work in theory. Just how far theory deviated from practice would become painfully clear over the ensuing months.

FROM THE MOMENT Johnathon and I shared our experience discussing conflicts of interest with Goldman's lawyers, everyone discussed the bank's lack of a conflict policy in every subsequent meeting; indeed, everyone was in agreement that this was a huge issue, one Johnathon and I would need to resolve as soon as possible. From time to time I could see fear in some people's eyes.

But the fear and desperation I saw in some of my peers was not restricted to what we were finding out at Goldman.

A few weeks later I finally had lunch with my old friend Paul Lin. As agreed, I found him in the cafeteria. We grabbed our trays and loaded them up with food while casually chatting like old times.

He and I had met a few years back when we were assigned to the same project. I was covering legal and compliance, and he had been covering the technology side. I still remember walking into that meeting in midtown Manhattan. Paul's boss sat at his office desk with a large window behind him. I shook hands with them, and then they grilled me for a couple of hours in preparation for their meeting with the New York Fed. It had not been a friendly meeting—it couldn't be, given the circumstances—but in the end it had gone well. His boss assigned Paul to work with me in support of the second phase of the project. We ended up having complementary working styles, and after the project ended, we had stayed in touch. He had a magnificent network—courtesy of his twenty years or so in the industry—and became a valuable, trusted, and reliable source of information.

Another clear memory was from August 2008, when I woke up around 5 a.m., dragged out of sleep by a phone that would not stop ringing. "Hello," I groggily croaked.

"Carmen!" I knew by the way he pronounced my name that it was Paul. I sat bolt-upright in my bed, immediately worried something was wrong. Calls that early in the morning were not uncommon for me—I was constantly working on projects with Europe and Asia. But a call from Paul at that hour was not normal. Whatever he was calling about, it was not good.

"Wake up!" There was panic in his voice. "Lehman is gone! Don't tell anyone I told you!" It took a while to register what he was saying. "Lehman. The bank. It's gone! Do you have cash?" I asked him what he meant by that. He repeated himself. I was in shock. On the third try my brain finally registered. That morning I went to the bank and withdrew as much cash as I could, just in case. Still, I had a hard time believing what he was saying. I scoured the news. Nothing. How did he know? A few days passed. Still nothing.

Soon enough the 2008 crisis came. Not long after that, my friends started asking me, "How did you know?"

Paul joined the New York Fed, and soon after that we lost touch. At first I thought nothing of it. People in the industry disappear for stretches of time as they get swamped with projects or adjust to new jobs. After a while, when he did not reemerge, I began to wonder if something had happened to him.

Now we were together in the cafeteria, both of us working for the New York Fed.

"What are you doing here?" A whiff of panic tinged his voice.

"I need to work. They made me an offer. I was available."

He looked around to see if anyone was looking at us. Then he shook his head. "You should not have come. I did not email you back for a reason." He lowered his voice even further.

"You have no idea what you have gotten yourself into."

My heart sank as he began filling me in on the nightmare his life had become. It had not started out right away. "I am losing my mind," he would occasionally interject. "You won't believe the things they have me doing." His words that followed did not, at that point, make much sense to me or even much of an impression. The jargon was just too technical, obscure, and removed from reality.

What stuck with me was the evident physical and psychological transformation. Gone was the happy, open, confident Paul I knew, ready to tackle any project big or small at whatever hour of the day. Gone was the Paul who understood and could explain complex things with remarkable speed and clarity. The man sitting in front of me was a tight bundle of stress and anxiety.

"Who are you reporting to?" he asked. I told him. "I don't know them," he replied. "Are they any good? Do people like them?" he asked.

"I don't know yet," I answered.

"Do you think you can put in a good word for me? Help me get out of my group? I need to get out of this group." His voice was full of anxiety.

"I will try," I promised, and my heart broke.

CHAPTER 7

The UK FSA

The following day Johnathon and I were scheduled to attend the weekly relationship management team meeting. Just prior to its start Johnathon said he would be telling the team what had transpired during our meeting with the Goldman lawyers pertaining to conflicts, focusing on El Paso and Capmark.

"What about Solyndra?" I asked him. He said that senior New York Fed management had indicated we should drop it. I looked at him. After a few seconds he added, "Look, from a continuous-monitoring perspective, one sample transaction is enough to issue a regulatory finding. We have two solid ones in El Paso and Capmark. We don't need Solyndra to move forward." At that point I had no reason to doubt him.

Still, I wondered what the taxpayers funding my salary would think if they knew. Solyndra had become highly politicized after its bankruptcy. Taxpayers had been left on the hook for hundreds of millions of dollars. There had even been congressional hearings. But New York Fed management wanted to drop Solyndra.

As we walked into the relationship management meeting and took our seats, I noticed that Michael Silva, the SSO, was in the room. Michael Koh, Silva's deputy, sat next to Silva. I sat across from them, next to Johnathon. Around us on both sides were the rest of the risk specialists and relationship managers. Taking the lead, Silva opened the "management update" section of the meeting, telling us about a session he attended with other SSOs stationed at the other large banks. According to him, the SSOs were not very happy that management—by which he meant

Sarah Dahlgren, New York Fed head of supervision—was insisting on them working together to figure out the new supervision structure.

He warned us, "Don't expect anything that Sarah wants to be implemented overnight."

Wait a minute. I thought the structure was rolled out in January. *We were now in November—wasn't it already implemented? Why were Silva and his fellow SSOs delaying the implementation?* I'd been at the New York Fed for only a few weeks, but I was beginning to figure things out. Then he casually mentioned that there would be a meeting later that day to discuss the IO—the institutional overview—but that he and the other SSOs were "pushing back on doing it." There it was again: delay, delay, delay.

The discussion then turned to a quick go-around so the risk areas could discuss what they had been working on. It was at this point that Johnathon presented on our conversation with Goldman, focusing on El Paso and Capmark. The reaction from the group was again one of general disbelief. Silva's mood darkened when Johnathon concluded that the consensus was that Goldman did not have a firm-wide conflicts-of-interest policy. Koh pursed his lips as Silva's demeanor changed.

The two Mikes did not like what we had learned about Goldman. To me this was surprising. I remembered Koh had flippantly stated in a previous meeting that "conflict is inherent in [Goldman's] business model." So what we learned about Goldman in the conflicts meeting could not have come as a surprise to them. Due to their reactions, however, it seemed to me that our suggestion that we look into it further was not a welcome one.

Silva *insisted* Johnathon and I schedule another follow-up meeting with Goldman's head of the conflicts group, Rachel Epstein. This time he planned on being there and encouraged others from his relationship management team to join. As he spoke, I began wondering just how many meetings I would need to go to before we could paper this and move on to other issues that needed our attention. Was this another delay tactic? And if so, why were members of the New York Fed relationship management team delaying *us*? Little did I know that this was only the beginning . . .

Earlier in the day Silva had asked Johnathon and me to meet with Mila, the relationship manager assigned to cover Goldman's Asset and Investment Management divisions. When the relationship management meeting ended, Johnathon asked Silva to confirm that he wanted us to go to that meeting. Silva answered to the effect that yes, someone from our risk team must be there. It was always interesting—if not frustrating—to see Johnathon asking for confirmation of requests that had been clearly stated. Later on I realized this is one of the many tactics he employed to protect himself.

On our way back to our desk Johnathon informed me that I would go to Mila's meeting by myself. This would be the first time I would attend a meeting without him. I wondered why he chose this particular instance. His excuse was that he had to go schedule the meeting with Rachel Epstein. In any case, I looked forward to seeing how members of Silva's relationship management team interacted at an individual level with members of the different risk teams.

As we sat in the big fishbowl conference room, I greeted the other attendants: Evan, who oversaw risk, and Analisa, my peer at NYSDFS. Mila, sitting with her notebook in front of her and both hands on the table, leaned toward me and started.

"UK FSA [regulators] had done a sweep review of firms in the private wealth management space. Pretty consistent themes and issues emerged from the sweep." The UK FSA regulators, she said, had "found weaknesses in the enhanced due-diligence space."

Enhanced due diligence is the process of asking a potential client for and obtaining answers to additional questions about who they really are before the bank does business with the client. These questions and answers are recorded and kept as part of the client file. This is usually required to verify that a potential client is not engaging in money laundering or is a specially designated individual—for example, a high-ranking politician, judge, or famous person.

Sending regulators to check the bank's records to make sure the bank has gathered and recorded the required information is how the government checks to see whether the bank is complying with the law. If information is missing from the file and the records are incomplete, the bank is not complying with the law. I remember thinking that, in light of my conversations with Johnathon, the fact that Goldman had issues—or, as Mila put it, "weaknesses"—in this regard was not unexpected.

With a shocked look on her face, Mila recounted that the UK FSA had "no exam team onsite [at Goldman]." Instead, the UK FSA had simply made an "information request," by which she meant the regulators had asked Goldman to provide records for them to review. To Mila's horror, upon reviewing the records, the UK FSA regulators "drew conclusions without asking [Goldman] questions." Goldman, she continued with full and sincere sympathy for the bank, "took exception" to this behavior from the UK FSA regulators.

The UK FSA, she concluded, with sincere and increasing horror, "did go ahead with the letter" against Goldman issuing findings. In other words, the UK FSA regulators, upon discovering that Goldman's records were shoddy, sent a letter telling the bank to fix the problem.

She paused and looked at me.

With that look I realized that sending me to this meeting was yet another test. Was Mila waiting to see if I was as horrified as she was at what she had implied was incorrect behavior by regulators toward Goldman? I could see exactly why the UK FSA would not bother to ask questions. Banks are expected to keep accurate and detailed written records. If the sample records the UK FSA had reviewed contained incomplete answers, there really was nothing for Goldman to say. It's that simple.

It was clear to me that Mila's horror was not about the fact that Goldman was behaving badly and had been caught with issues. I immediately recalled my interviews with Connor, Marylou, and Riley. The words "old guard" flashed through my mind.

I was not going to jump on her bandwagon. I was there to do a job. Instead of emoting horror and sympathy for Goldman, I looked back at her and patiently waited for what she would say next. Later—too late, in fact—I would figure out that my failure at that moment to share in Mila's horror toward the UK FSA's behavior and sympathy for Goldman was a big mistake. Still, even in retrospect, I would never do it. Our job was to regulate Goldman Sachs, not to protect it from regulators.

After a pause, in which her face expressed her disappointment in me, Mila continued, this time annoyed. She recounted that after the UK FSA sweep, Goldman's Internal Audit Department "did their own review and confirmed the findings" made by the UK FSA. Quickly changing to a more reassuring tone, she added that "as a result [Goldman] revised their forms and enhanced processes." She concluded, with a problem-solved tone of voice, the "intent is for audit to go back" in the first quarter of 2012 to "do some follow-up" testing, presumably to check if the fix had worked. *There you go*, I thought. *Goldman actually looked into it, and even they had to admit that the findings were true.*

At this point Evan, who had been quietly observing Mila during her monologue, interjected. With his eyes alternating between Mila and me, he said, with an "aw shucks" tone that made him sound as if he shared Mila's sympathy for Goldman, that the bank "had the same finding in Japan and Switzerland." The trouble was that his actual words made it plain that Goldman's anti–money laundering issues extended beyond their UK operations. Translated into plain English, he was saying that Goldman had anti–money laundering issues around the world. He was raining on Mila's parade, and her deflated look made it plain he had succeeded.

As soon as Evan pointed out the scope of the problem, I thought about SR 08-8. Anti–money laundering (AML) is one of the issues addressed in that letter. Large banks like Goldman, with lots of different divisions operating in lots of different countries, are supposed to implement an AML compliance program that covers the entire bank and complies with US federal, state, and international laws. For US banks this includes compliance with the Bank Secrecy Act of 1970 (BSA), the US federal law requiring banks to assist the US government in detecting and preventing money laundering.

In order to implement a corporate-wide compliance program, bank staff work together to understand the laws and come up with a strategy, after which the bank issues and implements rules dictating to employees how to go about doing their jobs so the bank can prove it is complying with the various laws.

It was obvious that we had to look into this.

But Mila had a different agenda, it seemed. Turning to me with a firm and chiding look, she informed me that she "feels like BSA and AML here [at Goldman] is strong."

What gave me pause was the juxtaposition between her telling me a few minutes earlier that the UK FSA had found serious AML issues that Goldman's internal audit team had confirmed and her assertive conclusion that Goldman's AML program was strong. This almost sounded like she was telling me, "There is nothing to see here. Move along."

As a lawyer, I was expecting her to provide evidence to back up her assertion. She didn't. Instead, she told me I had to look at the work that had already been done and how Goldman had made their customer and enhanced due-diligence procedures "universal and accessible." According to her, it was important for me to ask whether internal audit had gone the extra mile and to leverage off the work she had already done. She concluded by insisting I had to "check out the control validation review" Goldman had done. With a look of satisfaction, she announced, "They did their own sampling."

As I alternated between taking down notes and looking up at her, the same question came to mind: Why was she giving me evidence of AML issues at Goldman while simultaneously trying to convince me that AML at Goldman was strong? This didn't make sense. My mind kept flashing back to my conversations with Johnathon flagging all those AML issues. I decided I would need to discuss this with Johnathon, who, by now I knew, was supposed to go work for the team assigned to cover AML issues within our legal and compliance risk group.

I did not get a chance to reflect on or ask about any of this. There was a second Goldman Sachs asset management area with issues that Evan and Mila wanted to discuss. This time it was the US Securities and Exchange Commission (SEC) that had come in and done a sweep and found issues with Goldman's "Chinese walls" and improper crossing of information barriers.

The words "conflicts of interest" and "SR 08-8" came to mind once again. Chinese walls and information barriers are bank-speak for the physical and technological separation of people who work for the bank but who, because of a conflict, need to be isolated so they do not gain access to a bunch of information they must not know about. This is done so the conflicted people do not use the information to gain an unfair advantage. Think of it this way: when you are playing cards, you don't sit right next to your opponent and see their cards; you sit across from them. The invisible separation in front of both players is akin to a Chinese wall. As long as both opponents don't know the other person's cards, it's a fair game.

The fact that Goldman continued to have conflicts issues was, of course, a very big deal. Which made what Mila said next utterly baffling. She declared, in a dismissive tone, that the issues the SEC had identified at Goldman were "the same issues we see on the street," by which she meant that Goldman was no different from any other Wall Street bank.

Mila was implying that because every other bank had these issues, the fact that Goldman had them too was not a big deal.

Again I thought about Johnathon, who had flagged the conflicts issues as a very big deal for me as well. He and I were well aware of the general conflicts-of-interest issues on Wall Street. But Johnathon agreed that Goldman's issues clearly went way beyond what would have been considered an acceptable margin of error compared to the other big banks. My mind also flashed back to the articles and books I had been reading about Goldman as well as the congressional inquiries, all of which flagged this as a big issue at the bank.

Mila went on to add, with the disapproving tone of someone who thought wall crossing was and should be as normal as breathing air, "Compliance has been tasked with reducing wall crossings." Well, of course they were asked to reduce wall crossings and take steps to ensure that the bank complied with the many laws and regulations that had to do with potential conflicts issues. Once again, this was the type of thing that we as regulators were supposed to be looking into, particularly because it was detailed thoroughly in SR 08-8. We were not supposed to grade these banks on a curve.

As we got up to leave, I noticed that both Evan and Mila appeared more happy and relaxed. They must have been satisfied with how the meeting ended. I was not.

Besides the actual substance of the meeting and what seemed like Mila's agenda, there was one other element that concerned me: her tone and demeanor did not feel right. She displayed an unwarranted sense of ownership—as if it were her job to monitor the legal and compliance issues. But supposedly Johnathon had taken over supervising legal and compliance risk in June and now it would be my job. Why was Mila involved as if she owned this information and was being forced to share it with me?

THIS WAS ONE of the many meetings that would echo in my memory when I spoke with my colleague, Amy Kim. She oversaw legal and compliance risk at another big bank. One afternoon she casually approached me to discuss Goldman. She said Johnathon and other New York Fed managers had encouraged her to reach out to me. Like Johnathon, she was Korean American and an attorney. Unlike him, she had a bright and cheerful disposition. She dressed impeccably—suits, makeup, hair (which she kept mostly pinned up in an elegant bun), and shoes were just so. Her look screamed "money" and her demeanor "ex-Goldman employee."

I was correct on the Goldman point. Prior to joining the New York Fed she had worked at Goldman in compliance for three years or so. Now it was clear why Johnathon wanted us to speak.

Amy had been assigned to cover a European bank, and this puzzled her, as she knew nothing about real banking. She thought it would have made more sense to assign her to cover Morgan Stanley. I understood where she was coming from. Both Morgan and Goldman had become banks as part of getting bailed out during the financial crisis. They were direct competitors and the only large American investment banks to survive the crisis. The other two, Lehman and Bear Stearns, were gone.

What she really would have liked is to have been assigned to cover Goldman. She and her husband lived just a couple of blocks away from the bank, and she hated the one-hour-plus commute up to Stanford, Connecticut. Unfortunately, she had to wait at least a year before she could be assigned to Goldman—internal New York Fed conflicts rules prevented her from supervising the bank she had previously worked for.

I didn't need to prompt her to start talking about Goldman Sachs. She quickly went over the state of the legal and compliance functions at the bank—her own personal "institutional assessment" of sorts—to help me fill in the SR 08-8 gaps. I quietly listened and took notes.

In the Asset Management division "*no one* is doing blue sky checks," by which she meant the required checks to see if the securities being sold by Goldman were in compliance with applicable US state regulations established to protect investors against fraud.

I had never worked for or heard of a big bank not doing blue sky checks.

According to her, Goldman's outside law firm prepared the subscription documents and sent them on to the bank for the blue sky check, marked with a note that explicitly read, "blue sky check." However, she said, Goldman Sachs asset management "compliance is incompetent" and did not complete the required checks. To "compliance, the business is their client." Typically, for the compliance department, the bank is supposed to be their client, not the business people. To the layperson this may seem like a distinction without a difference, as both work for the bank. Sometimes it is. But sometimes it's not—like, for example, when the business person is stealing money from the bank or, as is more often the case, behaving in a way that puts the bank at risk.

Emboldened by my understanding look, she continued. The AML department "is a mess," she said. The "people doing the work [are] all incompetent. Management has never seen the system" used to make the AML checks. There was "no training for compliance whatsoever. No training on emerging legal issues and trends." The employees were just "cheap labor from temp agencies." The Goldman compliance departments were "pretty siloed in management style and in training across the board."

The "business people may be talking all the time. They are all connected. Improper flows [of information are] one of the biggest risks." There is "no client privacy." "Business people have complete disregard for compliance." With the lawyers, the relationship was a "little bit better because they need their documents," otherwise they cannot close deals Goldman has assigned them to work on.

There was no "legal-compliance" team approach, she told me. What there was, however, was constant "power struggles between all the divisional heads."

She wasn't done. Not even close. She moved right along to the issues plaguing Goldman's technology department. The "outdated systems" required "lots of manual calculations," she breathlessly declared. She went on to explain that only in the past year had they implemented improvements in the trade approval process—the improvement implemented was "the use of an Excel sheet."

Shaking her head, she added there was "no proactive planning" in compliance; instead, they all "go to the biggest fire," she said, gesticulating with both arms as she spoke. In my experience this was pretty typical in understaffed functions. Important work piles up and is left unfinished while the staff runs around trying to fix the problem of the day.

In the Investment Management division "their system cannot track the mandates for asset management for insurance companies." If this turned out to be true and they had no credible manual backup, this was a very big deal. Insurance companies usually have all sorts of rules they need to follow, including either not owning or having only a little bit of certain types of products in their accounts. For example, Amy explained, "corporate bonds are not coded properly," so Goldman "cuts checks to clients" because the bank "bought securities they should not have" bought for that client.

And yet the biggest issue, in her eyes, were the "cross-border" issues, which she described as "*huge.*" "Cross-border" is bank-speak for the laws and rules banks need to apply when doing international transactions. Goldman had a reputation for being shoddy. I assured her that Johnathon and I already knew this was the case. But she continued, "private placement reviews, licensing—no one tracks" anything. This, if true, was also a big deal. There are lots of federal, state, and international rules that require banks to keep track of who they offer or show potential investment opportunities to. Same thing with licenses.

She went on: "Lobbying is a mess. No one tracks." That was also bad if true. Banks engaged in lobbying do need to implement and keep track of campaign finance laws. She asked if I had already met or heard about their head of compliance. I said not yet. She said his name was Alan Cohen, and according to her, in her opinion, he was "incompetent."

By this point my head was spinning. I began trying to figure out how to schedule my week so as to have time to follow up on all this information. I asked her to summarize which areas were worse than the conflicts mess we were already dealing with. It was the only measuring data point I could use, as that was the one issue I had spent enough time working on.

She responded by saying that the compliance testing team, the investment management, asset management, and AML areas were worse than conflicts, with cross-border issues being as bad as conflicts.

Half of those areas were the ones Mila and Donna were tasked with covering.

I thanked her, and as we parted ways, I thought that if she was right, this was an even bigger mess than I expected. As I went looking for Johnathon to debrief him on the meeting, I also wondered why she had told me all this. Did she have an agenda? I could not say. She was, however, an attorney, and she knew I was too. We both knew I would factually cross-check her claims. This, in theory, was a deterrent to lies and exaggerations.

I eventually found Johnathon and quickly debriefed him on my conversation with Amy Kim. It was, for me, my first cross-check.

To my surprise, he nodded: none of this was new to him.

He suggested we add some of the issues she had raised to my annual supervision plan. "Why only some of it?" I asked. He explained with words to this effect: "There is only one of you. The New York Fed lacks the resources in the supervision area to cover such a wide range of issues." Having been there less than a month, I did not deem it prudent to point out that the New York Fed sets its own budget, moves around US dollars for a living, and sends whatever amounts it does not appropriate for its work back to the US Treasury.

All they had to do to pay for more personnel was reduce the amount of money they sent back to the US government.

But there it was: the order to look into some of the issues but not all of them. Or, as Connor had put it: make them feel pain, *but not too much.*

CHAPTER 8

Fly Paint

Walking to the New York Fed in the morning, I readied myself for the dizzying array of meetings where the same topics would be covered in the same ways, where people would rattle off acronyms running circles around empty centers, by humming one of my favorite U2 songs. *Yes, I thought, sometimes I felt "stuck in a moment" that I couldn't "get out of."* But even more appropriate was a later phrase in the lyrics. Meeting after meeting, delay tactic after delay tactic, it seemed increasingly clear that many of my colleagues believed that "later would be better."

That morning started like so many other Monday mornings. People wondering who would replace Marylou. People starting to talk about the holidays. And everyone asking about the conflicts-of-interest issues at Goldman, insisting this was an issue that needed to be addressed. And yet the next conflicts meeting with Goldman would not be until December, so there wasn't anything new to discuss.

Later that day we convened for yet another meeting. This time the usual routine of walking another ten steps or so into yet another room a few doors down from the previous one for another mind-numbingly repetitive meeting was interrupted by the request that we take the elevator and make our way to one of the more formal Fed conference rooms. Instead of the customary cheap ergonomic chairs and suspiciously flimsy tables, this conference room was full of wood, plush brown leather chairs, and soft overhead lighting.

Connor sat at the head of the table. Johnathon was seated to his right. I sat close to Johnathon. Everyone else gathered around the table.

After commenting on the ostentatious décor, Connor made a couple of unexpected announcements to the team. He had selected Craig to head one of the teams dedicated to anti–money laundering. The room responded with warm applause. A couple of people sitting next to Craig clapped him on the back. I thought I knew what was coming: Johnathon's official appointment to the AML team. I knew how much he had been looking forward to this.

But I was wrong. Very wrong. Connor announced that, instead of moving to the AML group at the end of the year, Johnathon would instead be staying on in the legal and compliance group. He would be taking over Marylou's job as team leader, reporting directly to Connor.

Johnathon would now be the team leader and on-the-ground supervisor of half of the risk specialists—including me.

I knew Johnathon had been looking forward to leaving this group. He had told me so on several occasions. In his own way he had been preparing me to take over his role not only as it pertained to work responsibilities but also in navigating the alarming dynamics in the Goldman group at the New York Fed. When I arrived he seemed relieved. And now he had to stay and deal with it at an even higher level.

So many questions: Why did management change their mind? Who made the decision? How would this affect the dynamic with the two Mikes and their team?

I smiled at him and tried to signal encouragement with body language—it was "not that bad, right?" He looked at me, then at Amy Kim, who also smiled and congratulated him.

I prepared to clap along with everyone else. Except no one did.

Surprised at the silence, I looked at the rest of the room. Some were stealing nervous glances at each other. Others tried to hide behind stony expressions. Why had no one clapped? Was the staff so polarized that they could not bring themselves to perform basic civil gestures? I remembered Paul Lin's warning over lunch: "You should not have come."

THE NEXT DAY, Thanksgiving was on everyone's mind as the risk specialists gathered for the weekly meeting with Michael Silva and his relationship management team in the big fishbowl conference room on the Goldman regulator floor.

Silva announced to the team that, with respect to the IO, "we may have to deliver one in March after all." It seemed that Sarah Dahlgren and her team wanted to continue "following the standard script." There were to be no adjustments for new products or processes. I looked around the room. A few relationship managers had slightly disappointed looks on their faces. Why, I was not sure. Perhaps because it meant there was work to be done.

He switched gears to the "Our Team" handout he had circulated. It contained his vision for how he expected his team to operate. He insisted that his team needed to "fly paint." His eyes shone with excitement as he went on to explain that the term came from the Blue Angels, the Navy's elite flying team, whose members fly in formation, keeping an eye on a letter or number of the neighboring jet to make sure they were moving in unison. These "fly paint" lectures would continue to happen periodically. One time he even showed us a Blue Angels' video.

Silva had graduated from the Naval Academy. Unable to fulfill his dream of becoming a fighter pilot,[1] he eventually became a lawyer and joined the New York Fed's legal department in 1992. Prior to becoming SSO at Goldman, he had been chief of staff to Timothy Geithner and Bill Dudley. As such, he must have been intimately familiar with the cultural problems at the New York Fed. His vision was an interesting choice, particularly as it seemed to reinforce the culture of herd mentality that the New York Fed was purportedly trying to fix: To be on the same page. To follow the lead. To fly paint.

With that, it was time for a quick go-around. Although ostensibly each person in the room was to discuss one thing they were working on, there was never enough time to hear from everyone. This time the focus was on tri-party repo. A repo is a contract in which a buyer agrees to purchase the assets of a seller on the condition that on a pre-agreed-upon date the seller will repurchase (repo) the assets at an agreed-upon price. Big institutions such as Lehman used this type of contract before the financial crisis to obtain short-term access to cash.

It works like this: an institution—say, Lehman—would borrow cash from another institution—say, Goldman—for a short time. Lehman would use its assets (securities or illiquid assets like real estate) as collateral (guarantee) for the short-term cash loan. Goldman would agree to hold on to the assets until the agreed-upon date, at which point Lehman would pay the money back (plus interest) to Goldman, and Goldman would return the assets to Lehman. The tri-party repo market is where securities dealers (big institutions like Goldman and Lehman) make money by entering into repos with all sorts of other institutions.

Repos became famous during the 2008 financial crisis because they were critical to Lehman's failure. Thus, the Fed had set up a task force to deal with them.

Silva was very familiar with repos. He had at one point been part of the group at the New York Fed, together with Dahlgren, Dudley, and Connor O'Sullivan, who dealt with the Lehman bankruptcy. His team was also very familiar with them. Many had been at the New York Fed during the 2008 financial crisis, and any sort of conversation or rumors about the tri-party repo market sent shivers down their spines.

We learned in this meeting that there was a rumor on Wall Street that the task force was looking to restrict less liquid collateral assets from being used in the tri-party repo market. Restricting less liquid collateral assets at the wrong time could trigger another round of problems in the financial system, which is why everyone was nervous about where this particular rumor was coming from and wanted to know more. How true it was—and how likely it was—had a direct impact on how they might need to spend their day.

Silva went ahead and confirmed that the rumor was true, adding, with a smirk on his face, that "the source of the rumor was Dudley talking to Jamie Dimon, and Jamie leaked it."

This whole exchange was fascinating to me. It was clear that some members of Silva's team—if not all—were still haunted by the financial crisis. More importantly, Silva's comments on Dudley and Dimon, the CEO of JPMorgan, indicated that Silva still had Dudley's ear. I wondered how Dudley would react if he knew Silva was sharing his secrets—particularly ones in which Dudley engaged in improper communications with the CEO of a big bank. Or maybe Dudley told Silva precisely because Silva would leak it? Impossible to say.

Michael Koh then took over the meeting. In his usual monotone voice he reminded everyone of their upcoming meeting with him to "discuss MRA remediation." We were to come up with our plan to check whether Goldman had fixed the problems identified in our MRAs, keeping in mind that the MRAs needed to be "addressed by the roll-up time." When roll-up time would be, however, he did not say.

In sum, I was supposed to review each of these MRAs and, if I determined Goldman had fixed them, close them. But Johnathon had not yet transitioned the MRAs that had been issued to Goldman in prior examinations to me. Because he had not shown me the list, I had no idea how long it was or what the issues were.

On top of that, I still did not have the systems training, so I couldn't get into the system and see the issues for myself. This also meant I could not document my work reviewing them, update the New York Fed data systems with my observations, or even close the issues if I determined they were fixed.

Until that day I hadn't worried much about not having access, as Johnathon had indicated this was not important to the legal and compliance risk group. But here was Koh saying that closing MRAs was the priority—rather than staying focused on all the issues bubbling up at Goldman and the New York Fed that had not yet been caught and documented.

I figured it was better to follow up and document the results of the follow-up as much as I could. I had enough experience to know that seemingly unimportant stuff like this has a habit of suddenly becoming very important at the most inconvenient time for me.

Following up is the weapons maintenance of the banking world.

Back to the meeting at hand, the conversation then turned to commodities. Anton, the chronically unkempt guy from market risk who covered the area, began the discussion by pointing out that Goldman's commodities group is "the one area that has not gotten the Volcker memo."[2] A general murmur and thinly disguised mocking gestures traveled through the room. And then he explained himself: "Goldman has physical presence in commodities because of the wealth of info they obtain. They can front run [the market] using material nonpublic info."

I quickly looked up from my notebook at him and the others. Anton looked around the room, satisfied. He had understood how things worked at Goldman and had shared his knowledge with the others. But the relationship management team did not seem interested in discussing the implications of what he had just said.

If what he said was true, it could mean Goldman was engaging in illegal activities, using their ability to own physical commodities and the critical insider information that came with ownership (like, say, insider knowledge of an upcoming supply shortage) to front-run the market. Front-running is the illegal practice of getting in front of securities-trading orders placed or about to be placed by other people so as to gain an unfair advantage.

This is how it works: if you know there is a supply shortage and, as a result, the price is about to go up, you go out and buy the securities while they are still cheap and no one knows their price is about to go up. When the price goes up, you sell and pocket the money. If you accidentally bought at the right time, good for you. But if you did it with insider knowledge that others in the market did not have, it's illegal.

A prosecutor can file charges (known as "insider trading charges") for illegally using critical insider information (the legal term is "material nonpublic information"). To a legal and compliance risk specialist, Anton's use of the terms "front-run" and "material nonpublic info" were red flags. So even though no one else wanted to discuss this further, it was obvious that I needed to take a closer look at Goldman's operations. And I would.

I looked at Silva, thinking to myself, *He is a lawyer. Surely he knows what this means.* But he seemed unperturbed.

I went back to my desk confused—frustrated, even. Why did Silva and the onsite team spend so little time on actual supervision work? The likely answers were obvious, but I still did not want to accept them.

———

AFTER THANKSGIVING I discussed some of my frustrations regarding the group dynamics with Elizabeth, my desk neighbor, and she shared some tips. When she took over her function as operation risk special-ist, she kept the monthly meetings with Goldman that her predecessor had been holding, but she changed them so that she, instead of Gold-man, set the agenda. She then gave Goldman a laundry list of issues and told them how they would spend the rest of the year going through them. So far it sounded remarkably similar to what Johnathon had told me. She did not say anything about pushback or obstruction.

She then told me how she used the different New York Fed com-puter systems to upload her work—the same systems I could not yet use. I remember mentioning my concern about my training being de-layed and how that might impact my ability to document my work and any issues I worked on at Goldman. Waving her hand, she said to me, "Don't worry about that." I looked at her, eyebrows raised.

With a smile she quickly added, "I didn't do anything the first year I was here."

Wow. I could not imagine myself lasting longer than three months at any banking job without doing anything. I had never heard of such a thing being possible from friends or colleagues in the industry working in any of the major financial centers—in London, Hong Kong, Singa-pore, or New York City. During my time in the industry there was just too much pressure to produce results, irrespective of your position within the bank. Lawyers, technology, compliance, risk, marketing, even the sales people are not hired by the bank because they want to hire them; they are hired because the banks have no choice. Banks invariably see all personnel as costs—the fewer people you have, the better. If you are there, it is because the bank needs you to do a job, and they need it done badly enough to part with their money and pay you to do it.

I knew the New York Fed was a private bank with a quasi-govern-ment function tacked onto it, and I thought this quasi-government aspect likely meant that things moved more slowly. But a full year of doing nothing was, I thought, a bit much—especially at the time I joined. The European crisis was in full swing. People were protest-ing all over the world. Postmortem reviews of regulatory performance during the banking crisis had been abysmal. If there was one thing that needed to change, it was certainly the speed at which work was done.

But Elizabeth's story was representative of what I was witnessing. This was part of the culture we were brought in to change. I wondered what it would take to actually change it.

———————

THE LAST WEEK of November began much like the previous weeks: another Monday, another round of repetitive meetings at the New York Fed. At the meeting with our legal and compliance team, Connor O'Sullivan announced an upcoming town hall meeting with Sarah Dahlgren. He told us this was a very important meeting for the group.

That much was true. Dahlgren had made a big splash earlier that month with her speech to the New York Bankers Association Financial Services Forum, where she openly talked about her view of supervision. In the speech she had spoken about the New York Fed's supervision objectives, which amounted to ensuring that the banks they supervised were "less complex, more resilient, and better managed." The entire group of New York Fed supervision employees reporting to Sarah were expected to attend the town hall.

Then, with a worried look on his face, Connor switched topics. It was time to address the relationship between us and the relationship management teams. He informed us that tension was building because our risk specialist teams had been embedded into the SSO teams and were assuming work that was previously done by them. He obviously meant that the relationship managers were unhappy that we, the risk specialists, were hanging out with them at the banks we were tasked with supervising and taking over their jobs. *Welcome to my life*, I thought.

As his comment got little traction, he moved right along. "We stopped exams in 2011," he declared for the benefit of those of us who were new. "The plan is to develop a yearlong [supervision] program for 2012." Perhaps because the plan was not ready, he then went on to point-blank ask the group for feedback regarding any tensions we were experiencing with the SSO teams.

I looked around the table. Everyone else was also looking around the table, trying to read each other's facial expressions and body language.

Slowly, responses started to bubble up. I joined the group of new employees—which was, at this point, about half of the group—who shook their heads "no." In truth, although I had experienced strange behavior from the relationship managers, I did not feel I was experiencing actual pushback—yet. I suspected this had to do with Johnathon being with me most of the time I had been at Goldman.

At the end of the month Johnathon and I met in his office to formally conclude my shadow-training period. This was earlier than originally planned, due to his new role as my team leader. He said he intended to be a hands-on supervisor and attend some of the upcoming meetings with Goldman together with me. We spent much of the meeting going over my work plan for the coming weeks.

Toward the end of the meeting he also brought up the tension between the relationship managers and us. With a serious look on his face, he said he wanted me to be aware that these people did not want me to do my job.

I knew he was right. Over the past few weeks I had seen how, in casual interactions, Lily, Mila, and Donna had behaved toward him. They took every opportunity to be condescending. They refused to share information with him. They misrepresented facts and tried to get him to say that things were different from what we had observed.

Donna had even gone so far as to accuse him of not inviting her to meetings with Goldman, which was a lie, as I had been with him when he had invited her to join us.

"What you saw happen to me will happen to you" Johnathon said calmly. "When the moment comes, make sure you come to me."

I asked him when that might be and how would I know. He answered, "When one of the two Mikes calls you in for a meeting and brings it up." He did not elaborate on what "it" was—but he did not have to.

I had been in the banking world long enough to know the tactic would likely be to accuse me of doing the things they were doing to me. There would be multiple rounds. The first round would be personalized and petty—something like accusing me of being condescending, and this would lay the groundwork for the second round, where the accusations would revolve around sabotage and not being a team player.

"Work closely with the other regulatory agencies" he said, adding that I should make sure to invite the FDIC and the NYSDFS to all my meetings with Goldman and, ideally, have them join me for all of them for cover.

"Stick close to Analisa," he said.

We agreed to keep our weekly one-on-one meetings going. It would still be another couple of months before I received the formal training, and Johnathon had laid out a pretty lengthy list of agenda items he expected me to cover as I supervised Goldman. As I left I asked him if he was happy with the new job. He hung his head, pushed his glasses up the bridge of his nose, and said no.

"I was really looking forward to leaving this group."

I felt simultaneously sorry for him and for me: the following day I would be at Goldman, almost on my own.

Almost, yes. You see, Johnathon had not been the only one looking after me. I had another guardian angel.

———

FROM THE MOMENT I arrived at the New York Fed the secretary assigned to the two Mikes, Delilah, had been observing me. I had been observing her too, noticing how she was the type of proactive secretary who took pride in her job. For example, she always made sure new people had the pens and the notebooks they needed. She sat at a desk right across from the two Mikes, not far from me.

One day I happened to be passing by her desk when she called me over with a casual remark, something like, "Do you need a new notebook?" As I came closer to answer her question, she looked down at a pile of papers on her desk. On top was a printout that happened to have the name of a person she wanted to warn me about.

She took her right index finger and placed it right below the name while simultaneously looking up and giving me a meaningful look.

I was so surprised that I wasn't sure what to say. Delilah was expecting my reaction. Smooth as silk, she said in a casual yet deliberate way, "Let me know if you need anything."

This was a risky thing for her to do. The open floor plan, with its constant stream of people milling about and incessantly watching each other, posed a formidable challenge. Walking out with me to grab a cup of coffee or lunch was not an option. It was evident to me from the start that the New York Fed office culture looked down on social interactions with all administrative staff.

I was too new to push the envelope much, but in my own small way I always made a point to say hello to her and all the other administrative staff I worked with and respected. She used those opportunities to share information and warn me.

She did this on four separate occasions. The first three people she warned me about were the ones Johnathon had mentioned: Mila, Lily, and Donna. But Delilah also warned me about someone Johnathon chose not to mention.

Michael Koh.

CHAPTER 9

You Didn't Hear That

The December holiday season was in full swing. Decorations peppered store windows and restaurants across Manhattan. Despite the pretty streets, festive music, and party invitations, I was having trouble soaking up the holiday cheer. Because Hendrik was in his busy season at work, we would not be taking time off to celebrate and visit his family in the Netherlands; we would do that in February. Instead, we hunkered down for a month of intense work, and I made peace with the fact that we would barely see each other.

Inside the Goldman regulator floor Delilah had taken it upon herself to add seasonal touches to the office. Her efforts did little to lighten the mood. The European crisis continued unabated and was finally starting to pop up in casual conversations. Delilah's warning about Michael Koh had deepened my understanding of the SSO team dynamics. Day to day it was pretty apparent that Mila, Lily, and Donna seemed to be going about their strategy under the guidance and leadership of Michael Koh. At first I didn't want to believe it because Johnathon had kept him out of our conversations. But after Delilah warned me about Koh too, I wondered how high it went.

Meanwhile I started to piece together their possible motivations by learning more about the recent history of the supervision structure. And it was clear that we posed a threat.

THE SUPERVISION FUNCTION was, when it came right down to it, very small. Very few people were tasked with the job of supervising the large banks. The way the annual ratings worked, our small group of ten legal and compliance risk examiners was in charge of producing one of the four components that, when added up, would determine the ability of each of the ten banks we supervised to borrow money from the US Treasury via the New York Fed's discount window and, in turn, use it to make money.

There may have been fifteen other people (it would eventually grow to over twenty) on the SSO onsite team at Goldman as relationship managers, but in theory the few people working in each of the four risk areas were the ones responsible for doing the actual work—that is, data gathering—that mattered in terms of rating the bank. I was in one of those four risk areas—in charge of the legal and compliance risk rating for Goldman.

The New York Fed's decision to leave onsite as relationship managers Koh, Mila, Lily, and Donna—the people who had previously been in charge of supervising and producing the bank's annual ratings— made my job very difficult.

Before the new supervision plan was rolled out—we were told—in January 2011, the risk people reported directly to the SSOs, who in turn reported to Sarah. The supervision change led to risk groups reporting up to Sarah directly—independently of the SSOs. In theory this meant the ratings went from us, through to Sarah, and on to the Fed in Washington, DC, as they had retained the power to appoint the risk supervisors, completely bypassing the SSO teams. Because Dudley was both president of the New York Fed and a member of the Fed board, in practical terms the ratings went through him—although if they went first to him and then to the board or to the board and, through that mechanism, up to him, no one seemed to know. What everyone agreed was that, in effect, the SSOs and the people directly reporting to them were not in charge of the ratings.

In practice, as it related to me, this meant that the relationship managers who had my job before me now had a lot of time on their hands to worry about what I was doing.

Which is not to say that was the only thing they did or worried about. There was the matter of figuring out what their day job was now. But it was easy to conclude that, if I found issues at Goldman that those former legal and compliance risk supervisors had not found or if I discovered they had overlooked important things or done things wrong, well, that could reflect badly on them.

The same went for the other members of the legal and compliance risk teams. Connor and his leadership team, which now included Johnathon and Riley, were being pretty consistent in telling us at our weekly meetings that we were to follow the supervision plan that they were going to give us and that we were to do it by ourselves. They kept telling us the relationship managers had their job, which was different from our job.

In practice it was an undercover turf war.

When I asked whose idea it was to leave our predecessors on the onsite teams, I was told it had been "senior management's idea." Who, exactly, no one would say. It took a while, but eventually I came to understand that "senior management" was a term everyone deliberately used to avoid pointing fingers directly at one person in senior management.

It would not be until several months later, while talking to other current and former Fed employees, that I was told the new supervision structure had apparently been Sarah Dahlgren's idea and that Bill Dudley blessed and supported it. Inexplicably, Dudley had kept Dahlgren on as head of the supervision function, despite criticism from both within and outside the New York Fed about the performance of the supervision teams she led both in the run-up to and during the 2008 financial crisis. Dudley protected Dahlgren, and she could do no wrong.

In effect, her plan to "fix" things had amounted to a few cosmetic changes—putting lipstick on the pig. Dudley supported her revised plans and signaled that support by taking a hands-off approach. The fact that he never showed his face at supervision functions that gathered the entire group was his way of demonstrating that Dahlgren, not he, was in charge of the supervision function.

Well, the fixes didn't seem to be working. The pushback from the SSOs and their relationship managers against the new risk specialists was further delaying all current work. As Silva himself announced at one of his SSO meetings, management was trying to figure out how to improve risk-side hiring. Risk was still bleeding people, and it became harder and harder to bring in the right kind of people. I was one of the few who had accepted the job and was still there. And there was work to be done.

———

As I prepped for the December 8 meeting with Goldman about their conflicts-of-interest issues, I reflected upon Silva's actions. In the last SSO meeting he had made it clear that he was attending the meeting and that he believed Goldman was taking a huge reputational risk by engaging in transactions like El Paso and Capmark. He insisted he wanted to take a look at their conflicts program.

Meanwhile his team was not being helpful as I strived to prepare for the meeting. In fact, they were the opposite of helpful: they constantly interrupted me with inane questions and unprompted discussions on irrelevant subjects. For example, at some point every morning Lily would get up from her desk and, standing with her head and shoulders poking over the computer monitor, would begin, "Oh, hi! I didn't see you there!" At which point she would ask me what I was doing. I would explain I was preparing for the Goldman conflicts meeting. With a smile on her face she would say something like, "Why?" or "Did Goldman give you anything to read?"

And she wasn't the only one—far from it. Min Sung, Michael Koh's deputy, would stop by my desk and ask me what I was up to as well. When I gave him the same reply, he would start giving me his own opinion on Goldman, which was full of ridiculously glowing, over-the-top assessments on some of their reports. No one asked him—and, again, not helpful.

It became so absurd that, one of the times Sung was talking to me, Lily interrupted him to tell me, "Sung is Goldman's greatest cheerleader.

He should be Goldman's employee of the year. They need to hire him!" I reminded myself that Sung worked for the New York Fed.

When it was Donna's turn to interrupt me, I made a point to ask her, loud enough for Lily to also hear, if she would be joining us at the meeting. For good measure, I stood up, moved to one side, and asked Lily if she would be joining us as well. This was my small way of letting Donna know that I was not Johnathon: I would not let her falsely claim I had neglected to invite her to a meeting with Goldman. Donna looked at me seriously, her face uncertain. Slowly she broke into a smile, saying of course she would be attending.

Michael Koh interrupted me. Even Michael Silva interrupted me.

I was reading a section of a book dedicated to describing how Goldman dealt with conflicts, which seemed to suggest that the bank used conflicts to make money, when Silva made his way to my desk. He casually looked at both me and the book. He began with a casual "How are things going?" followed by other forgettable chit-chat before focusing on what had brought him over. "What are you doing?" he asked.

Once again I answered something to the effect: "I am preparing for the conflicts meeting," throwing in a "This is still something you want us to look into, right?" for good measure.

"Yes," came the reply.

He glanced at the book and quickly back at me. He then asked me what I was reading. I replied along the lines of: "A recently published book about Goldman."

Slowly, a look of suspicion fleeted across his usually passive face. "Where did you get it?" he asked me.

"From the New York Fed library," I answered.

He stared at me blankly. He then spoke about the importance of considering the source of the material I was reading. I casually pointed out that it had a section dedicated to Goldman and conflicts, which seemed to echo the very concerns he had raised a few weeks ago. Flattered, he looked at me silently for a few seconds, as if considering what to say next.

"In that case," he suggested, "we should share what it says with the rest of the team."

I did. Whether anyone read it or not, I would never know.

You might think that after day three of this song and dance I would have started to show signs of exasperation, but no. I deliberately kept my eyes open and kept my cards close to my chest. Johnathon and Connor had warned me about pushback. I also knew that, to a certain extent, their curiosity was inevitable. These people had not had the chance to interview me before I joined the New York Fed. They had no idea who I was and did not seem to be busy with actual productive work. Johnathon's constant presence had previously kept them away from me.

Examining me was way more interesting and important to them than examining Goldman. Over the ensuing weeks I watched them do an eerily similar version of this regulator inspection waltz with every new person who joined the regulatory team.

The Monday morning meeting at the New York Fed on December 5 was all about the upcoming Christmas office party at Harry's Italian Restaurant in downtown Manhattan—where the restaurant was, what type of food they served, and why they had picked it (something about having the space for a big enough table to fit the entire team and the ability to crank out enough pizza for everyone).

Finally Connor and his deputies, Riley and Johnathon, moved the conversation to the three challenges facing the risk function. The reorganization challenges were due to retirements. The staffing challenges revolved around the need to staff up the risk function. The examination challenges were due to a lack of resources and the reclassifying of risk.

By this time I had started looking forward to coffee breaks and lunches. After all, it was the interactions with my colleagues during these times that provided the more interesting color. By now my fellow risk examiners were starting to show signs of exasperation at the endless repetitions from Connor, Johnathon, and Riley. Nothing big yet—a roll of the eyes here, an annoyed look over there. It had the virtue of building up trust between us and allowed the more experienced members of the team to let their guard down and talk to us newbies more about what was really going on.

Invariably, when I brought up Sarah Dahlgren, my colleagues were hesitant and went off on different tangents. Some mentioned she was close friends with Erin O'Brien. Others that she was close friends with Tammy Rosenbaum, the SSO of the JPMorgan Chase team.

I decided to give it one final try. My online research yielded critical articles openly describing Sarah Dahlgren as "technically incompetent" alongside more flattering pieces. I casually brought up the flattering articles with my colleagues. A few people smiled or even guffawed. One of the veteran risk examiners told me the New York Fed had extensive contacts with the media and worked closely with various publications when necessary or prudent to improve the public profile of their senior management—to "make them look cooler than they are" or something like that.

They told me there is a club within the New York Fed dedicated to teaching employees how to talk to the media and do public presentations. They even teach how to do television interviews. Anyone could join, but really it was for senior management.

Midway through the week I met with Johnathon one on one. After quickly updating him on my previous week's work, he asked me if I had experienced pushback. "Not yet," I replied, "but I did experience incessant interruptions." I filled him in on the odd routine of visits at my desk as well as the protectionism and fear of Goldman I had witnessed. He nodded silently in recognition and reminded me to keep my eyes open for pushback.

As it turned out, I didn't have to wait long for the pushback to begin.

A FEW DAYS LATER I joined Johnathon, Lily, Analisa, Tom (FDIC), and others in one of Goldman's smaller conference rooms for an overview of the compliance department supporting Goldman's Investment Management division, which held the assets of large pension funds from the United States and other countries. Their clients included the

Mississippi Public Employees Retirement System pension fund and ABP (at that time the largest pension fund in the world) under its Asset Management subdivision. Their private Wealth Management subdivision included wealthy individuals like Facebook's Mark Zuckerberg and Mitt Romney.

The job of Goldman's compliance department is to make sure the Goldman bankers interacting with and selling financial products to those large pension funds and wealthy individuals adhere to company procedures designed to ensure they are complying with the law.

Leading the presentation and sitting across from me was Alexander Lambert, the head of the Compliance division. His job, and that of the Compliance division he ran, was to make sure Goldman complied with the law when making and selling the company's financial products to its customers. Under SR 08-8 Lambert was senior management. As such he also had an obligation to lead by example, communicating and enforcing a culture of compliance with the law—and making sure his employees were going about their day complying with the law.

Lambert had thick, dark hair cut short and combed sideways. His perfectly coordinated blue shirt and blue tie highlighted his pale skin and prominent red cheeks. Whether they were naturally that red or reflected some sort of nervousness on his part was impossible to say.

Johnathon and Analisa sat at either side of me. Erin, Sue, and two new Goldman employees I had never met before—Colin O'Maley and Kate Vogel—joined us in short order. As I readied myself to take notes, I wondered if Lambert would be as entertaining to watch as James Muller had been.

Sitting back on his chair, holding a pen with both hands, Lambert began by telling us, with a half-serious, half-mocking look, "I don't want to confuse you with all the legal entities." He then proceeded to give, aided by the slide decks in front of him, a rather detailed overview of how the division was structured and staffed on both the business and the compliance sides.

He then calmly stated that he did not "believe that there is a need to comply with consumer compliance laws with respect to the [private wealth management] clients due to the size of their portfolios."

Oh oh, I thought, here we go again. Another meeting with Goldman lawyers, another enormous SR 08-8 red flag.

I glanced around the room. Johnathon, Tom, and Analisa looked shocked—as I was. Lily seemed unperturbed. Committed to his presentation, Lambert continued with a hint of annoyance in his voice: "We don't view the [private wealth management] business as retail because of the high net worth of the individuals involved." Then, reading our faces, he paused.

I looked at him intently, wondering whether he realized that telling a group of lawyers and regulators that Goldman believed it did not need to comply with the law might not go down well.

His brow showed a trace of sweat. After swallowing, he added, "Even though, technically speaking, they are retail." Of course, they are retail. And of course, the bank needs to comply.

Lambert then proceeded to calmly lay out in detail a veritable laundry list of the legal and compliance problems plaguing his division. Added all up, they spelled "Merry Christmas" to us. He had just delivered the list of MRAs and MRIAs I needed to issue for his division— and include in my annual report. His list went well beyond confirming the problems already identified by other employees at the New York Fed. From conflicts to anti–money laundering, through suitability to confidentiality of information, and all the way to best execution of product sales, there did not seem to be a point in the product chain that wasn't in serious need of repair. Particularly troubling was Goldman's limited understanding of how international laws applied to their international clients.

Lambert eventually broke away from his list of problems to offer his views on supervision: "We in compliance do not want to be the supervisors" of the business, he insisted. He added, with a perfectly serious face: "Our job is to make the business people better supervisors." Another SR 08-8 red flag, this one raising questions about the independence of his staff. I stifled a laugh and kept writing down as much as I could, thinking to myself that the issue-finding part of this job was going to be easier than I thought.

Once the meeting was over and we were out of Lambert's earshot, Johnathon, Analisa, Tom, Lily, and I looked at each other. Johnathon,

Analisa, and Tom had "what a mess" looks written on their faces. I am quite confident I did too. Lily smiled and laughed.

Someone—Analisa or Tom—said something should be done. They were both clearly in favor of moving forward, but they interpreted Dodd-Frank as curtailing their ability to act independently without the New York Fed.

Apparently they needed us to concur. Otherwise they would not be able to move forward.

Johnathon and I concurred. Lily remained silent. In Johnathon's mind we did not need her approval to move forward with our work. As she was now a business-line specialist focused on corporate functions, in theory she no longer had the power to determine the ratings, and we did not report to her.

Before returning to our desks Johnathon gave Lily a serious look and then turned to me. He asked me to transcribe the meeting minutes. He stressed that I had to circulate them to the group and within the New York Fed and come up with a first draft of the list of follow-up issues that might eventually turn into regulatory findings. Lily smiled and stuck a pen in her mouth.

———

LATER THAT DAY, in his SSO meeting, Silva seemed to have a problem he wanted to share. He began by telling us how unreasonable the employees from the Federal Reserve Board were, going so far as to describe one of them as a "control freak beyond all reason." He crossed his hands in front of him. Both Michael Koh and Sung, who were sitting beside him facing me, nodded approvingly. I glanced around and noticed Lily, Donna, and Mila also nodding in agreement. I got the feeling they had heard this before and understood that his statements were meant for the team newbies.

For me it was quite arresting to hear an SSO talk like that about the board in an official meeting. And to have his whole team nod approvingly.

He continued. Our lives would become much more difficult if we shared information with the board or other Fed employees who worked in Washington, DC. But he made it seem as if it was not worth the bother. I looked around again. The number of nodding heads increased. Two words came to mind: flying paint.

I felt my stomach tightening: Did Silva just tell us not to share information with the Federal Reserve Board?

I had been at the New York Fed long enough to understand these were dangerous waters. My official appointment as a legal and compliance examiner came directly from the Federal Reserve Board in DC. Johnathon had made it clear I was to meet with Bob, the board employee assigned to cover Goldman, once a month and share information with him. Sharing information with the board was part of my job.

Silva looked around the room. With a face full of fear, he spoke of the "sudden push to be much more open with foreign supervisors and the SEC." His team collectively gasped and recoiled at his words, the way a believer recoils at a heresy. Silva went on to pointedly voice his fear—the risk that the SEC will take the information we give them and go file lawsuits against Goldman.

He paused and looked at his team, driving his unspoken message home. He then reminded the team that should a situation arise, internal proceedings called for both the SEC and the New York Fed to each write a memo.

"Our memo and their memo need to agree," he said, adding that only "then an action moves forward."

Again he looked meaningfully around the room. More nodding. He went on, "I have enjoyed pushing on information sharing." Whether he was pushing for or against information sharing was left for us to figure out. He closed the topic by saying he was focused on ensuring that Morgan Stanley and Goldman Sachs "are getting coordinated messages."

Once again I could not believe what I was hearing. Afraid my facial expressions would give me away, I did the only thing I could think of at that moment: put my head down and focus on taking detailed notes.

A few minutes after the meeting ended, Analisa walked over to my desk, notebook in hand. Between preparing for the conflicts meeting and figuring out next steps to address the Investment Management division's compliance issues, we had a full plate. She immediately brought up the Investment Management division compliance meeting. She still could not believe Lambert's statement about Goldman not needing to comply with the consumer protection laws.

Just as I was about to agree with her, Lily rolled her chair away from her computer monitor and, looking at us, stated, "You didn't hear that."

Stunned, Analisa and I looked at each other, then back at Lily. She stared right back at us, with a half-smile. "Yes, we did!" Analisa and I retorted, in near unison. Analisa quickly opened her notebook, looking for the page where she had written what Lambert had said, telling Lily, "I wrote it down."

I added, "So did I."

Lily looked back at us and broke into a brief chuckle. Her eyes hard, she dropped the gauntlet: "I did not hear that."

Analisa and I looked at each other again, then back at Lily. I remember looking away from Lily and telling Analisa: "Let's get to work. Our conflicts meeting with Goldman is tomorrow. We need to have our questions ready."

After about thirty seconds, out of the corner of my eye, I saw Lily get up and head over to Esther Abramson's office. Esther Abramson, who had recently returned to the New York Fed after working with Timothy Geithner. Esther Abramson, who less than three years later would be hired by her friend Erin O'Brien to work at Goldman Sachs.

Esther Abramson, Lily's boss.

CHAPTER 10

Gaslighting

Oh, if that were true, then from the beginning there would have been nothing. Nothing real from the beginning.

Ingrid Bergman's voice accompanied me as I got my first coffee that morning. It was a heartbreaking line from a wonderful—if terrifying—1940s film. I smiled as I recalled it, because it somehow fit my current situation. Unlike Bergman's character, however, my eyes were wide open and I knew exactly what Lily and her people were trying to do. The title of the George Cukor film was the answer: *Gaslight*.

Gaslighting is psychologically manipulating someone into questioning their own sanity. I was intimately familiar with the many ways a perpetrator goes about weaving that web—one step forward, two steps back, three steps to the side. My first close encounter with gaslighting came early on in life, courtesy of family members. I have to admit that in my pre-Fed experience it was also a daily workplace challenge. I came to think of it as one of the inevitable by-products of making a living cleaning up other people's messes. From what they told me, friends and colleagues experienced it as well.

After listening to countless stories and participating in many conversations, I had long ago concluded that the best antidote to gaslighting was to create a written record.

For my entire pre-Fed career this was a pretty simple task. All I had to do was follow five basic steps: (a) document everything—every step I took, every conversation I had, every relevant fact—using meeting minutes, documents, and email; (b) avoid using the gaslighter's preferred methods of interacting: one-on-one meetings, one-on-one calls, and voicemails; (c) prepare management for the inevitable gaslighting; (d) produce the written record as soon as the gaslighting was set in motion; and (e) hunker down and steel myself for the "gaslighter shuffle"—the vicious reaction triggered by exposure to facts, including frantic attempts to deliberately inflict pain and suffering on anyone implicated in the fact gathering.

The hardest step was the last one—not because I was not willing or able to handle the repercussions but because I wanted the ordeal to end so I could get the unpleasantness over with and move on to more entertaining things, like dinner with friends, a classical music concert, or binge watching *Buffy the Vampire Slayer* reruns. I could never figure out a way to make it happen faster.

My experience notwithstanding, I simply could not stop replaying in my mind the conversation with Lily. Eventually I archived it and moved on: this was a marathon, not a sprint. And the next day we had the next meeting at Goldman to discuss conflicts of interest.

That morning Silva, Lily, Esther, and a few other members of Mike's SSO team joined Johnathon, Tom from the FDIC, and Analisa from the NYSDFS as we made our way through the Goldman offices and into the conference room where the conflicts meeting would be held. Goldman had chosen for the occasion one of their more impressive-looking rooms, located in the upper floors close to the C-suites. We arranged ourselves around a long, dark, wooden table, with the regulators on one side and Goldman on the other.

As luck would have it, I ended up sitting directly opposite Rachel Epstein, the head of Goldman's Business Selection Group. To her left and right were Erin O'Brien, Bruce Acton II, and a few other Goldman employees I had never met. Everyone took turns introducing themselves. Sam Goldstein was from the legal department. He had pale skin and dark hair combed over to disguise his receding hairline. The others turned out to be some of Rachel's direct reports. Donny Koh and Indira Lakshmi were physically present in the room and sat far away from Rachel, as befitted their junior rank. A few other Goldman colleagues were on the conference call line.

Rachel looked like she was in her early sixties, with short hair, a bit on the sparse and dry side, dyed a dark shade of brown. Her makeup did little to hide her pale, sagging skin and large bags under her eyes. She began her presentation by giving historical context for the business selection function: the "function started a hundred years ago ... in the context of [mergers and acquisitions]. As business evolved, it grew from a merger to a firm-wide function" and had been covering the entire firm "since 2004." With growing confidence she informed us she was a member of the Goldman Sachs Management Committee and reported directly to Gary Cohn, Goldman's president and chief operating officer.

I took notes as she went slide by slide, describing different aspects of their process, occasionally answering increasingly pointed questions posed by Johnathon, Analisa, and Lily. Yes, Lily was actually asking Goldman relevant questions. As Rachel answered them, however, the atmosphere in the room began to change. I glanced around. Lily and Esther now seemed troubled.

Interesting.

Suddenly Silva spoke up, asking Rachel to tell us how Goldman ended up in the Kinder Morgan–El Paso situation and how they had resolved the conflict. She replied that Goldman was the sole adviser to El Paso and Kinder and, for a long time, to the contemplated spinoff. Kinder had made the approach to El Paso. She then added, with a tone of disbelief, "No one could have anticipated that El Paso would do that."

She paused a few seconds for effect. Again I glanced around. The other regulators—even Lily—had *Really?* written all over their faces. Goldman had a multi-billion-dollar stake in Kinder Morgan and two seats on their board and, as she said, was sole adviser to both companies. Two of the biggest American companies in the oil and gas marketplace combining forces to become the biggest of all players and, in the process, generating millions of dollars in fees and profits for Goldman—and no one could have anticipated that? Really?

Rachel continued, "Then we had the conversation. We laid out for the board in excruciating detail the situation. There was a debate."

I looked at her and asked, "Do you have documentation?"

She stared at me and didn't answer. Sam Goldstein spoke up, "We have board meeting minutes and email confirmation."

Immediately my mental liar detector went off. I quickly put my head down to avoid tipping him off and went back to my notes, thinking, *What happens when we ask for copies of the notes and it turns out they don't exist?*

Later I did ask for the documents. And they did not have them.

Rachel resumed her explanation of how Goldman resolved the Kinder Morgan–El Paso conflicts: "We discussed the recusal with the [business] head of the [Merchant Banking] and [Investment Banking] divisions [of Goldman Sachs]." Unapologetically, she added, "Compliance is not involved in the consultation process."

I glanced left and right at the other regulators. I read the same expression of disbelief on every one of their faces. *Good,* I remember thinking. *I am not the only one.*

Sam, perhaps sensing Rachel had "stepped on it," stated, in his best salesman's voice, "They only get involved in the implementation of the decision." I was about to intervene with another question when Silva took over, asking about Goldman's "open seating arrangement."

Rachel, Sam, and Bruce looked at each other for a few seconds, exchanging puzzled looks.

For many nonlegal professionals, open seating arrangements are a cheap way of cramming together a lot of people into a smaller space. As regulators, we saw it in a much different, more problematic way. Banks have an obligation to maintain client confidentiality and privacy. An open seating arrangement makes it difficult to prevent people sitting around you or walking by your desk from overhearing conversations you may be having with a client or from reading papers on your desk or documents open on your computer screens that should remain confidential.

The problem becomes worse if, let's say, two lawyers, or two bankers, or two analysts working on opposite sides of a deal find themselves sitting close to each other.

In that situation the typical firm would implement what the industry calls Chinese walls. In short, individuals on opposing sides of a transaction would be physically separated so as to ensure they could not inappropriately communicate or share information for as long as the transaction is open. This serves the dual purpose of making sure the negotiations between the parties and the terms and price of the deal are fair and that the individuals complied with their obligations to maintain client confidentiality and to act in the best interest of their client.

Over the years, as a corporate lawyer, I had found myself occasionally sitting behind one of those walls. I had also participated in conversations about them and knew of many firms that went to great lengths (and expense—which they passed on to their clients, of course) making sure computer systems were isolated and personnel sat on different floors with special access keys. If the individuals were socially friendly, such friendships would be put "on hold" until the transaction closed.

After a few seconds Sam waded in first, matter-of-factly: "Different lawyers from different divisions sit together."

Bruce Acton added, "There are no Chinese walls within the legal department." Sam quickly rejoindered, "We don't separate compliance people either."

Rachel, not wanting to be left behind, added, while looking at the regulators with a look of disbelief on her face, "It would be terrible if they were separated."

Viewed from their perspective, Rachel, Sam, and Bruce's statements made perfect sense. Each one of their lawyers and compliance officers may have been assigned to work for different company divisions. From their vantage point they all had one client whose interests they were paid to put above everyone else—Goldman. But that's not how conflict laws work.

I looked around at the other regulators. Eyes were popping out of sockets like ping-pong balls.

Rachel returned to her presentation, bragging about the progress they had already made in implementing what they called conflicts checks. They had already rolled them out in the Securities, Merchant Banking, and Investment Banking divisions, adding, "The next frontier is the Investment Management division."

Wait—what? I remember thinking. *Did she just say they currently do not have policies and procedures for conflicts checks in one of their divisions?* If that was true, this was not just a question of not having a firm-wide conflicts-of-interest policy. This meant they did not have a firm-wide conflicts-of-interest program in place. I looked around at my colleagues, gauging their reactions. Half-open mouths and looks of shock blanketed the regulator side of the table.

At this point Silva voiced his concern that the "Fed is worried about the perception that the game is rigged, that the public's confidence in the financial system is not there." Rachel looked at him. Her face darkened. Her eyes went hard. In an offended tone, she declared, "We stand by the Kinder transaction. Everyone benefitted, as determined by an independent auditor."

"Who was the independent auditor?" I asked.

Rachel quickly replied, "Morgan Stanley and Evercore"—the two other investment banks that took part in the transaction.

Yet there was a rumor making the rounds that Morgan Stanley was upset—about what, exactly, no one knew. But before I could follow up, Esther intervened with a question: "Can you walk us through a declined transaction?"

Rachel looked at her team, a question mark on her face. Nervously Indira waded in with a response, "Some are based on reputational risk—for example, pornography." Rachel interjected, "The bulk of our issues are [Investment Banking division vs. Investment Banking division] issues." Esther nodded silently, as if considering whether to believe them.

Lily asked casually if they had financial information on hand when making a conflicts decision. Rachel, looking at Lily as if she were dumb for even asking that question, replied, "Yes, we have it and take it into consideration." She arched her eyebrows and somehow managed to not utter "duh." Looking around at the regulators, she added, "We are not a legal or compliance function. We don't hold ourselves to be that kind of a function."

Even Silva looked upset now. It was becoming clear that what Goldman meant by "business selection" had little to do with conflicts of interest.

There are two ways you can look at the phrase "business selection." You could say business selection is about figuring out which side of a deal you are going to be on. That interpretation could be aligned with conflicts of interest, which is about avoiding being on both sides of a transaction. If you have to select one side, then you want to make sure you pick the winning side.

That's not exactly what Goldman was doing. Goldman was using business selection to figure out how to successfully be on every possible side of a deal.

This is, of course, a cynical interpretation of both the phrase "business selection" and the legal concept of conflicts of interest. As if he heard my thoughts, Sam added, "This is why it's called business selection." After gauging our reaction, he added, "They do both."

Rachel, perhaps sensing she should try again, added that if it is a true conflict, "I don't let money guide me."

Johnathon slowly and deliberately asked, "Who determines the group's compensation?" Rachel looked at him for about a second before responding "the finance group."

Silva intervened again, "We have a similar issue internally. We have certain routines that we enter into to determine breaches of the law. What is your system for doing this?" Rachel replied, "Internal Audit does backcheck." She then added, "We find out occasionally from committees, from clients who complain."

I bit my lip to refrain from asking, *From lawsuits too?*

Rachel continued, "The most severe ones end up in Employee Relations. Sometimes it's inadvertent—the intent factor is important."

Silva asked how often these cases end up in Employee Relations. Rachel refused to answer at first, going off on a tangent about how the "trickiest ones are where the position is very small." He did not like that answer, so he asked again. Rachel looked at him, thought for a moment, and replied, "One in four or five years."

Rachel wasn't done. She went on to explain that sometimes "a deal takes place that is different from the deal we had originally cleared or approved. Dormant deals 'wake up' and the bankers never tell us."

Silva, looking at her with an *Are you kidding me?* expression, tersely asked, "What happens [to the banker]?" He then added, more as a statement than a question, "Bonus gets docked."

Nervously Rachel answered, "The bankers are supposed to refresh. Once authority is given, they keep it. What we may consider dormant may not be what the client thinks is dormant."

Johnathon spoke up, "So you don't have any time stop on a project."

Rachel replied, "People view us as commercial partners. We are not perceived as cops. We are woven into the business. We want them to come to us early. The smartest bankers come to us early because of client trust."

I glanced around the room. Some of my colleagues looked like they had heard enough. Perhaps sensing this, Rachel went on to remind everyone that she founded the group and "has been in charge of it the whole time." Pausing for effect and looking straight at me, eyes hard and full of malice, she continued, "I have been in charge [of this group] longer than some people in this room have been alive," while simultaneously dropping her upheld hand in front of her, pointing at me. I felt everyone staring straight at me. I sat perfectly still, looked straight into Rachel's eyes, and held her gaze.

For about a second I contemplated whether I should be flattered or insulted, but I quickly discarded both options. The presumptions about my age and experience I've had to face on the job have been so frequent that this one wasn't even that bad. But I quickly emptied my mind in the hopes of maintaining a blank facial expression. It worked. With a hint of disappointment in her voice, she turned her attention to showering love on her small team.

Esther then asked, "How do the team separation procedures work? Does it come to your shop and influence the setup?"

Rachel responded that "in Kinder we separated the information and the team. Other times we will make a disclosure. Sometimes the clients make us agree that if a team works for one side, it will not work for the other for X period of time."

A member of Rachel's team, Manny, said they didn't keep meeting notes of their internal meetings. "Solutions, however, are captured in the CABS system."

Johnathon asked him, "Can we have copies of whatever you have?" The faces on Goldman's team made me immediately think whatever CABS system records they had would probably not amount to much.

The meeting ended shortly thereafter. We walked out of the conference room and made our way toward the Goldman regulator floor. As
soon as it was safe, the words "They don't have a conflicts-of-interest program," "Can you believe it?," "Yikes," and "Wow" flew in every direction.
We were all in agreement at that point—Silva, Esther, Lily, Johnathon,
Analisa, and me. On top of not having a firm-wide conflicts-of-interest
policy, Goldman didn't seem to have a firm-wide conflicts-of-interest
program. Panic and worry washed over the group in waves.

Personally I was not at all surprised. After all the reading and preparation I had done, I expected to see and hear from Goldman pretty
much what I saw and heard. Given the reactions I saw from the other
regulators, a little hope began to spring up in my heart that something
would be done. Everyone seemed so determined.

My worry was that in all the excitement, all the focus would shift
to conflicts, at the expense of the growing list of issues I was encoun-
tering in other Goldman divisions. Issues that seemed to point at problems just as big if not bigger than conflicts of interest.

Johnathon, Lily, Analisa, Tom, and I quickly broke away from the
main group. We had another meeting to go to with Goldman—this
time to go over their risk assessment system.

By this point a pretty consistent pattern had begun to emerge.
Johnathon had asked for the meeting to be scheduled based on some
already-identified issues—in this case insufficiently developed risk assessments. The meeting would be led by a senior person—in this case
Erin and her colleague Wendy, who was in charge of risk assessments
at Goldman.

A list of problems plaguing the unit—all worthy of follow-up and
tagging as MRA or MRIAs—would promptly follow. Specifically, in
the case of this particular meeting, they went from the low number of
countries whose laws were being tracked through the decision to not
use rankings to ensure consistency when dealing with issues all the
way to the lack of a system audit trail.

Disagreements would be voiced—particularly, when Johnathon asked how Goldman knew they had captured everything so that the company could measure and track its compliance with every law it was supposed to be complying with. Erin and Wendy tag-teamed to answer, "The objective is to capture the key ones. We took a look at the reg[u-lation]s and decided which were the relevant ones."

For example, they said, Regulation E (wire transfers) and Regula-tion B (equal credit opportunity) were left out, as they "are not appli-cable to us." I took copious notes and composed my list of follow-ups.

The meeting demanded formidable displays of self-control on the part of regulators. I bit my lip again as I watched Johnathon's efforts to hide his snicker behind an intentional cough when Erin claimed, "I talk to colleagues and benchmark with competitors." She may very well have done so, but the risk-assessment infrastructure she was try-ing to impress us with seemed at second glance to have more in com-mon with a buggy than with the fancy cars we knew their competitors were driving.

A dash or two of arrogance for drama was always included in these meetings. For instance, Erin insisted that "we know what we do." The performance ended with regulators walking out and telling each other that this division seemed to have some serious issues that needed to be addressed.

As we walked back to the Goldman regulator floor after this meet-ing, Lily ventured a casual compliment, something along the lines of: "Wow, Goldman has done a lot of work building that system and set-ting up those thirty-four countries, right?"

Luckily, Johnathon, Analisa, and Tom were around. Each one took turns pointing out that one of Goldman's competitors tracked some-thing like sixty countries, and two other competitors tracked over seventy. I jumped in to add that yet another competitor tracked eighty-nine. Ever suspicious, Lily asked me how I knew that.

"Because I worked on a similar project," I answered. "It took our team one year to build the system, complete with an audit trail, and pull the eighty-nine legal opinions together. According to Erin, Gold-man has taken two years and completed maybe thirty-four countries? Not good enough. They need to get a move on this."

Lily's face grew serious. Out of the corner of my eye I saw Analisa smile.

The second we walked onto the Goldman regulator floor I knew something was wrong. The New York Fed team was gathered inside the fishbowl conference room. As I got closer to my desk Delilah signaled me to join the meeting immediately. Although I joined fifteen minutes after the meeting had started, it took just a few seconds for me to open my notebook and start taking notes.

Silva was clearly in a bad mood. Sitting as usual at the center of the table, face red, blue eyes blazing, he was forcefully rattling off a list of instructions on how he expected the risk specialists—us—and his relationship managers—in this case, the business-line specialists—to behave: the way a military leader would. "When there is a disagreement as to a meeting, whether it goes forward or not, the risk specialist always wins." The exception was meetings with the forty-first floor—Goldman's C-suite. For those he had "the last say as SSO."

After a brief pause he added, "It is helpful for the risk specialist to understand that they can go forward. We do expect the risk specialist to always touch base with the business specialist. I want the business specialist to share with the risk specialists what is going on." Again he paused, looking around the room. I glanced up at the silent and sullen faces around the room.

"If it's the case that a particular risk stripe creates a pattern of interactions with the firm that is not the best, then that is another story. We will revisit the situation if it turns into a problem." I wondered what he meant by "not the best."

He wasn't done, though. Weighing his words, he reminded the team, "There are consequences regarding our interactions between the state and the FDIC." My mind inevitably flashed back to the meeting where he first warned us about this. "You do get more out of the firm if you let them talk." I wondered whether this morning's meeting had anything to do with his mood. "Be careful about taking an interrogatory attitude—it may not help you."

He continued, "As for the firm, we are seeing more grumpiness, but in the end we get what we want. Goldman over time will get more annoyed with us, and I plan on annoying them quite a lot."

This last bit was clearly an attempt to lighten the mood a bit. But it fell flat. No one smiled.

Silva then tried a different tactic. He said he was positive, casual, and complimentary in his interactions with Goldman but had "zero tolerance for threats or bullying." "Don't engage directly" he warned us, if we encountered any threats or bullying from Goldman. "Do let me know so I can engage them."

I kept wondering, *What happened?*

Finally someone pointed out that quite a few people in the room had no clue what had transpired. *Thank you,* I thought. The two Mikes alternatively spoke up and tried to explain while simultaneously attempting to disguise things a bit. Apparently a couple of risk specialists had wanted to question Goldman. Ryan O'Hara, the relationship manager in Silva's team, had tried to stop them. A fight had broken out. I followed everyone's eyes and, looking toward the right side of the room, focused on Ryan. The contrast between his white shirt and his deep red head made him look like a really angry cherry-flavored lollipop. Not far from him sat other risk specialists, less red but almost equally as unhappy. A few months later one of those risk specialists would end up leaving the New York Fed.

The internal pushback had become palpable. People inside the Fed were defending the interests of Goldman Sachs to the point of obstruction.

I again thought back on the movie *Gaslight,* as Ingrid Bergman walks into the house. "It's all dead in here. The whole place seems to smell of death."

This time I didn't smile.

CHAPTER 11

How Do You Think They Are Getting Ahead?

"We don't share information with the board."

I had just invited Donna and Lily to my second monthly meeting with Telephone Bob, our designated contact in the Federal Reserve Board. Terry was going. Lily was going. But Donna wouldn't go—her reason: "We don't share information with the board." By now that did not surprise me. As I made my way to the conference room I briefly glanced back at her desk. She was not there. She was already on her way to Mila's office—her boss.

Terry, Lily, and I sat in the conference room with Telephone Bob on the line. He started the meeting by announcing that he was interested in ensuring that "consumer issues are found and corrected and followed to completion." He complained about not receiving information since July and was concerned about inconsistencies he had found "in terms of the info posted into the databases."

There were "sixteen, seventeen ITRAK issues, fifteen were Litton related," but he could no longer see them in the system. Bob wanted to know what was going on.

Silence reigned. There was no way for me to answer Bob's question: I did not even have system access yet. I looked meaningfully at Lily. She sat there silently, chewing her pen, considering what to say. Eventually, after some hemming and hawing from Lily and Terry, Bob was told that "Rob had the Litton issues taken out of ITRAK." Rob was Terry's boss.

Bob immediately asked, "Are the issues gone, or is it still open [be-cause of the] lookback? The consent order still remains."

Excellent question, I thought. I had watched Johnathon fail at get-ting clarity around the Litton issues and the consent order from Lily, Mila, and Donna. Again I looked at Lily. She sat there smiling, saying nothing. After a few seconds of silence Bob said he wanted an answer. Because I now had Johnathon's job, it fell to me to get him the answers.

I told him I would try, privately wondering how on earth I was go-ing to do that.

Bob then brought up another MRA in the system—this one for a violation of Regulation B (equal credit opportunity). *Wait—what?* I re-member thinking. My mind flew back to the moment during the morn-ing's risk-assessment meeting when Wendy and Erin said Goldman had specifically left Regulation B out of the risk-assessment system, as it did not apply to them.

Yet here I was, hearing from Bob about their Regulation B issues.

According to him, the issue had been identified in Avelo Mortgage, a Goldman subsidiary. Lily just chewed on her pen and remained silent. Once again Bob asked me to find out what was happening. I left the meeting with more detective work to do—on top of my actual work.

I had been back at my desk for a few minutes when Silva walked over, asking Lily and me to join him in the fishbowl conference room. He looked like a man fighting back waves of panic. For a second my thoughts flew to Johnathon and his warning about "the meeting." I quickly grabbed my notebook and pen and followed him and Lily into the conference room, steeling myself for the worst-case scenario I could imagine—which had become, over the years, my default mental state.

Esther joined us just as Silva took his customary seat. Outside the window the sky was quickly growing dark. He began by telling us that he wanted to discuss the Goldman team's performance in the conflicts meeting. As he looked at each of us in turn, he alluded to the "vampire squid" metaphor part of Matt Taibbi's recent *Rolling Stone* article about Goldman, saying he agreed with it.

He then professed his deep concern that Goldman did not seem to have a conflicts-of-interest program. Esther and Lily, looking at him with pleasant smiles on their faces and bright eyes, nodded in agreement. So did I.

Although he did not bring up recent history or upcoming events, his panic seemed to have a factual basis. On July 15, 2010, Goldman paid $550 million to the SEC and promised it would reform its business practices in order to settle charges that Goldman misled investors in its marketing materials in the Abacus collateralized debt obligation deal and agreed to a ban on committing intentional fraud in the future.

The following April the Senate released a 640-page report, the results of a two-year inquiry, which concluded that Goldman, rife with conflicts issues, had misled investors about positions it took against their clients when betting in the housing market. The Senate asked the Justice Department and the SEC to look into violations of law by Goldman and possible perjury charges against Lloyd Blankfein, the bank's CEO.

Yet here we were, barely six months later, looking at Goldman's handling of transactions like Kinder Morgan–El Paso and getting the sense that the bank's conflicts program was riddled with doublespeak designed to mask its failure to tackle the bank's conflicts. On top of that, Goldman's lawyers and senior management were talking out of both sides of their mouth in an attempt to mislead and confuse the regulators.

In the past, when Goldman wasn't a bank, this would have been bad. Now that it was a bank—and one that had been bailed out by the public—Goldman's continued failure to fix this could, under the right circumstances, turn into much bigger sanctions against it.

His voice full of disbelief, Silva expressed shock that only "one employee [had been] let go in four years" due to conflicts violations. With a brief laugh he noted that Goldman "choked on the backchecking issues."

Why these two issues? I remember wondering.

He then asked Esther and Lily what they thought.

Esther glanced at Lily before answering. She started by saying that it "resonated with her that the deal clearing is different from the one that was approved." Michael nodded and quickly went on to state he was "skeptical" that they were managing their conflicts. He believed they were not "being managed well at all."

All three of us nodded in agreement.

Esther went on to voice her concern that "there are no walls within the merchant banking law." Lily agreed. I quickly looked at Esther. As far as I knew she was not an attorney—I presumed that was why she was not articulating this quite the way an attorney would. I decided to give her the benefit of the doubt. I looked at Silva. It seemed from his facial expression that his mind was following my train of thought. He said that Goldman was being "disingenuous [when saying] that they are just like other firms."

Silence. It seemed like Lily had no follow-up to her boss's comments. Silva then turned his attention to me, asking what my initial thoughts were. I considered my answer for a moment, trying to come up with the best list I could. I paid particular attention to not repeat anything I had already heard so as to move the conversation forward and not take credit.

I ran through a list of issues, among them Goldman's lack of a real conflicts check, no compliance involvement, and no clear documentation. Silva, Esther, and Lily sat in silence, looking at me. Their expressions went from serious to puzzled to panicked. I guess they didn't expect to hear the truth.

After a few seconds he nervously announced that he didn't want Goldman to "fail in a [disorderly] way." Indeed, he was afraid that "conflicts of interest will lead to client runoff."

Looking straight at me almost pleadingly, Silva asked me what Johnathon thought and what my next steps would be. On my left, out of the corner of my eye, I could see Esther and Lily honing in on my reaction. That's when I sized up the situation. This being a conversation, I only had a few seconds.

Silva's comment about a disorderly failure could be interpreted as implying that if the New York Fed took action against Goldman for their conflicts issues, somehow we may be deemed "at fault" for triggering the failure and shutdown of Goldman and, potentially, another financial crisis. By "we" he seemed to mean the New York Fed in general and the individuals assigned to supervise Goldman in particular. But then again, our job was to regulate, not to worry about a bank's well-being if they were not complying with the law.

Still, longtime New York Fed employees may see things differently. An event like that, coming after the New York Fed had stepped in to bail out Goldman, could add another layer of embarrassment and complexity for the New York Fed.

We could end up losing our jobs.

His fear of client runoff could mean that if, somehow, current and future Goldman clients found out how badly the bank managed its conflicts, they could pull their money out or refuse to hire or do business with them in the future. If this were to happen quickly, it could turn into another Lehman situation, with Goldman collapsing in a matter of months.

Oh, please!, I remember thinking. Whenever there was a risk of a disorderly failure, regulators historically have arranged for bigger banks to step in and absorb the collapsed bank. There were plenty of bigger banks around who sold the same products Goldman did that could be asked to step in and absorb it.

As for client runoff, that was extremely unlikely. My mind quickly flashed back to the last time massive client runoff and a criminal conviction had quickly brought down the accounting firm Arthur Andersen as collateral damage in the collapse of Enron, the energy company. I quickly concluded the situation was not exactly analogous. Arthur Andersen's reputation in the market was different from Goldman's. The government had not stepped in to save it before the scandal, as it had done with Goldman. Having done so, letting the bank fail so soon after would not look good.

Lastly, I thought of my position within the New York Fed. My job as senior bank examiner and legal and compliance risk specialist was to find issues, document them, and work to get them fixed. Taxpayers paid for my services. They were my client. My loyalty was to them. If Goldman did not fix the issues I found, the Justice Department or senior people at other regulatory agencies could perhaps one day use the record I built to support a legal case against Goldman. This is not to say that I did not understand the political dilemmas Silva's comment seemed to be hinting at. The bottom line was that they were all above my pay grade.

Not liking any of my options, I decided to take the most obvious and safest route out. I told Silva that Johnathon and I had only briefly touched base due to the nonstop meetings I had been in since we left the Goldman conflicts meeting. I added that during our brief meeting Johnathon had expressed deep concern about what he had seen and heard coming out of Goldman. I finished by saying I would be discussing the meeting with both Johnathon and my legal and compliance team to determine next steps.

Silva answered "Okay" and gave me as a takeaway some points he wanted me to follow up on. He asked me to talk to Connor O'Sullivan and Johnathon about following up with Goldman on whether Goldman should have a firm-wide reputational-risk and/or ethics officer and whether they thought an attorney instead of Rachel should head the conflicts group.

He studied my reaction to his requests. I sat there, impassive, not betraying my thoughts or emotions. It seemed to have worked: Silva's demeanor changed from panic to a somewhat calmer seriousness. He declared he had "not got the sense they have something that will explode." In a way that seemed to try to get me on his side, he mused that the "Fed has the impression that they are on both sides on every deal." The question, he wondered out loud, was "do we decide as a policy matter that Goldman is too big to manage these conflicts?"

I repressed a smile, quickly looking down at my notebook, and took notes.

———

THE FOLLOWING DAY Johnathon and I walked into Michael Koh's office for our meeting to go over Goldman's current list of pending MRAs and MRIAs. After a brief discussion about my possible assistance with preparing the annual report's institutional overview, Koh moved on to Litton. According to him, three things were open and being worked on: (a) the lookback; (b) the consent order, for which Goldman had chosen Navigant as the consulting firm to assist them with cleaning up the issues; and (c) the memorandum of understanding issued to Goldman before it became a bank holding company. Michael indicated that due to some internal back-and-forth, the contract with Navigant had not yet been signed.

I addressed Koh directly: "Bob said he went into the ITRAK system and could not find the Litton issues. He asked if the consent order was still valid."

Without missing a beat, Koh told me to ask Bob "if he is coordinating with Owen," adding "Owen is in charge of the Litton consent order." He could not remember Owen's last name and suggested I ask Lily or Donna for it.

He then went on to explain that Goldman had been "issued a consent order focused on postsale environment." One MRIA was relevant—it pertained to late fee remediation. "All the other ones go away and are closed," he said, adding that "we will make Donna owner for the Litton ones, and she will be in ITRAK."

Wait, I thought, *Didn't I just tell you Bob said he could not see those Litton MRAs in ITRAK anymore?* I focused on taking notes to hide my growing unease. Something was not adding up. I looked at Johnathon. He remained silent, his face placidly serious. Then again, I already knew he was trying to protect Koh because he did not warn me about him.

Michael went on to explain that for the Regulation W MRAs I was to work with Johnathon, Mila, and Donna; for the Bank Secrecy Act and AML MRAs I was to work with Irene; and for the MRA issued as part of the 2009 roll-up he would eventually assign a person for me to work with.

I privately wondered what Johnathon would say about me continuing to work with Mila and Donna on closing MRAs.

I asked Michael what the expectations were for me to complete this work in light of the fact that I would not have access to ITRAK until my training was completed. The first of the two mandatory training sessions would not be until the end of January and beginning of February. I knew ITRAK system access was crucial if I was to (a) issue new MRAs and MRIAs to Goldman, (b) monitor Goldman's progress in addressing existing open MRAs and MRIAs, and, once Goldman had fixed them, (c) close open MRAs and MRIAs.

Addressing only the first part of my question, he explained that transmittal letters with the MRAs and MRIAs, the bank's responses, and the due dates—that is, the date the bank was due to have corrected the issues—were posted in BOND. BOND was another New York Fed computer database I did not yet have access to. As for the Goldman team, the secretary "inputs MRAs into ITRAKS." She then informs Koh and he "ensures accuracy."

He then instructed me to go into ITRAK and BOND to get the due dates and to set up in ITRAK "to get email to remind you to follow up" on the issues. I could then put together my project plan for closing the issues. "Keep in mind," he said as he concluded that part of the meeting, "some are closed by exams, others with a simple meeting."

Michael quickly moved on to the annual report (for which he used the Fed-speak term "roll-up"). Speaking to me as if he were my boss, he began: I was to take a look at the June 2010 letter issued to Goldman, which highlighted three issues. The bank had responded and was in the process of addressing them. At some point we needed to respond to that letter, saying whether the issues were corrected.

"Given that Litton is gone, and considering the ongoing work," I was to consider a series of six factors when thinking about the roll-up: (1) what new MRAs and MRIAs had come up, (2) how they remediated the open issues, (3) the severity of the new MRAs issued, (4) weigh Litton in, (5) any issues identified by internal audit, and (6) issues that came up during continuous monitoring.

As he went through each of the factors he wanted me to consider, I took notes. I wondered how could the Litton issues be gone if Navigant, the consultant Goldman was going to hire to clean up the mess, had not yet begun work? To me this was illogical. Somehow I needed to figure out what was going on.

Also, what was Johnathon thinking? Michael Koh was acting as if he were my boss in front of Johnathon, my real boss. I occasionally glanced up at him, trying to get a read on his face, looking for just how seriously he wanted me to take Koh's instructions. But I couldn't tell.

Michael closed the meeting with his take on the institutional overview. He insisted we would not be updating it. I wondered what Connor would think of that, as he had instructed me to offer my services, and here was Michael rejecting the offer.

In any case, neither Johnathon nor I committed to follow his orders, as he was not supposed to be ordering us around. We had Connor's orders to follow, and those had to do with SR 08-8.

Once at my desk Johnathon suggested we discuss the MRAs later and instead focus on the Goldman conflicts meeting. I updated him on my meeting with Silva, Esther, and Lily. He said he was already working on setting up a meeting with Connor on Monday. We quickly agreed on the basics for our Monday morning team meeting presentation. Looking around to make sure no one was within earshot, Johnathon then asked how things were going with Lily, Mila, and Donna. I replied along the lines of "pretty much as expected." I told him I had a few stories. He replied he was looking forward to hearing them on Monday afternoon.

———

WHEN MONDAY CAME AROUND, Johnathon took the lead in the legal and compliance meeting. He noted that one of the criticisms of the New York Fed was that it took too long to verify whether the banks had properly fixed the MRA and MRIA issues. As a result, the issues remained open for too long. There was pressure—and an expectation—that the currently open MRIA and MRA issues "will be cleared off by the end of this year. Remember, some may need exams to close. Keep in mind that this feeds into the RAP and the roll-ups."

I quickly glanced around the room. Some of my colleagues looked slightly uncomfortable. Other shifted on their seats.

Connor O'Sullivan added that we should "look at the materiality of the issue and whether or not you feel you have information that is sufficient for you to be comfortable to close the issue. If after it's closed it blows up, we own the blow-up too."

Something along the lines of, *That explains why so many issues are still open,* ran through my mind. With respect to MRAs, Connor said that "when you write them it needs to be clear what you want them to do. But not so detailed—we are not their consultants." I thought, *There he goes again.* Be clear, but not so detailed. Make them feel pain, but not too much. Still, he was the boss, so I wrote it down.

Finally, Connor indicated that each of us was to "have a discussion with the SSO so they have a sense of your game plan in January—not before." That was because our legal and compliance annual supervision plan was "still being fleshed out, and we still need to customize [it] for the institution." By this he meant that the other risk embeds and I were to take today's additional input and create a tailored annual supervision plan to guide our work at our respective banks. We were also to let our team leader know how much time we were spending weekly on SSO requests. So from now on, I had to inform Johnathon how much time I spent on requests by Silva and his team. That would be interesting.

It was still the much-needed coffee breaks that helped keep my sanity, as I continued to meet with other people and gather additional color. I happily bonded with my fellow embeds, who shared a lot of my concerns regarding how to make this work, especially if we got stuck on an issue in which those sitting above us had differing views. A few voiced concerns that they had too much to cover to handle it all by themselves. I also discussed with them what happened during the conflicts meeting with Goldman. A few agreed to get me copies of what they had seen at their respective institutions.

I also continued to meet and bond with colleagues working outside my risk group. They plugged me into the goings-on in other areas of the New York Fed. Some of their anecdotes—such as women getting paid less than men—were entirely expected. Others, if true, were even more disturbing. For instance, there was the female employee who said that a couple of months into the job colleagues had bullied her. She had been forced to give up her password to a subscription the New York Fed had purchased under her name so everyone in the team could access the information. Upon discovering the New York Fed was not paying their fair share, the provider threatened to sue the New York Fed. Furious, management allegedly responded by reprimanding her and threatening to fire her. She was terrified because she could not afford to lose the job.

I also met former New York Fed employees who began sharing their own anecdotes. "Have you gotten any good trading tips yet?" one of them asked.

"What do you mean?" I answered.

According to this former examiner, what a lawyer would refer to as "insider trading" was more than common; indeed, it was a side-gig of sorts. The trick was to meet and hang out with the right people, which, according to this examiner, were those assigned to the different trading desks. All sorts of information was apparently being improperly passed around between the banks and within the New York Fed itself.

The former examiner was, of course, not a lawyer. I pointed out that improperly using insider information to make money could, you know, get you into all sorts of legal trouble.

"What? That's illegal?" the former examiner retorted.

"Yes" I answered—apparently, neither ethics nor basic legal concepts had been part of this former examiner's fancy academic degree.

After considering it for a moment, the former examiner stated, "Not if you don't get caught."

"What if somebody throws you under the bus?" I asked.

Without skipping a beat the former New York Fed examiner answered, "Why would they do that? They are doing it too. Why else do you think they are working there? How do you think they are getting ahead?"

CHAPTER 12

Record Tampering

As we approached the end of the year my days were split between the mundane and the eyebrow raising. My next meeting with Johnathon could be classified as mundane: business as it should have been. I started by retelling my close encounters with the business-line specialists. His reaction, in so many words: *I told you so.* As the two Mikes had not yet called me into their office for a one-on-one meeting, he decided it was best to wait until that happened before moving forward. He then gave me new issues to look at within Goldman—as if I did not already have enough on my plate.

We then turned our attention to conflicts. He expressed shock at how he walked out of the conflicts meeting with the impression that Goldman had practically admitted they can't do business if they are not on both sides. I then told him about Michael Silva's meeting and his follow-up requests. Johnathon said we needed to discuss this further with Connor.

He then instructed me on the list of items he wanted me to follow up on. These included figuring out why Goldman didn't have conflicts policy documents, why no conflicts checks were being done, and why there were no Chinese walls.

He also asked me to analyze the lack of qualifications of Rachel and the other Goldman employees tasked with handling conflicts. Finally, he asked me to look into the problematic employee reporting lines. For instance, Goldman's CEO had been personally involved in the conflicts decision-making process of the Kinder Morgan–El Paso transaction.

This was a clear signal to us regulators that the most senior Goldman person making conflicts-of-interest decisions was the person everyone reported to. Complicating the conflicts issue was the fact that the CEO had stock in and is a client of the bank. I wrote it all down.

Johnathon finished by instructing me to get ready to present to our legal and compliance risk group on what transpired during our conflicts meeting with Goldman. Right before I left, Johnathon reminded me to follow up with María, our group's secretary, to set up a meeting with Connor to bring him up to speed. I left with the feeling that something would come out of all this. But I was wrong.

The following day I was back at Goldman. Silva seemed once again to be in a state of panic, this time because of Europe. "Be prepared for the crash," he told us with a red face and a moist brow, adding, "Remember, if you are on vacation, bring your computer home with you" as well as any materials we felt we needed to have close by to do our work. We should look at any existing issues and think about "which metrics you would want to get, where to find it, and so on." We should "have handy contacts for the general counsel, chief compliance officer, divisional legal, and compliance heads." I glanced around. Fearful faces blanketed the room.

Silva then informed us that management was considering a change in the process used to rate supervised institutions. They were "talking about moving to quarterly ratings as opposed to annual." I quickly glanced up from my notebook and swept my eyes across the room. Eye rolls, smirks, and half-smiles popped across the board.

He then gave us another fly-paint lecture. He reminded us that we "are expected to fly paint," adding we were also "expected to fess up to our mistakes." The team listened silently and nodded here and there, seemingly in agreement. When it came to nodding, Silva's team flew paint to perfection.

The next day, just as I had settled in to work on transcribing meeting minutes, I got pulled again into the fishbowl for a quick, previously unscheduled SSO meeting. It was time to announce promotions.

Silva enthusiastically told the team that the Board of Directors met. After pausing for effect and looking around the room, he continued, they "elected Mila an officer of the bank!" A round of applause greeted Mila, who happily smiled and bobbed her head up and down, her hair following along.

After the applause died down Silva continued, telling the team the board also promoted "Michael Koh to assistant vice president." Another round of applause followed. Koh cracked only the briefest of half-smiles.

Mila and Koh got promotions. So much for getting rid of the old guard. So much for implementing a new supervisory structure. So much for changing a culture that was rotten to its core.

"Carpe diem," Silva said in closing, sending us back to work.

DAYS LATER, on December 19, the legal and compliance group meeting began with a presentation from the AML subgroup. They would be conducting an AML exam at all the big banks. The point was to get a sense of the AML operations and get "some view into what the AML risk is." They were looking to "partner" with the legal and compliance risk specialists in order to obtain a "temperature check" for our organization. Work was to begin in the new year.

From now on, all AML-related communications pertaining to our respective banks needed to be sent to Ellen, the leader of this group. At the end of the presentation she asked for feedback on the status of each of the banks.

Johnathon replied that Goldman was particularly high risk with respect to their AML operations. I concurred.

I then gave my presentation on Goldman's conflicts issues to the legal and compliance group. When I finished, I sat in silence, waiting for them to respond. I had worked with Johnathon and discussed the topic with almost all the other risk embeds the previous week. They all knew what was coming and made supportive comments. So I focused my attention on Connor, Emma, and Riley.

Riley voiced his opinion in favor of issuing findings. Connor looked back silently with a face full of fear. He asked whether I had been experiencing pushback from Silva and his team. I answered along the lines of "not on this issue." I did mention other things I had seen and experienced that I thought fell under the category of pushback.

Connor asked me how Silva had reacted to the meeting. I relayed what he had said in the postmeeting, complete with his reference to the "vampire squid" comment, and included his follow-up requests. Connor then waited, perhaps searching for something else. I studied his face: something seemed to be wrong. Eventually I was given in- structions to dig deeper into Goldman's conflicts files and to report back if I experienced any pushback.

After encouraging us to go full-in on using the enhanced continu- ous-monitoring process to engage in abbreviated bank examinations, Connor brought the meeting to a close.

During the thirty-minute break in between meetings I headed to the coffee room for my second cup. On the way there a couple of other risk embeds caught up with me. One of them brought up the topic of conflicts. "What did you think of Connor's reaction?" I asked him.

"He was afraid," the risk specialist answered. "Michael Silva is very powerful," he added.

After checking to see if no one he deemed untrustworthy was over- hearing, he continued, "Michael Silva has the support of the high- est echelons" at the New York Fed—by which he meant Bill Dudley. Connor was new to his position, having come over from the legal de- partment not that long ago. According to my colleague, Connor didn't know how the politics worked yet.

As other people began gathering in the conference room, he leaned over and warned me to be careful: "Even Connor is afraid of him."

My next meeting started with Emma, another of Connor's dep- uties, explaining that the new "enhanced continuous monitoring" process meant we could issue MRIAs and MRAs to the bank on the fly, needing just one or two examples of identified problems. *Good,* I thought. *This would work for the Kinder Morgan–El Paso and conflicts issues. Maybe we can issue a dozen MRIAs and MRAs and move on to the other issues.*

Riley then warned us about closing old MRAs and MRIAs: "Don't rush to close something just because there is pressure to do so. The pressure is a carry-over from the previous [supervision] model. We now own the risk, so we need to be comfortable—not the SSO team." I wondered what the two Mikes would think of this advice. I remembered Johnathon had delivered a very different message to the team just a few days before, and I privately wondered if Connor and his leadership team were on the same page with respect to this particular topic.

At some point Riley asked if anyone had any questions. I used the opportunity to voice my concerns surrounding my ability to close the Goldman MRIAs and MRAs. I lacked both the tools and the information to really move forward. I also talked about what I had noticed over the past few weeks: how a number of the Goldman SSO team members often leapt to the bank's defense and worried how Goldman would react to negative criticism from the risk specialists. I noted that the two Mikes were telling the team to withhold critical information from the Federal Reserve Board and other regulatory agencies, emphasizing the need to protect Goldman.

Riley glanced at Emma and at Johnathon, looking like a man desperately trying to stop himself from saying something. To my surprise, he didn't say anything. No one did. All I saw was fear; all I heard was silence.

Shortly after that meeting we headed out for the Christmas lunch at Harry's Italian Restaurant. We sat next to whomever we chose around the large table, which made for some strange pairings. The awkwardness dissipated when the pizza arrived. I nervously looked around for a slice I could eat—I have food allergies that make eating out a bit of a challenge. For a little while we all put thoughts of work aside and talked about our respective holiday plans.

On the way back to the office I asked some of my colleagues what they thought of what I was seeing at Goldman. Again, it was the fellow risk specialist who warned me about Silva who provided the clearest explanation. He said that I should not be surprised, as Goldman was an incredibly divisive topic within the New York Fed. There were a lot of people who felt Goldman was getting away with things it should just not be getting away with. I asked about the other banks—surely they were getting away with stuff too.

"Goldman is different" is all he would answer. Everyone agreed.

THE FOLLOWING DAY began with an overview of the compliance function supporting Goldman's Securities division. The presentation was
led by Dick Glass, head of this compliance division at Goldman Sachs.
He was a thin-boned, compact man. His frame was wrapped in a
tight-fitting, buttoned-up suit. He spoke as if to an empty room.

During the next hours Dick went through the organizational structure of the compliance division and what they were working on, reassuring us that Goldman was "very good at risk management." Dick
had a section in his presentation dedicated to conflicts and another to
Chinese walls. It seemed the word had spread around Goldman about
the questions we were asking.

Regarding conflicts Dick volunteered his take on what he called
Goldman's "perceived conflicts." "Market making automatically requires us to be on the opposite side of half of our clients," he said.
When they have multiple clients in different parts of the firm, he explained, "we are shorting [the position] at the same time, typically because another client has requested we short it. We know this ends up
in the press." He punctuated this last statement with a "we don't care"
look on his face. I wrote it all down.

After a dramatic pause he looked up at us, contorting his face into
an insincere expression of horror. "The amount of new regulations is
astonishing," he complained. "We won't be able to comply with [them]
completely due to [the] velocity [and] ambiguity of the changes."

He looked around the room, probably unaware that he looked like
he was trying to get away with something.

I quickly put my head down and bit my lip to stop myself from laughing out loud. Our reactions must have had an effect: when Dick turned
his attention to the issue of Chinese walls, he became considerably
more reserved. But that didn't make us forget his claims. Meeting after
meeting we were hearing Goldman's senior management brazenly tell
us that they would not comply with regulations.

After grabbing lunch, it was time for the weekly meeting with Silva
and his team. New York Fed management's focus that week was on giving out evaluations and merit increases. I was still in my probationary

employment period and had not gone through the evaluations cycle because I was still too new.

The roll-up was still "up in the air, but it looks like June." After another warning to make sure our contact list, computers, and all material necessary to do our work was with us just in case Europe went haywire, Silva pointed out that the "board [is] complaining the SSOs are not cooperating." But then he added, "The exception was [the Goldman team]."

After the meeting I walked back to my desk, unsure what to think of this. Maybe the board was misinformed? I had witnessed a few members of the SSO team—including Silva—make it clear on a few occasions that they were not going to cooperate with the board. Or was he perhaps talking about the Goldman Board, not the Federal Reserve Board? I remember casually flipping back through my meeting minutes, looking for reassurance. Then I remembered that perhaps this had something to do with the fact that I had been sharing information with Telephone Bob. After a few minutes I put that aside and went back to transcribing the ever-growing pile of meeting minutes.

That Thursday I met with Johnathon to again talk about conflicts. I would end up having over twenty-five meetings over the space of seven and a half months on the topic of conflicts. He wanted to make sure I added two more items to my list of follow-ups with Goldman before conflicting holiday calendars would prevent us from touching base.

The first one was to find out the New York Fed's policy on Chinese walls for legal and compliance people. He added that "this was important because if the Fed doesn't require it, then we can't force anyone else." The second revolved around "why the compliance division was not part of the conflicts of interest determination. Does the Fed require it? We may need to challenge that as well." I wrote it down.

"I am almost finished with the meeting minutes. I should be done by early next week," I reminded him. He told me to go ahead and email them out when I was done. We wished each other Merry Christmas and went our separate ways.

———————

I RETURNED TO WORK right after the holidays, on December 28. The Goldman regulator floor was quiet. Most people were away for the week. This gave me a chance to work on typing up the meeting minutes without the incessant distractions of meetings and interruptions from various members of Silva's team. Right after I finished transcribing I queued up the email, copying everyone who had attended the meetings, attached the meeting minutes, and hit "send."

Relieved, I looked away from my computer toward the door and contemplated getting up and going for a second cup of coffee.

At that moment I noticed Esther walking out of her office. She looked directly at me and walked into Silva's office. After a few minutes she came back out, looked at me again, and returned to her office. After a few more minutes Silva walked out of his office.

He looked serious. He looked ... *furious*.

He walked toward me and, assuming a friendly tone, asked me if I was available for a quick meeting in his office. "Sure," I answered. Grabbing my notebook and pen, I walked back with him. I sat down by the table, with my back facing the door. Instead of joining me there, he sat in his desk chair, in a pose reminiscent of Amenemhat II's Egyptian statue at the Metropolitan Museum of Art, keeping as much physical distance from me as he could.

He began by saying he had received some troubling feedback about me from a few people on his team. I looked back at him with my best poker face. "I wanted to give you some mentoring feedback," he continued.

Here we go, I thought, Johnathon's warning blaring in my mind.

Silva began by telling me how important credibility was at the New York Fed. "When you say something is wrong you want them to give that respect. ... Be careful that you are sure we have evidence on hand." He paused. "Credibility at the Fed is about subtleties, perceptions as opposed to realities." And then he warned me, "They will freeze you out" if they don't perceive you as credible.

Of course, he did not say who "they" were.

I finished writing and looked up. He had stopped until I did just that, so I could admire the meaningful look on his face. After a moment he pointed out that the New York Fed "respects most people who are deeply analytical and gather facts and appear unbiased in gathering them. You must be perceived as analytical." Looking straight at me, he concluded, "New people don't perceive how the organization is perceiving them."

Rereading these meeting minutes all these years later, I can still feel as if it was happening for the first time, the mixture of anger and nervous anticipation I felt as I waited for him to be done with his "mentoring" advice. As he spoke, my handwriting changed, as if to reflect my mood. It is not as smooth as it was at the beginning of the meeting.

After a pause Silva continued, "The ones that are taken most seriously are the most quiet ones."

Looking straight at me, he obliquely brought up his team. "Make sure your experience comes out in an unthreatening way, unclouded by biases." He must have felt my simmering rage, for he quickly added, "or, in this case, perceived bias." He then stated it was important that his team "perceives you as very analytical, very team oriented," adding he wanted me to "make sure they feel you respect them." He reminded me that at the New York Fed, "if you want to move to other areas, they ask your colleagues" about you; they "don't look at the [performance] reviews."

The words *flying paint* flashed in my mind.

I decided this would be an excellent opportunity to jump in. I did not write down what I said at that moment in my notes, but the conversation proceeded something like this: "I have spent the past few weeks discussing a number of individuals on your team with my legal and compliance risk management. Johnathon told me what to expect from each of your team members and prepared me for this moment. He said that at some point you would call me into a meeting based on things they had said to you about me."

As I spoke Silva grew increasingly pale.

"Could you give me their names?" Silva asked, while making as if to grab a pen and paper to write them down.

"I am pretty sure we are talking about the same four individuals," I responded.

He pursed his lips and returned my gaze.

"Johnathon instructed me to make sure I went everywhere with other regulators and to never be alone with any of those four individuals." I then added, "I am an attorney. Just because I was not hired to be one does not mean I don't know how to gather evidence."

He looked a touch surprised, as if he did not know I was a lawyer. At first I surmised this had to do with how young I look and how small I am. Then I realized that maybe he had never seen my résumé; after all, he had not interviewed me, and neither had his team. The New York Fed was well known for hiring young people, particularly women, straight out of college. Quite a few people were probably walking around thinking I was one of those young people.

Moving on from his confrontation, I turned my attention to work. I told Michael that Johnathon had added a couple of additional items to the list of evidence we were gathering on conflicts. I asked him if he was okay with that. He quickly agreed.

Having nothing left to say, I thanked him for his mentoring advice. I then asked him if he ever considered mentoring others within the New York Fed. "It is not often that one sees a Latino in such a senior position as you," I told him.

He had revealed that detail about himself a week or so earlier while defending the New York Fed's decision not to punish an employee for posting racist opinions on Facebook. He told us during the team meeting that one side of his family had illegally crossed over the Mexican border many decades ago, back when the United States did not police it. He was aware, he told us, that not looking like he was Latino had been of great help to him in his military, banking, and legal career, but he was still half-Mexican, and the comments had offended him. The law, however, he had argued, was the law, and the employee had exercised his freedom of speech.

"I can't climb any higher," he said to me, matter-of-factly.

"Why?" I asked, expecting, I confess, to hear all about the Hispanic glass ceiling from his perspective. I am always curious to read and hear about other people's experiences.

"I've made too many mistakes over the years," he replied.

On my way out Silva asked me if I could print the meeting minutes I had circulated—Delilah, his secretary, was not around. I did it as soon as I got back to my desk.

Sometime before noon Esther walked up to my desk. "Hi," she be-gan. I looked up, noticing the fake smile. The conversation, accord-ing to my minutes, went something like this: "Where did you get the meeting notes template?" she asked. Something about her casual tone made my stomach tighten. I told her I got it from colleagues—Ana-lisa, I think; Johnathon had told me to ask her for samples. But then it was clear that Esther wasn't interested in templates. Trying to sound casual, she continued. "Isn't it interesting how different people hear different things in a meeting?"

I looked right at her, waiting for the punchline.

"I don't recall hearing a lot of the things noted in your meeting notes." I arched my eyebrows and gave her a half-smile, as if to say, *Of course not.* She was taken aback. Whether by the look on my face or by my silence, I could not say. Esther went on, "I did not mean to imply that you have not taken proper notes. It's just that it must be difficult to take good notes when you are leading a meeting."

I knew where she was going with this. I did not want to believe it—but if I am honest with myself, I knew it at that very moment. She seemed to be looking for an elegant way in which to present her re-quest and get me to go along with the plan.

What she seemed to be implying was that she wanted my meeting minutes stricken from the record.

At this point in the conversation I believe she expected me to throw her a bone. But her ask, in my view, amounted to record tampering. The question for me was: How do I let her know that she messed with the wrong person? This being a conversation, I had only a few seconds to decide.

"I did not lead four of the five meetings whose notes I posted. I was shadowing Johnathon. The one I did lead was only perfunctory. Johnathon asked me to focus on taking notes." I tried my best to look at her meaningfully as I said this. She shifted her body from a half-sitting position on my desk to a fully standing one, facing me.

"How can I make corrections to them?" she asked, using a tone and facial expression that seemed to more appropriately match the words, *You need to delete them.*

"You can send me a redline version," I answered, using a polite tone and emphasizing the word "redline." She stared at me in disbelief. I continued. "In the past, when I have circulated documents, people mark them up using redline," I added. This is a common practice among lawyers working on preparing documents because you can track exactly who wrote what and when. It is, at its core, a tool for transparency and accountability.

I could tell by the look on her face that she got it. She smiled back enigmatically. I quickly added, using a *just doing my job* tone of voice: "It wasn't hard to take meeting notes. I was just transcribing what Goldman was saying. I didn't think about what was said until after I had taken down notes. My goal was to gather evidence"—which was what my legal and compliance team had asked me to do.

"Okay," she answered and walked back to her desk. I watched her go and kept my attention focused on her door. Esther never sent me a redline version of the minutes. This made it even clearer what she had been trying to get me to do that day.

A few years later she was hired to work for Erin O'Brien at Goldman Sachs.

Once Esther returned to her office I waited at my desk for her next move. After a minute or two she walked out of her office and into Silva's. Again. This time she sat down across from him. A few minutes after that, she walked out again, looked at me again, and disappeared into her office.

Not long after, Silva walked out of his office. He stared at me. Was that anger I saw? Or was it desperation? Whatever it was, it was intense. I looked right back at him. After a few moments he headed out of the Goldman regulator floor.

I opened my notebook and quickly jotted down some notes on my conversation with Esther. I instinctively sensed the clock was ticking.

As I wrote, my first thought was, *I need to talk to Johnathon as soon as possible.* And then, a more pressing thought.

I need to talk to a lawyer.

CHAPTER 13

The Spy Store

Time moved slower than it ever had that afternoon. I knew I needed to reach out to my friends and get legal advice, but I couldn't talk about this at the office. Not many people were there that day, but Michael Silva and Esther were—and they were watching me. So, while the minutes passed like hours, I racked my brain thinking who within my network of friends I should reach out to for help. I quickly prioritized my friends who were lawyers. But really, most of all, I wanted to see Hendrik.

I discreetly consulted my Blackberry contact directory. About halfway through I realized that no one on my contacts list seemed to have the necessary experience to advise me. I could feel an amorphous wave of panic beginning to take shape somewhere in the pit of my stomach. I took a deep breath and kept going. Toward the end I found two names I thought could point me in the right direction.

I quickly emailed each of them. Short, casual, urgent-sounding but innocuous emails—something like, "Hey! Happy New Year! Are you around?" No details to tip them off or get them in trouble should things go wrong. I prayed they would come through. Next I reached out to Johnathon, but I could not connect with him. I tried to work and kept my eyes on the clock. I left as soon as I could.

After what felt like ages but was maybe a couple of hours, both of my contacts answered. Wilson responded by directly suggesting we catch up early in the New Year. *Shit,* I thought, *I need advice way sooner than that!* Then my friend Samuel got back to me. Luckily he did have time for a quick chat on the phone.

Samuel and I had known each other for about five years. A mutual acquaintance had introduced us when he moved to New York. We quickly bonded over the fact that we were not from New York. I was born in Indiana and raised in Puerto Rico; my parents were from the island. After finishing his medical residency as chief resident, my father relinquished the opportunity to continue practicing medicine in Indiana as well as his role as honorary team doctor to one of the Indy 500 race car teams for the chance to practice medicine in his place of birth. I was three and a half years old when I left Indiana. Samuel was born and raised in Florida. We shared a bit of the same perspective on life in New York City.

Samuel was a "don't mess with me" lawyer with the unusual ability—for a lawyer—to work through complicated math calculations in less time than it takes an average person to blink. I found this out one day when we were both at a meeting. Arguments and negotiations had been going back and forth for a while. At some point someone made the mistake of assuming they could easily pull one over on Samuel. Perhaps it had something to do with his southern drawl or his excessively polite manners. Who knows. Samuel decided enough was enough and orally worked through three calculations in a row in the time it took everyone in the room to blink twice. Smiling calmly, he took a victory lap, drawling something like, "Well, I suppose you will need some time to verify that. Why don't you go ahead and do that right now. I am happy to wait."

The other key feature about Samuel is that he had a passion for government and politics. He was one of those die-hard believers in the government's obligation to use its power to make life better for all of its citizens. The kind of person who walks the walk with such committed sincerity that it would lead a committed government skeptic like Hendrik to immediately label him as "the devil incarnate." This belief trumped Samuel's passion for math and motivated him to go to law school.

Given that we were only a couple of years apart, I would say it even trumped Samuel's common sense.

Unusual for a Gen-Xer, at a certain point Samuel chose to veer away from the private practice of law, a field that, at the time, had better employment prospects due to a relative shortage of warm bodies to do work. Instead, he chose to go into government, an industry overflowing at all levels with healthy, active baby boomers who weren't going anywhere. This meant, in practical terms, that there was an extremely high statistical probability that Samuel would never go as far as he could have gone if he had chosen to continue to work in a field with labor shortages. But Samuel was a believer.

Surprisingly, this belief in the duty of government survived the 2008 financial crisis, better known in certain circles as "the great Gen-X massacre." Prior to the crisis Samuel and I as well as others had gotten to know each other well enough to become friendly and had formed a loose, informal group I like to call the Gen-X Network. We came from different backgrounds and worked in different sectors of the economy. What brought us together were our shared generational experiences.

After just about all of us got laid off during the 2008 financial crisis, we had plenty of time to get together and commiserate. The conversations usually followed the same pattern. First, we would ask each other if we knew of any Gen-Xers who had not gotten fired. Some would then lament that when they got laid off, the price of rent and food was going up and their savings were dwindling down. It fell to me to explain how all three were not only correlated but also the foreseeable consequence of how the government had handled the crisis.

At some point during the conversation the words "government is totally screwing this up" would inevitably pop up, at which point we would turn to Samuel. Unfazed and undaunted, Samuel's attitude and opinions could be summed up as follows: "Not on my watch." Someone—whoever happened to be at that moment going through a bad bout of cynical depression—would point out that it would take a while for all those baby boomers working in government to retire or die. "I am happy to wait my turn," Samuel would respond, with the same smile he gifted those lawyers after rattling off the mathematical calculations.

On top of all this, Samuel had a knack for networking. It came as naturally as breathing. During and after the financial crisis Samuel used that extra time of his to deepen the bench, which now amounted to an incredibly vast nationwide network of contacts from all walks of life and all levels of the seniority ladder.

As I waited to speak with Samuel, I walked in circles around my apartment, pondering how to approach what I imagined would be an unpleasant conversation. After all, Samuel had been one of the few people who had encouraged me to take the job at the New York Fed. I steeled myself for what I expected would be a negative reaction to my story—something along the lines of *I don't believe you.*

Finally, the time for our call arrived. I was alone at home. The years in New York had dulled the southern drawl a bit, but it was still very much there. He asked me what was happening. I started to fill him in, but after a couple of minutes he interrupted me. Apparently Samuel had heard enough.

"I see. This doesn't sound right. You really need a lawyer. ASAP," he began, quickly adding in a concerned, bewildered tone: "This doesn't sound right at all."

"Yeah, that's what I thought," I answered, too surprised and relieved at being believed to question why. "That's why I called you. I know you don't practice in this area, but do you know anyone I can talk to?"

"Have you reached out to anyone else?" he asked.

"One other person so far," I told Samuel and shared the name.

"Good," Samuel responded, adding, "That was one of the names I was going to suggest. I don't think Wilson is the right person, but someone in Wilson's network probably would be. Definitely."

After a pause Samuel continued, "I know just the person you need to speak to. Let me see if this person is willing to meet with you. I will get back to you as soon as I can."

Soon after I hung up, Hendrik walked through the door. As he had been traveling a lot the previous month and a half, I had to spend quite a bit of time on the backstory. This was not easy, as he had a propensity to tune out when I veered into what he referred to as "French historian territory." However, three-quarters of the way into my account of the meeting with Michael Silva he perked up and stopped complaining. And then, halfway through my account of the meeting with Esther he abruptly interrupted me.

"Don't do it."

He was referring to Esther's request that I delete evidence. I informed him that I hadn't done it.

"I didn't think government was that evil. You need a lawyer."

I smiled and told him about my conversation with Samuel. "Good," he said, nodding. We spent the next couple of hours racking our brains, trying to come up with other names to call.

A few hours later I heard again from Samuel. When all was said and done, his message amounted to this: "My contact has agreed to meet you. I will reach out with the exact venue closer to the meeting time. Assume it will be somewhere like a midrange restaurant or pub, and dress to blend in. Do not tell anyone about the meeting."

I took a deep breath and let the message sink in. I had never been invited to a meeting under such secretive parameters. I am one of those people who proactively works to confine drama to music, plays, books, and movies that have nothing to do with lawyers, doctors, or banking.

Real-life drama, like real-life conflict, is an unwelcome, inconvenient guest to be ushered out at the first opportunity. The faint smell of it is enough to make me queasy. But here were drama and conflict, barging into my life.

———

BACK IN THE OFFICE after the holidays I went into my meeting with Johnathon with some trepidation. He had signaled over the past couple of months that he would have my back when the time came, and the situation had evolved pretty much the way he had said it would. I wondered if he would walk the walk.

When we finally met I began with "Congratulations, you were right" and proceeded to tell him what had happened with Silva and his team.

"I am not surprised," he answered, gloating the way only a person who has lived through the same experience can. He continued along the lines of: "I know from personal experience what that team is like. No one should be asking you to delete evidence from the record." He then told me he would personally speak with Silva and "intervene on

[my] behalf." *So far this seems to be going rather well*, I thought, allowing myself to believe the conversation was about to end. But Johnathon was not done.

"I want you to know," he said, "that, as you know, I have been visiting the other legal and compliance risk examiners in my charge. I want you to know that you are being treated differently from your other colleagues."

This was a deliberately loaded sentence. We both knew it. After a few seconds I managed what I hoped was a noncommittal "Oh." He did not elaborate on his meaning, leaving it up to me to work it out.

I can't do math calculations the way Samuel can. What I can do is connect an impressive amount of data points and extrapolate a large number of scenarios in the same time it takes Samuel to do the math calculations. My mind had already been endlessly working through numerous ones since I had left Silva's office. Johnathon's comment added a new, enormous data point to consider. What did he mean by *different?* We were both minorities and attorneys. I can't speak for him—I can't speak for anyone—but based on my personal experience, a minority attorney who hasn't experienced discrimination is like a unicorn: I have yet to meet one.

Was this why he told me this? Why now? Why at all? Why him?

More importantly: What did he want?

———

A FEW HOURS BEFORE the meeting with Samuel's contact I was finally given the meeting location. I quickly let Hendrik know—hoping he would be able to join me—and, as instructed, dressed to blend in. It was cold and dark outside, one of those New York City winter nights filled with frost coming out of people's mouths as they walk by. The subway ride felt much longer than it actually took. Half my brain could not quite believe what was happening.

As I got closer to the restaurant I spied Hendrik waiting for me outside the door. *He made it!*, I thought. I breathed a sigh of relief as we walked in together. Despite a light color palette, the place was rather dark. It was very busy and would remain so for the duration of our meeting.

We had been given a name for the reservation—Xander—and a brief physical description for us to identify him: a skinny man of average height with short salt-and-pepper hair. We gave the name to the host and waited. After a few minutes a waiter discreetly led us to a table located toward the back. There we found two people, one of whom matched Samuel's description. The other—Yates—came across as a slightly younger, more robust version of Xander.

After brief introductions, which were effusive so as to make it appear we were already friends, Xander began with: "I picked this place for a reason." After the waiter had distributed the menus and left, he continued, "It's highly unlikely anyone with any interest or connection to the topics we will be discussing is going to wander into this place." I had concluded the exact same thing the second Samuel had communicated the meeting location and said as much. "Excellent!" Xander said.

The waiter came around to take our orders—this being Manhattan, there was never much of a wait. Xander and Yates took great care to place their orders in such a manner so as to guarantee things would take a while, buying us more time at the table. They also somehow managed to make it clear that the waitstaff were not to hover over us. *Clever*, I thought. With that, we settled in.

Xander and Yates began by introducing themselves. I will keep details scarce. Suffice it to say that their credentials included partner at one of New York's biggest law firms, head of a government agency, and extensive litigation, banking, securities, human resources, and regulatory experience. They were the right age, moved in the right circles, and were able to talk to the people who mattered. They were, in short, the right people to provide advice.

Xander rearranged things in his pockets and on the table, where he placed his Blackberry and key chain. He then took the lead. "I already know what I am going to say. But I do want to hear the story first. From the beginning." What followed was, from my perspective, a systematic, relentless examination. Xander and Yates took turns rapidly firing off questions. First they tackled the facts. No detail was left untouched. Every scene you have read about—and many more I left out—was discussed in minute detail. The New York Fed org chart. Dudley, Dahlgren, Connor O'Sullivan, the two Mikes, Johnathon—everyone I worked with. Every meeting with Goldman. What I had seen and heard.

As we progressed I noticed their expressions change. By the end they were clearly in shock.

Next they tackled my personal background. Again, every detail was put through a microscope. My childhood. My education. My dating life. My tax returns. Who I used to hang out with. The jobs I had held. What I had done at those jobs. Who I had worked for. Who I had worked with. Who I hung out with. I felt like a witness on the stand. The whole thing must have lasted about an hour and a half. Maybe two. Drinks came and went. Food came and went. I barely touched anything—my stomach was in knots. All the while they tag-teamed and kept up the pace. Occasionally they would look at each other. Finally, silence.

Taken aback by the degree of concern in their faces, I asked them why they looked so upset. They explained that they had separately done some informal, network-style due diligence of the Federal Reserve Board, the New York Fed, Bill Dudley, and Sarah Dahlgren. They were expecting to hear something bad, along the lines of incompetent employees behaving badly perhaps. What I was saying was worse than what they expected to hear. Much, much worse. The behavior appeared so deliberate. They expected this level of deliberateness from other parts of government, but not from the Federal Reserve Board or the New York Fed. Not after the 2008 financial crisis and Dodd-Frank. And I had proved to be a credible witness—which, from their perspective, made the whole thing worse.

"You have a problem. You have a big problem," said Yates. With the table now cleared, we huddled in closer. To buy another hour and a half, we placed dessert, coffee, and after-dinner drink orders and requested they be delivered separately.

Playing with the key chain, Xander and Yates began a systematic legal analysis and extrapolation of a large number of possible scenarios and outcomes. The issues I was facing were no mere ordinary human resources complaint; they were of a totally different caliber. There were both potential civil and criminal violations involved. Everyone at the table was a lawyer and knew this was true. The conversation quickly got technical. My head started spinning as I heard them walk through everything from me finding a way to successfully push back on Esther and Michael Silva to them getting me fired.

They even weighed the chances this would blow up in such a way as to get me killed. From their perspective it was logical to consider this angle. They were aware that Goldman had a group of people composed of former CIA operatives and private investigators working out of their 85 Broad Street office who were dedicated to dealing with inconvenient issues faced by partners. I had read about it in William D. Cohan's *Money and Power: How Goldman Sachs Came to Rule the World*—one of the books I read in preparation for the conflicts meeting.

After what was probably an hour of this but felt much, much longer, Xander brought the conversation to a halt. "Here is my advice," he said. Then he placed the key chain he had been fiddling with all night right in front of me. I looked at it and back up at him. I signaled I did not understand. Xander smiled.

"That is a USB recording device. Don't worry—I have not been recording this conversation. But as you know, New York is a one-person consent state. As long as one person in the room consents—and that person can be you—the meeting can be recorded. I suggest you get yourself one and use it."

Xander paused and looked at me meaningfully, letting me absorb his recommendation and all the unspoken points that went along with it. After a few seconds Yates went on, "You are in a dangerous situation. Meeting minutes may not be enough." Another pause ensued. I again absorbed what they said—and what they meant. I knew they were right. As an attorney, I knew recorded evidence was more credible than meeting minutes or personal testimony. Xander jumped in: "Best-case scenario, you use the recordings to do your job better. If things take a turn for the worse, you will regret not having the additional evidence."

"You don't need to decide what to do with the evidence now," Yates added. "Evidence gives you options. No evidence, no options."

Xander continued along the following lines: "After all these years, after all that I have seen and heard, I have learned from experience.

There are plenty of bad people out there, in places and positions they should not be. Able to get away with things they should not be allowed to get away with. I am surrounded by them in my line of work. I have seen them destroy good people. I don't trust anyone in my line of work. I carry this," Xander said, raising the recorder with one hand and holding it in the air, "to protect myself from those bad people."

I kept silent, listening and staring at him as he detailed certain experiences that, frankly, left me horrified. "I could be wrong," Xander said, looking at me sadly, "but I do believe they will ask you again. When that happens, you will have to make a choice." I did not want to believe him, but I understood it was a real possibility.

"I'm so sorry," Yates added, signaling agreement.

"Don't be afraid to record," Xander continued. "No one will notice if you do it. Think about it. We have been sitting here for what—three hours? My recording device has been on the table all night. No one has said a word or even noticed it." *Good point,* I remember thinking. Xander hammered on, "None of these people give someone like you a second thought." I knew what he meant—and I knew he was right.

It was very late by the time we walked out of the warm restaurant and into the frigid, windy winter night. Hendrik quickly signaled for a cab. We sat silently holding hands all the way back to our apartment. After Hendrik fell asleep, I headed for our living room.

I sat on our couch, put on some classical music, and sat alone, thinking—until it was time to get ready for work.

THE UNIMAGINATIVELY NAMED Spy Store was located on the second floor of a building about a block away from the subway station. I had a bit of trouble finding both the building and its entrance, which, I figured, made sense. I carefully looked around before walking into the building, making sure no one I knew was around. I made my way quickly up the long flight of stairs and walked into the store.

I browsed for about five minutes before a gentleman came up to me and asked if I needed help. He was tall and portly, with white hair and blue eyes. I asked him if he could show me a few of the recording devices I had been eyeing locked inside a glass case. He looked at me for a moment, as if considering why I would need a recording device. He then turned to the display and walked me through three of the options.

The first was a very expensive and sophisticated one. It looked like a true professional wiretap device. It was way outside my budget. Next he showed me a slightly less sophisticated device. *Solid*, I thought, *but a bit too bulky for someone as tiny as me.* It worked as a wearable, but I would not be able to wear it with all my suits. I asked him for the price. It was better but still outside my budget.

I am sure my face said as much, as he immediately pointed me to a USB stick–like device, similar in size and look to the one Xander had shown me. "It's small, as you can see. You can't wear it, but it does fit on a key chain. You can attach it to your Blackberry case too," he added, eyeing the Blackberry in my right hand. He explained how it worked.

"How much is it?" I asked him. The price was right. Still, I looked at it, unsure if it would work. It looked so tiny and not too sturdy—not unlike me. Reading the look on my face, he leaned over slightly and got closer to me. I looked up into his eyes. He looked worried and a bit sad.

"Don't worry," he said, gently.

"I promise you, it will work. You will catch him."

CHAPTER 14

Counting to Twenty

During the first week of January 2012 the world outside the New York Fed was preoccupied with Europe's financial crisis. Occupy Wall Street was busy planning another protest in front of the New York Fed, which they would hold sometime in mid-January. Meanwhile the banks we were supervising were busy with bonuses, promotions, firings, and wrapping up end-of-year transactions.

I headed to work that week armed with the recorder. As I rode the subway to work, I focused on the device. I knew so little about it. It came with very few instructions. I had not had enough time to practice using it. On my way to the office I racked my brain trying to figure out how to discreetly turn the recorder on and off. The on-off button was located toward the top. The button itself seemed a little bit fiddly and hard to activate.

I also worried about how long the recorder could be left on. I had no idea. I knew it did not last all day, but what did that mean exactly? How far away did I need to be from the microphone for it to work? More importantly, how clearly would it capture the voices in a conference room? No clue. Obviously the closer the person's voice, the clearer it would be, but what if I happened to be too far away from the person whose statements mattered the most in that particular meeting? Worse, what if I turned it on and the device failed to work for whatever reason?

I figured I would need to just give it a go and hope for the best. As a backup plan I decided to redouble my efforts at taking meeting minutes. It would have the added benefit of giving me something to do, which would calm my nerves and help me concentrate on my work.

The morning started quietly. I grabbed my usual cup of coffee and sat at my desk on the Goldman regulator floor. I was so focused on what I was doing that I failed to notice Analisa making her way over to me. "Happy New Year!" she said.

"Happy New Year to you too!" I replied. She grabbed the chair next to me, sat down, and we began going over some of the overlapping issues we were working on.

Analisa began by informing me of the results of an internal audit Goldman had done of one of the compliance programs in its Wealth Management division. It had just come out. This was one of the divisions whose head of compliance, Alexander Lambert, had so memorably told us that they did not feel they needed to comply with the consumer protection laws because of their clients' wealth. But the internal audit had revealed so many problems that Goldman's internal audit team had taken the rare step of giving the audit a "qualified" rating—which was the lowest they would go.

This was a red flag for the regulators. Both Analisa and I were already well aware the division had problems. Analisa wanted to use the results of the internal audit to push for permission to move forward and take a deeper look at the Wealth Management division. I told her that I would ask Johnathon and Connor, but based on the fact that Johnathon had already pointed to issues in the division, I suspected it would not be difficult to get his buy-in.

We wondered how Mila and Donna would react to the audit results. After all, they were assigned to cover this division.

The second issue was a potential market manipulation issue—a rumor involving a potential business transaction—Analisa had spotted involving Goldman and another global financial services provider. In her opinion there were two reasons she wanted to follow up on this rumor. First, the rumor fit the profile of the type of false rumor one sees in market manipulation cases. And second, she wanted to verify whether the pressure of recent high-profile scandals had pushed Goldman's compliance department to improve its monitoring and surveillance activities.

It was not my place to tell her what to do. That said, if she wanted to look into it, the question was whether I wanted to join her. This was obviously a great opportunity to use that one rumor to spot check if and how Goldman's surveillance and monitoring worked in 2012. I encouraged her to move forward and told her I would circle back with Johnathon and Connor to see what they would say.

The third issue Analisa wanted to look at was Goldman's controls around insider trading—specifically, the type of insider trading Rajat Gupta had been accused of. Again, I agreed with her. If we were going to look into Goldman's surveillance and controls around market manipulation already, it was easy to add the surveillance and controls around Gupta's type of insider trading to our to-do list.

To move forward, we agreed to start emailing our respective teams.

After she went back to her desk I thought about how the element of surprise had prevented me from turning on the recorder. I wanted to practice using the device so as to gain confidence. This was a missed opportunity. I brushed it off and figured I would be sure to turn it on at the next opportunity—the weekly SSO meeting.

I SPENT FIFTEEN MINUTES before walking into the SSO meeting preparing myself. I toyed with the device while reflecting on my meeting with Xander and Yates. When the time came I grabbed my notebook, pen, and phones. I had one of the phones in my hand. The other—the one with the recorder—was tucked into my open purse.

I fiddled around inside my purse and activated the "on" button just before walking into the conference room. I sat down and placed everything in front of me, hoping for the best. I quickly opened my notebook and focused hard on writing down everything I heard.

After recounting his holiday weekend, Silva announced, "The board took notice that [the SSO] teams did not file the IOs [institutional overviews] at the end of December." With a disdainful tone he added, "I don't know how a midlevel staffer gets away with talking like that to a bunch of senior SSOs." I quickly looked up and around the room. Serious looks and silence.

"I expect to be written up in some sort of report," he concluded.

He then went on to give his take on how 2011 had gone. "I got the right deputy," Silva said, signaling to Michael Koh sitting beside him. "We then moved to get all of you," he added, looking around the room. "As someone new to bank-sup, it was very important for me to learn the job, so to speak."

Bank-sup was Fed-speak for bank supervision. After a brief pause Silva added, "I feel like I made a lot of progress learning about bank-sup and Goldman Sachs. My biggest 2012 goal is to make the new [supervision] structure work," he paused and, with a slightly furrowed brow, continued, "I do think it's going to be hard to make it work. The risk side faces the biggest transition because they are figuring out what it means for risk to own risk."

I focused on my notes and tried hard not to write down what I was hearing as "Michael is afraid the SSOs won't be able to control the work output of the risk function."

Silva then asked his team if anyone had "any thoughts on our relationship with the Board of Governors." I looked up and around the table to see who would take the bait. By now I was used to the fact that he preferred to use these meetings to gossip about the politics and inner workings of the Fed—as opposed to, you know, supervising Goldman in a data-driven, quantifiable, measurable way. His team was always happy to oblige. People looked at each other, trying to figure out who would speak first.

After a few seconds Ryan O'Hara spoke up. Affecting a serious, detached tone, he said that "over the last ten years I've seen the environment shift from 'let the NY Fed do their own thing' to the opposite." Silva agreed that "members of the OC [operating committee] seem very interested in the new business-line approach, supervising and controlling it. Below that the bureaucracy [has] no intention of changing a single thing in terms of what they do."

This, he claimed, was his concern. He went on to give an example: "that the IO incident has come to this, this is the least of the things we want to push back on," he said as he waved his right hand.

Someone then brought up the 2008 financial crisis. Silva addressed it by saying the Federal Reserve Board of Governors "had to find someone to blame, so they blamed the New York Fed. Their way to deal with it was to suck a bunch of power away from the New York Fed." He then added that he did "think this is an exciting time. I have been waiting my whole career to push back on things. If they are going to try to fire me for making things better, I know all the severance formulas." As he spoke he tilted his head slightly back and raised both hands, as if he were holding a piece of paper and checking through a list of formulas.

Koh, circling back to the IO issue, added that the "board felt that we have scaled down the requirements dramatically; they still got blown off. SSOs basically got together and said that they would hold the line on this issue. We will talk about this tomorrow in the roll-up RAP [annual ratings review] process."

Silva intervened, "All this hopefully means for you guys is some entertainment." After a pause to absorb the smiles from his team, he added, "This is the best chance in a long time to see change."

Silva then told us: "If you weren't a team player, you wouldn't be here." Silence immediately descended over the room. Everyone looked around. Perceiving the reaction, he added, "That sounds more ominous than I meant. It's more about accepting the package you got. Once you give support, you will be amazed how the team blossoms."

I stifled a laugh. I thought, Next time just address me directly, Mike.

With that, he ended the meeting. I carefully grabbed my things from the table and headed over to my desk, wondering if and how the recorder had worked.

That night I got home and plugged the device into my computer to see if it had worked. Alas, it had not. I was extremely disappointed.

I reread the instructions and reflected on why that could be. Had I not charged the device long enough or failed to properly turn it on? Either way, I was glad I had stuck to taking detailed meeting minutes and, in light of this incident, made a mental note to keep doing so.

The hardest part was to actually go into the meeting and sit there, thinking all the time the recorder was working. Even though it had not worked, the drill gave me confidence to try again the next day. Before going to bed I plugged the device in for overnight charging. I made sure the computer's hard drive did not spin down and go into sleep mode.

EARLY THE NEXT MORNING I found myself alone on my side of the office. Sitting across from me was Lily. No one else was around. Because of my height, I was almost completely concealed behind my computer, even when I was standing up. I quickly glanced around to make sure no one saw me, and I turned on the recorder. This time I made sure the red light flashed on.

I then made myself visible to Lily by peeking out to the right-hand side of my computer monitor, leaving the recorder in front of me on the desk. I started to chat with her about the weather. This gave me the chance to test distance and audio quality. After a couple of minutes, with nothing left to say, I moved back to my desk and quickly turned the device off. Although I would not be able to listen to the recording itself until I got home, this time at least I was sure I had done everything correctly.

The conversation Analisa and I had had the previous day about potentially looking into the false rumor for market manipulation had led to a series of emails. The messages were written by Donna, copying Mila, Analisa, and Silva. Donna and Mila had confirmed the rumors Analisa had told me about. However, they insisted it was not an issue we could look into because rumors can't be tracked using systems.

At some point during this exchange Donna stopped by my desk to tell me I was not to look into any insider trading issues until after the Rajat Gupta trial. Silva then wrote that what Donna and Mila were saying made sense.

For whatever reason, it seemed that Silva and his team were asking me not to perform my job. After all, my management team and Analisa's all agreed that we should be looking into these issues at Goldman.

I then sent a detailed email back to everyone that included references to sections of the law about rumors, market manipulation, and bank surveillance systems. Silva replied-all, saying that what I wrote made sense, but we should not copy other regulators—meaning Analisa. He ended his email arguing that this was how we can all learn from each other.

Mila then followed up, wondering whether Goldman's peers had something similar, including the surveillances that I mentioned in my email to the group. Donna sent response emails detailing what she believed I should do.

I forwarded the email chain to Johnathon and walked over to Analisa's desk, recorder in hand, to get her take on how things had developed. A lot of people were seated at their desks in her area. I struggled to turn the recorder on, fearing someone might catch me doing it. Eventually I managed. I went about the conversation as naturally as I could, hoping I would capture some of it.

During the afternoon I had a choice to make. First, I had a long training session with the two Mikes about the upcoming annual report "roll-up process." After that, I had to rush over to the New York Fed for my one-on-one meeting with Johnathon, which could also potentially turn into a two-hour meeting. I was afraid the recorder would not last through the afternoon. I decided to not take it into the annual report meeting and save it for my meeting with Johnathon.

Once everyone settled, Koh began by stating that the slide presentation would be a high-level overview of the annual review process. He began with a brief explanation of what the IO was. According to him, the content of the IO came from summaries prepared by the bank for use in their 10K and 10Q SEC filings, which were then inserted into the IO.

As I listened to Koh's explanation, I realized that the SSOs' months-long stand against the board's request to put together the IOs for the too-big-to-fail banks amounted to a refusal to do a copy-and-paste job from a public document that would take one examiner with basic computer skills maybe half a day to put together. I kept my head down to hide the look on my face.

Koh then moved on to the RAP, explaining that the risks being assessed in the annual report were credit, market, liquidity, operational, and legal and compliance risks. He then spent a long time explaining how things were done last year. It was a convoluted explanation, full of half sentences that began in one place and ended up in another. I literally could not take meeting minutes.

This was not unusual for Michael Koh.

I sneaked looks left and right to see how others were reacting. Although I saw serious faces focusing on Koh, I also got the sense that not much was sticking. I ended up writing about seven questions that came to mind as I heard him speak and made a note to ask Johnathon about them.

Perhaps sensing the meeting was not going well, Silva interrupted his deputy to remind everyone that "the bread and butter of supervision revolves around the RAP process." In his view this "forces a discipline on us to assess risk and on the firms to stay on top of it so as not to blow up. We are in the middle of a shift. Risk heads need to work together and consistently across all stripes."

He then ceded the floor back to Koh, who proceeded to ask the risk stripes to use their document when moving forward with our work. Which document he was referring to was not clear.

Indeed, why were they going to come up with a document? Isn't it the job of the risk stripes to come up with the annual ratings, anyway? Why would I use *their* document? Why would any one of us use their document?

I did not get a chance to dwell on this further because of the pleading look on Michael Koh's face. It would turn out to be the only time I ever saw him lose his composure. I was, in fact, so stunned at hearing him plead with us that I literally stopped taking meeting minutes and stared at him.

After he was done speaking I simply wrote down: Michael Koh pleads with us to use his team's documents. I wondered what Johnathon would say to this.

Koh then turned the conversation to the question of closing the MRAs and MRIAs. At this point Mila jumped in to say she did not want to do any testing to close the MRAs and MRIAs; instead, she wanted to read what Goldman's internal controls had done and, if it was okay, use that to close the MRAs and MRIAs. She calmly sat and looked at us, as if what she was suggesting made perfect sense. The room went quiet.

Wow. Here was Mila saying we should follow Goldman Sachs's lead as to whether they had complied with the MRAs to close them. This was unreal.

As for me, I still had no access to the systems—and would not until I had completed the two training courses. So I could neither close old MRAs and MRIAs nor issue new ones based on the work I had already done. My first training course would not be until the beginning of February.

Probably sensing that Mila had been too direct in showing her cards, Koh recovered enough to suggest that "perhaps some limited testing of higher risk MRAs might make sense."

Nice try. What was going on was still clear as day.

He then moved on to his next slide in his presentation, which listed the various elements of the "sup plan" (the annual supervision plan). He highlighted from the list enhanced continuous monitoring and pointed out that "the meaning is now changing." My mind immediately thought back to my legal and compliance risk team, who had directed me all this time to use enhanced continuous monitoring and continuous monitoring as the basis of my supervision work at Goldman. They had not mentioned anything about the meaning changing. Perhaps Koh meant to say that he wanted the meaning to change. Or was he trying to plant the seeds of confusion so we would stop using these examination methods?

Clearly hijacking Koh's meeting, Silva interrupted him again. And this time in a completely unexpected way.

"I want to talk about an email exchange between Carmen and Donna," Silva began. I swallowed hard and gripped my pen a bit tighter. "Carmen had identified a rumor about a business purchase. Donna confirmed that it was a rumor. Carmen then indicated that we may want to follow up on false rumors. Donna asked her a question."

Wrong, I said to myself. Donna did more than ask me a question. She insisted that we could not look into this.

Silva continued, "Carmen stuck to her guns and indicated that we needed to follow up on market manipulation and insider trading. Mila and Donna then responded with advice on what things to look for."

That was not true, either. Mila and Donna actually made it clear in writing and in conversations that I should stop looking into these issues.

Still, Silva continued with his version of the events: "Carmen will do what she will go ahead to do. Donna was edgy in her communications." After a pause, he added, "Carmen was so polite that she was clearly counting to ten before she hit reply and sent the emails."

Everybody laughed. I did my best to hold back a smile, all the while thinking to myself, *I counted to twenty.*

"I congratulate everyone involved in the situation," he said in closing. The congratulations annoyed me because, in effect, he was congratulating Mila and Donna for trying to block me from doing my job. I could sense everyone's eyes on me. I kept my head down and took notes, lamenting that I did not have the recorder on hand to capture the moment.

Koh wrestled the meeting back from his boss. If he was upset at Silva's interruptions, he did not show it. He remained calm as ever, in complete control of his tone and facial expressions. Next he focused on the last slide: the roll-up and bank holding company ratings.

Suddenly the atmosphere changed. This was the purpose of the meeting.

Koh went about making his points with great care. "Overall composite bank rating was done together with New York State," he began. "Again, Goldman is going to want to know what that rating is based on. A one or two rating has no impact. Three or lower ... and there are impacts. Right now there is an MOU on the bank, and management rating is a three, and that limits acquisitions and the ability to expand. Certainly, for legal and compliance, it was weighted heavily and led to threes."

I looked up quickly at Mila. She was shifting anxiously in her seat. Next I glanced at Koh. My intuition told me that singling out the legal and compliance risk stripe was no accident: Mila was the person in charge of that function when Goldman's rating went down.

Now I was in charge of it.

He continued, "Getting rid of Litton was a way of alleviating the risk. We told Goldman that is good, but there are other issues—for example, corporate governance—where you have some additional work to do." Koh quickly looked at Lily and Esther, who were in charge of corporate compliance, as he was saying this. They sat there looking back at him, smiling and nodding.

My mind flew to the pieces of data I had been able to gather on Litton so far. Litton was Goldman's mortgage servicing company. Goldman was under a consent order from the Federal Reserve and had a legal obligation to clean up the mess the servicing company had made. The plan was to hire a consulting company to do it. Even if Goldman sold it, Koh and his team had admitted in prior meetings that Goldman would remain on the hook for the clean-up. Apparently, the contract with the consulting company had not yet been signed, which could mean the clean-up had not begun.

Mila, Donna, and Koh had been withholding regular updates on the progress of the consent order from me, just as they had from Johnathon.

It was difficult to know for sure, but it seemed safe to say Litton was not an issue that could be deemed as having gone away yet. But Koh and his team had closed it.

The meeting ended with an extended discussion of the final slide, which he called the Homer Page. The Homer Page was a one-page summary of how the bank ratings were produced under the new supervision model rolled out in January of 2011. The document indicated that the risk lines—not the business lines—were responsible for coming up with the bank ratings. In other words, risk specialists like me would be coming up with the bank ratings, not Silva's team.

However, the Homer Page Koh showed us had been redacted. According to Koh's Homer Page, which Koh's deputy Sung had modified by inserting the business-line specialists in Silva's team, the risk specialists would be providing the information to and work for Silva's team, who would be the ones coming up with the bank rating. This was wrong, as it reverted back to the old pre–January 2011 model of supervision. It was also completely unexpected. But this is clearly what the two Mikes had been pushing for since I had started working there.

You could feel the tension in the air. I glanced around at the other risk specialists to gauge their reactions. They were serious and seemed taken aback by this turn of events. Koh then indicated that he wanted the risk specialists to use last year's rating as the baseline for this year and refresh the existing rating by using the most recent exams and the closing of MRAs, MRIAs, and any new issuances of letters. As I heard Koh rattle off the factors he believed we should use when determining this year's ratings as well as his renewed plea that we use his redacted version of the Homer Page, I kept glancing at him, Mila, and Donna. Michael kept his tone steady, but Mila and Donna had anxious looks on their faces.

If it wasn't clear earlier, everything was obvious now: Silva and Koh's team was looking to raise Goldman's ratings, and they were targeting the legal and compliance rating as a means to do it.

Though they had not come out in the open to admit this, it was, to me, the only logical explanation.

I need to tell Johnathon about this as soon as I get to his office, was all I could think.

This went way beyond pushback. This could be obstruction.

CHAPTER 15

The Fed's Way of Doing Things

I was looking forward to talking to Johnathon. Even though he had never mentioned Michael Koh as someone to look out for, he had clearly warned me about and tried to protect me from Mila, Donna, and Lily. So I still trusted him—to the extent that I could trust anyone at the New York Fed. And he was my boss.

As I made my way to his office I tried to connect the dots. I knew Johnathon had had my job since July. Prior to that it was divided among Mila, Donna, and Lily. When Johnathon had transitioned his work to me in November he had made no mention of having issued new MRAs or MRIAs based on his work. Nor had he spoken of working on any letters that were going to be issued to Goldman containing findings.

Connor O'Sullivan had mentioned that they had suspended full-blown exams. I had spent the final two months of the year gathering data during continuous monitoring that could certainly be used to support issuing MRAs and MRIAs, but because my training had been delayed, I still couldn't document them in the way the New York Fed wanted them documented.

Johnathon had only shown interest in me going out and gathering data. When I had pushed both him and Connor to turn this data into actionable items, such as MRAs and MRIAs, they had indicated I should just wait until I had taken the training and then I would know how to do it. Why the constant delay?

However, once we started our meeting, instead of answering my direct questions, Johnathon spent about fifty-three incredibly frustrating and inconclusive minutes meandering through three topics: my IO training session with the two Mikes, my end-of-year meetings with Silva and Esther, and how to work with the business-line specialists going forward.

Johnathon's advice for how to handle Silva's team amounted to: "the thing that I say to myself is, how do I work with them and how do I make myself effective without, um, creating unnecessary battles." Was he now intimating that I was the one creating battles? I decided to change the topic.

After a few minutes I tried asking for advice on how to respond to Mila's question as to whether Goldman's peers had similar market-manipulation and insider-trading surveillance systems in place. Not responding was not really an option; she had been promoted a few weeks ago to officer of the bank, and at the New York Fed, hierarchies were very important. She had initially tried to stop the inquiry from going forward and was now trying to derail it by pushing me to go off on a tangent. I was there to evaluate Goldman's behavior against laws, rules, and regulations, not in comparison to other banks. But no matter which angle I took, I could not get Johnathon to give me a straight answer. I wondered if he was delaying giving me feedback until he'd had time to circle back with the two Mikes.

At the end of the meeting he agreed to read the emails I had forwarded and to continue the conversation at the end of the week.

"No, NO, NO! You can't correct my meeting minutes!" exclaimed one of my legal and compliance colleagues. He was reacting to my account of my exchange with Esther after Christmas. Everyone who listened to my story agreed that the request was unacceptable. "That is your evidence for issuing findings!" someone else exclaimed. "No one has ever asked me to do that," said a third risk colleague.

I was happy to receive their support. Johnathon had already given the same feedback, but it was good to have his perspective validated by other legal and compliance risk colleagues, especially those who had worked at the New York Fed longer than Johnathon had. They encouraged me to push back. They also suggested I manage the situation very carefully. I told them how the SSO team at Goldman went about their daily business, asking them if they were experiencing similar dynamics within their own SSO teams. After they recovered from shock, they said things worked differently at their teams and filled me in. I was surprised at just how different things worked. "Who is on that team?" they asked me. I rattled off some names.

"Mila is very familiar" with how things should work, voiced one of my risk colleagues, with a facial expression that fell somewhere between incredulity and *what is she up to?* The others concurred.

———————

THE FOLLOWING DAY I met with Erin O'Brien and her assistant, per Goldman's request. Presumably it had been Erin's idea. She had insisted I come alone. Officially the purpose of the meeting was to discuss something to the effect of "postings on various legal and compliance-related events." The part about coming alone had raised immediate alarm bells in my mind. I gave Johnathon and Silva a heads-up and voiced my concerns. Neither of them was thrilled about the request, but both encouraged me to attend and report back.

I casually mentioned the meeting request around the Goldman regulator floor, trying to get a feel from others just how usual or unusual this meeting request was. I discovered that it was, indeed, unusual. Erin O'Brien only met alone with Silva, once a week, in a conference room next to the back exit of the Goldman regulator floor.

I walked over to her office, thinking back to our first uncomfortable encounter, wondering what this was really going to be about.

Erin first made me wait outside her office until she wrapped up another meeting—just long enough for me to read the newspaper articles covering the inside glass wall of her office. She then invited me in and directed me to sit at the round table next to her desk, facing the door. As we settled down she closed the door. Hanging behind it, directly in front of my face, was a long, luxurious fur coat. I made a point not to comment on it.

With the most charming, professional tone she could muster, Erin informed me that going forward I was to work with her and Sue as my point persons for all areas of compliance. *As opposed to whom? There hasn't been anyone else,* I remember thinking. She continued, "We will confirm Bruce Acton for legal," she added.

Erin then spent some time detailing her coverage area. She informed me that Goldman expected to receive a letter from the Consumer Financial Protection Bureau (CFPB) "pretty soon" announcing that they would be coming to examine Goldman. She then insisted we set up a weekly one-on-one meeting so we would have a regular opportunity to deal with any scheduling or information flow issues coming down the pipeline. We then wrapped up so we could both attend the previously scheduled overview of Goldman's compliance department supporting the Investment Banking and Merchant Banking divisions.

Clever. I wondered how Johnathon and Silva would react to this meeting turning into a weekly affair.

I rushed back to the Goldman regulator floor and did my usual walk-through, asking everyone if they were joining me for the next Goldman meeting. All the regulators sent people to cover it. This was not surprising. These were Goldman's bread-and-butter divisions. This was the compliance team working for the divisions that generated most of the Goldman scandals (Abacus,[1] Kinder Morgan–El Paso, Solyndra, Capmark) and SEC investigations (Massachusetts government bond underwriting kickback scheme[2]) that the press had been writing about since the 2008 financial crisis. This was the team who supported the Investment Banking division run by David Solomon, one of the Goldman executives being groomed as the potential CEO.

It was eerie. As the meeting progressed, it appeared—from the topics Goldman covered and the way they covered them—that somebody from our team must have read my meeting minutes and informed the bank of the items I had been flagging for follow-up. One by one, the Goldman representatives mentioned almost every issue I had flagged internally, adding for each item that they were "already working on fixing it."

Back at my desk I fought the feeling of despair that crept up as I made my follow-up list. Not only did this division have a lot of issues, but Goldman was also trying to use the fact that they had admitted to them and the claim that they were "working on it" as a defense against the New York Fed issuing them a finding. I wondered if my fellow regulators would go along with it. Regardless, I knew I would not.

THE FOLLOWING DAY I met again with Johnathon. Just like our previous meeting, the conversation meandered. A new pattern was emerging: Johnathon seemed to be running circles around certain issues having to do with Silva's team. He was also becoming increasingly ambiguous.

He started by providing more backstory on the new supervision model. The structure had been rolled out in early 2011, but the implementation had been phased in. Johnathon had only arrived onsite at Goldman in September. According to him, the team assigned to Goldman had a different supervision model from that of teams assigned to other banks. At that time I did not have access to exactly how the other SIFI (systemically important financial institutions) supervision models were different, but the fact that Goldman had a different model was the subject of many conversations at the New York Fed.

"It's amazing how different the Goldman supervision model is," Johnathon added.

Johnathon then talked about what he had done to address my situation with Silva's team. Referring to me, Johnathon said he told Silva: "I have somebody that I'm relying on, and I'm giving her all sorts of deference because I trust her capability-wise. Skills, experience—right? All these things—right? It would be really helpful if you gave Carmen a little bit more breathing room—right?"

He then explained to Silva that the kind of challenges I was experiencing were not dissimilar from those he had experienced with Silva's team. Johnathon wanted to make sure I could come up with a rating without being challenged in the way Silva's team was challenging me.

He said Silva responded with, "You know what? I agree with you."

Silva then told Johnathon he would talk to his people and reiterate to them that I had a lot of experience and a lot of knowledge and that he saw it. According to Johnathon, Silva said that this would mean to his team, "in an indirect manner, back off."

I really wanted to believe Johnathon. But I knew I couldn't. Why wasn't Connor O'Sullivan in that conversation? Why was Johnathon stammering as he told me about this conversation?

Johnathon then gave me some advice: "You don't have to fight every war," he said. "In your interactions with Mike, you know, my recommendation to you is that, um, you, um, you treat him as almost, like, an ally to you, right?"

There it was. I heard the warning loud and clear: watch your back. Keep your friends close; keep your enemies closer.

Just as I was wondering why he had not brought Connor into the conversation with Silva, Johnathon casually mentioned that Michael had called him directly, bypassing Connor.

Of course. *Clever man,* I thought.

And he wasn't done. Johnathon then told me that he had admitted to Michael that I needed to "calm down a little bit, right? In terms of the way she presents her facts, right?" But, he said, he gave complete deference to me because I was capable and experienced. I just hadn't mastered Fed-speak.

Wrapping up, Johnathon said that he told Michael he was focused on making sure I understood "the Fed way of doing things, which is, even for me, I said, it was difficult, right? Especially coming from the private sector, because you see this giant *Titanic* slow to move, right? And the whole time sinking."

I connected the dots and concluded that Michael Silva and his team were not really going to stop blocking me.

I then asked Johnathon a practical question: Could I treat audit reports as data points to use as evidence to support issuing findings and the annual rating? Johnathon did not let me finish the question. "Yes, you can," he said emphatically. I then explained that the audit reports I was referring to had been issued by Goldman's audit team and were highly critical of the Goldman compliance divisions that he, the other regulators, and I had already identified as having serious problems.

I expressed my concern that Mila and Donna had dismissed these reports in various conversations that had taken place among regulators at the Goldman regulator floor earlier that week. I didn't go into the details, but I told Johnathon that they had tried to dismiss them by stating that the reports could not be relied on because everyone knew Goldman's audit team had issues.

I told Johnathon, point-blank, that I thought Mila and Donna would try to stop me from using the reports as the basis for issuing findings and the annual rating. He scoffed at the idea, saying, "What are they going to say? That it didn't happen? They are not going to be as stupid as—"

"Let me tell you something," I interrupted. "Yes, they may be. These are people who are proactively saying, 'please delete evidence, please don't investigate insider trading and market manipulation.' These are Fed employees who are getting upset because I'm hinting at wanting to do stuff that is incredibly obvious. So they are going to say that it isn't true, and they are going to question my data points, every single one of them, even though they may be crystal clear to an unbiased observer."

Johnathon insisted that it wasn't going to happen because he was going to be there and Silva was going to be there. *We'll see about that,* I thought.

I hid my dissatisfaction by changing the topic, recounting what had transpired in the previous Goldman compliance overview meeting. I relayed my observation that Goldman was trying to use the excuse of admitting to an issue and claiming to be working on it to stop us from issuing findings. Privately I thought Silva's team would support Goldman's approach, and I wanted to get a feel for how my risk stripe saw this tactic.

Johnathon's response was "No, they can't do that." We agreed that if Goldman was in fact working on it—a claim we would have to check to see if it were true—we could lower the penalty or the severity of the finding but not the finding itself. I thought this, in theory, sounded correct, but in practice, again, there were no clear guidelines he could point to that we could use to defend our perspective from an attack.

I went home that Friday evening and straight into what turned into three days of meetings with different attorneys, seeking additional feedback about my situation. In between, Hendrik and I spent time running around New York City, apartment hunting. We needed to leave our apartment by the beginning of February and were running out of time to find one.

On Sunday night I finally checked my work emails—to see if anything had come in. Goldman's legal counsel had sent an email late on Friday, when no one would be expected to pay attention to it. Its purpose was to alert the New York Fed supervisors to a "fast moving transaction" Goldman was about to close with Banco Santander, Spain's largest and most international bank. By the time I had checked my email that Sunday night the transaction had already closed. I noticed that neither Silva nor anyone else copied from the New York Fed appeared to have responded to the email Goldman had sent the New York Fed before the transaction closed.

My heart sank. My intuition told me this transaction was going to be a problem. As if I did not already have enough of them. I went to bed, not looking forward to work on Monday.

BACK AT THE NEW YORK FED on Monday I met with Connor in his office. I communicated to him directly the pushback I was experiencing from Silva's team and asked him to intervene before the tensions surrounding the upcoming production of the annual report and ratings boiled over. I discussed the challenges Johnathon and I were facing due to the lack of clarity with respect to the new structure and the fact that four of the relationship managers—Koh, Mila, Donna, and Lily—were holdovers from the previous structure and had refused to transition the entire legal and compliance work portfolio.

Connor replied that he had been head of legal and compliance risk for six months and had spent the first month working on the document that captured how the ratings were going to be produced. Simply put, the two-page document made it clear that our risk team takes the lead in assigning the rating. Thus, he thought this issue had been resolved a long time ago. I then brought him up to speed on Koh's meeting on the annual report ratings process, where it was obvious they were extremely anxious about not having control of the ratings and were looking to take over the process.

Connor then asked me if I thought that part of the issue had to do with the holdover employees from the previous structure not coming from the same type of professional background Johnathon and I came from. I said that was definitely part of the problem, but it was not the whole problem. A bigger issue was that although Johnathon was very good at pointing out the challenges, he had failed to escalate, leaving me to do the clean-up job.

I then told him that Mila and Donna were holding meetings with Goldman and not including me and that Esther had asked me to redact the meeting minutes. I also recounted how Mila, Donna, and Lily had been gaslighting me and blocking me from following up on issues. Connor silently took the information in but limited himself to saying that Johnathon should be the one telling me what to do.

I made it clear that there was a lot of anxiety and frustration among Silva's team about not having a say in the ratings. They were pressuring the risk stripes, and this was making my life extremely difficult. Connor silently took it all in. I then relayed that Koh had made it clear that they wanted to have control over what happens and how the ratings are done. Connor avoided giving me a straight answer and instead summarized the responsibilities of the SSO team and the risk stripes—again.

Finally, he said that in my case it sounded like the fact that "some of the business-line specialists still feel ownership for portions of the year" before Connor and Johnathon had come in midyear was complicating the situation. "They still feel ownership for the mortgage foreclosure," by which he meant Litton. And it "sounds like it may also be complicated by the fact that since they don't clearly know what they are responsible for, and they have probably professional pride invested in this, that leads to some sort of desire to still retain responsibility."

His clear articulation of the problem, however, was not a solution to the problem.

So I pressed him. Again. I made it clear that Silva's team wanted to raise Goldman's legal and compliance ratings and that Johnathon and I disagreed with that assessment based on the evidence we had been gathering for months. I reminded him—again—that I had only been there for a very small part of 2011, so if they were going to base the ratings on just 2011 data, I was happy to get out of the way and have Johnathon step in and cover the second half of the year, but I made it clear that management needed to step up now and bring clarity to the process and the parameters that would be used for coming up with the ratings.

He signaled that he understood and told me what I was telling him was helpful. He indicated he would float some potential solutions and revert. I privately prayed he would get on it right away.

———————

BACK AT GOLDMAN the next day I noticed Donna had arrived early. She and I were supposed to meet in a few minutes with some other regulators, including Analisa, in one of the conference rooms on the Goldman regulator floor to go over the open Litton and other regulatory findings Donna was supposed to transition over to me. The meeting had been originally scheduled for the previous week, but Donna had postponed it.

Meeting with other regulators present was something I very much favored. There was nothing I was working on that other regulators weren't also working on, so including them was more efficient. Besides, I needed witnesses. Both colleagues at the New York Fed and the other regulators had consistently advised me to never go into a meeting alone.

Donna did not want the other regulators to join us and asked if we could meet early, just the two of us. She explained that she only wanted to discuss New York Fed MRAs and MRIAs—the ones she was supposed to transition to Johnathon and me and that Bob was asking about. "I think that the report that was run unfortunately pulled a lot of items that are closed. So I can tell you that all of the MRIAs with the exception of one are all closed," she explained.

"Are they closed because you closed them?" I asked.

"Yes," she quickly answered, adding, "I have one that we can talk about that is based on whether or not they can prove reparations." She added that she also had notes on all the open findings that had been assigned to Johnathon. I immediately noted that this was not part of the original meeting agenda.

As I walked over to meet with her one-on-one I wondered what she really wanted.

"You know I have no problem with Analisa being a part of any of these discussions as long as they're not Fed-specific things we are dealing with," Donna began with a smile.

"I hear you," I replied. "It's just that when I'm dealing with specific issues that she's also working on, my management has indicated that I should work closely with her."

"Oh! Absolutely," Donna said, "and as far as resolving things or remediating things, that's fine. These were specific to our consent order."[3]

"So in other words," I said, "New York State does not have an opinion on the open issue." My question was designed to smoke her out. The open issue was a foreclosure issue related to Litton. According to Analisa, both the New York Fed and New York State had done extensive work together on Litton.[4]

"No," she answered, "they had their own foreclosure exam." With findings, of course.

I looked at her, a half-smile on my face. The issue amounted to Goldman remaining on the hook for cleaning up the mess. New York State definitely had an opinion about that. In fact, they had signed an agreement with Goldman conditioning the approval of the Litton sale to the bank fixing the issues. Both agencies wanted to make sure Goldman fixed the issue.

To me this was confirmation that what Donna wanted was to tell me something she did not want the other regulators to know. Having got what she wanted—me, alone in a room with her—Donna did not miss a beat, explaining why the one open issue was unlikely to be closed anytime soon. Even though Goldman had sold Litton, it was still on the hook for the MRIA (for cleaning up the mess). I already knew this. Again I asked myself: *What is this really all about?*

So I asked, "With respect to Johnathon's issues, is there anything in particular you think he would appreciate that you add your thoughts to?"

She looked straight into my eyes, "Um, well I don't know." She broke into a small laugh, then she wondered out loud whether "there's any way I could close the findings in a better, more efficient fashion."

There it is, I thought.

What Donna wanted was for me to ask Johnathon to ask her to close the open Goldman issues for him, even though they had been assigned to him. The question was, of course: Why?

I of course had my suspicions. Closed MRAs meant fewer blemishes on Goldman's record. Fewer blemishes could be used to justify raising their annual ratings.

Then again, Donna worked for the New York Fed. Not for Goldman Sachs.

CHAPTER 16

Santander

"Approximately by when do we need to, I guess, have, like, some kind of submission of, like, risk materials for our topic?"

The two Mikes had just finished providing additional information on the upcoming ratings process. Elizabeth Alfonsina from operational risk was trying to ask the SSO team a very simple question about the timing of her report.

She was struggling to come up with a name for the section of the annual report she was responsible for producing. Not because she couldn't remember the name but because management could not agree on what to call whatever it was the risk stripes were supposed to submit.

Clearly, I wasn't the only risk stripe at Goldman facing issues with the SSO team.

We all looked at the two Mikes, waiting for an answer.

Koh looked at her for a beat or so, with his customary expressionless face, his Gordon Gekko haircut gelled perfectly in place. You never knew what kind of answer you were going to get when you asked him a question. The one type of answer he had a propensity to give—and the one everyone dreaded—was the long, pointless, meandering monologue that did not answer the question but that New York Fed culture expected everyone treat seriously. Koh was not the only employee prone to these types of pointless monologues, but he was the one we most interacted with. On this particular day Michael Koh stepped up to answer Elizabeth's question. For about three minutes he wove partial phrases with acronyms and left out verbs, spinning artless non-sentences with each other.

In other words: he didn't know.

Silva took a different, more animated, approach in an attempt to manage their lack of concrete information: "I think it's a very exciting time. I think that both the business-line specialists and the risk specialists are … it's a brand-new day to figure out how they're gonna risk manage this, how they're gonna harness this, this whole new thing. Now, the risk stripes, you guys have a wide open, you know—how are you going to assess these things? How do you wanna do it? How do you wanna write it up?" In other words, Silva was saying that it was up to us to decide how we wanted to approach the process. Did he mean in terms of method? Or was he referring to whether or not we chose to focus on Goldman's lack of compliance?

"It's all up to, you know, do you wanna use exams? Do you wanna use continuous monitoring? Do you want to go out and do spot—whatever, you know, whatever you're comfortable, um, signing off on, is, is how it's going to be. And I think that's, that's kind of neat. It's a chance to really reinvent the process." Silva looked at me. But the process *had* been reinvented—it was supposed to have been already implemented for a year now. More importantly, nothing in that rambling response answered Elizabeth's simple question.

Two full seconds of silence ensued as everyone surreptitiously checked out everyone else's reactions.

But we had little time to ponder how to handle all this toxic combination of political maneuvering and obfuscation. The Santander transaction over the weekend had somehow caught Silva's attention. He told his team and all the risk stripes to add this transaction to the laundry list of things we had to do.

Banco Santander was a big, old, diversified Spanish bank—much bigger, older, and more diversified than Goldman Sachs. Santander had managed to maintain its standing relative to other large, big, complex, diversified banks on the world stage despite the 2008 financial crisis. But then the European crisis came along to threaten it—and all other European banks.

Following the October 2011 downgrade of Spanish sovereign debt, Fitch Ratings had downgraded Santander and a number of other large Spanish banks.[1] Like many other large European banks on the world's top-fifty list, Santander was under pressure from European regulators to hold more capital in its balance sheet to meet European capital requirements. Santander had responded by, among other things, selling its Colombian subsidiary in December of 2011 and using the cash to strengthen its balance sheet.[2]

This helped, but it was not enough.

The entire situation continued to deteriorate. Santander wanted Goldman to temporarily take some of their noncash assets off their balance sheet prior to the next round of bank stress tests, and Goldman was interested in doing that transaction. The banks got together and hammered out a deal. It boiled down to a repo, the type of transaction critical to Lehman's failure.

As Silva saw it, "Basically, Goldman's lawyer Bruce Acton gave us notice last week that they were going to be entering into a transaction with Banco Santander that might attract some press notice, and I, being a lawyer, scanned it for any application requirements and didn't see any and . . . I didn't really think too much beyond that. But fortunately there's people on this team that do look at these things more closely than I do."

Indeed, Silva hadn't seen anything wrong with the transaction, but prior to the SSO meeting a few New York Fed employees had reached out to him expressing their concerns. This made him look at the Goldman email in a different light. He continued, "It's pretty telling if you think this thing through that it's basically window dressing designed to help Banco Santander artificially enhance its capital position, and, um, it appears to be perfectly legal." He then said that they asked Goldman whether they thought they should do this and why, and apparently Goldman had provided an explanation that justified the transaction.

In other words, Silva was upset because the transaction's purpose seemed to be to help Santander appear to be a healthier bank than it actually was. He had asked Esther Abramson to prepare a quick presentation for the SSO team meeting.

Silva added that he had no doubt that there were many banks out there right now marketing ways for European banks facing stress tests to game the system. He then asked Esther Abramson to walk the SSO team through the mechanics of the transaction. Esther proceeded to present her understanding of it. An animated discussion ensued. The different risk stripes began to analyze the transaction from their respective angles.

Silva interrupted the conversation to let everyone know that the New York Fed had asked Goldman to produce the legal opinions. I would look at them, and once we had reviewed the terms and conditions of the transaction, we would meet with Goldman.

This much was true. Prior to that meeting Silva had emailed Goldman demanding a meeting with them to discuss the transaction. I in turn had forwarded Goldman's email to my legal and compliance risk management team, saying I agreed with Michael and asking for guidance on what to do next.

I knew this was no ordinary transaction. There were clear international and geopolitical implications to the transaction, so this was above my pay grade. Recognizing the uniqueness of the situation, Johnathon and Connor quickly got involved. Silva asked Goldman to email us the documentation. Johnathon, Connor, and Silva all wanted me to look at it. Johnathon and Connor both suspected that Goldman had not completed all the required steps to execute this very complicated transaction legally.

The legal documents arrived in multiple batches due to the complicated nature of the transaction, which involved the United States, Brazil, Spain, the UK, and the Middle East. I dug in.

By the time I had my weekly one-on-one meeting with Erin O'Brien and her assistant, Connor had identified the Supervision and Regulation letter issued by the Federal Reserve that provided guidelines he believed Goldman needed to follow in order to paper the transaction correctly. I did not discuss it in detail with Erin, but I did follow up with her, inquiring about the status of the additional documents we were still waiting for.

I kept in constant contact with Johnathon and Connor, who both took a hands-on interest in the matter. Connor told us about an analogous transaction Morgan Stanley had done, to which the New York Fed had objected. He seemed to be implying that because the New York Fed had logged an objection to Morgan Stanley, we could use that precedent to push back on Goldman if they contested our efforts to object to the Santander deal. Connor and Johnathon instructed me to focus my attention on understanding how Goldman implemented the transaction from a legal and compliance perspective. I proceeded to do just that.

I had several premeetings with Silva and his team before our meeting with Goldman. The first was a brief one with Silva, right after my meeting with Johnathon and Connor. During our conversation he mentioned he had met with his friend Tom Baxter, the general counsel of the New York Fed; Silva had worked for him earlier in his career. Baxter had apparently told him to back off pressing Goldman on whether they should have done the Santander transaction. According to Baxter, there was no legal basis for pushing back on Goldman on this.

I spent the rest of the afternoon and evening at home getting ready for the Santander meeting. I stayed up late into the night, sitting on the sofa, classical music playing in the background, reading up on the transaction and looking up all the applicable laws and regulations, making sure I understood how everything fit together.

In the process I realized that Esther had not explained the transaction correctly.

THE MORNING OF our meeting with Goldman I was reviewing a batch of documents when I discovered that Santander had required Goldman to obtain prior approval from the New York Fed in order to complete the transaction. The problem was that Goldman had notified the New York Fed about the transaction late afternoon on a Friday, too late for the New York Fed to review and approve the deal before the transaction closed on Sunday. If the deal ever went bad, the New York Fed would be dragged into the mess because the paperwork made it look as if the New York Fed had approved the transaction. I alerted Johnathon, Connor, and Mike Silva.

The last premeeting was with Silva and the SSO team. It began with Esther Abramson amending her initial description of how the transaction actually worked. The team silently took in her updated presentation.

Silva then turned to focusing the group on the task ahead. He presented his view and goals for the upcoming meeting with Goldman: "My own personal thinking right now is that we're looking at a transaction that's, uh, legal, but, uh, shady. I want to put a big shot across their bow on that. I don't think we have a legal basis to oppose it; however, if by poking at it maybe we find something to, you know, object to, if that makes sense, um, and maybe we find something even shadier than we already know, uh, so I do want to poke at this thing."

So that was his tactic this time around. His team, especially Esther and Lily, nodded in agreement.

Silva's main concern—despite Baxter's warning to back off—still revolved around whether Goldman should have engaged in this transaction. He offered his thoughts on that: "The one thing that probably wouldn't be productive is we know already right now, that, the two sides are just way apart on should. They look at it from a very narrow client perspective; we look at it from society's perspective. And this meeting isn't going to close that gap—that's going to be a matter of Federal Reserve policy."

Still, he was determined to have the team look into the matter: "So let's poke at this thing, ah, let's poke at it with our usual poker faces, you know, um, I'd like these guys to come away from this meeting confused as to what we've"—he laughed briefly—"I wanna, I wanna keep 'em nervous," followed by more laughing. "Does that make sense?"

Again Mike's team signaled their approval by emphatic nods, sprinkling his statements with the occasional "right," "yeah," "exactly," "okay," and "yes!" The only sign of approval missing was "Amen." It was ridiculous. I didn't nod.

I then brought the team up to speed on what I had uncovered: a sentence in the term sheet stating that Goldman needed to post and obtain a "no objection" from their prudential regulator on or before January 6—the Friday evening when they sent us the email.

A term sheet is a list of the material terms and conditions of a contract. When it becomes part of the final agreement, the list of terms becomes binding, which means that if you don't comply with a term on that list, there is a breach of contract. The prudential regulator was, of course, the New York Fed. I went on to explain that although they had posted us on January 6, we had not had enough time to review the transaction and provide the "no objection."

What followed was a snapshot in time of what it was like to work with Esther and Lily during my time at the New York Fed. The only difference was that they did it in front of Silva and the SSO team.

First Esther pounced, defending Goldman. With a confident smile and a smooth voice, she stumbled at first. "Well, I don't think that, I, my unders—I mean"—she paused, considering for a second and a half what to say next—"Goldman doesn't have a requirement, right?" by which she meant that Goldman did not have a legal requirement to obtain a "no objection" from the New York Fed.

"Sure," Lily quickly chimed in, agreeing with Esther, her boss.

Esther continued, "It was an internally required thing to notify the, the ..."

I interrupted her. "No, Goldman has an understanding with the other party," Banco Santander, by which I meant Goldman had agreed on the term sheet to Santander's condition that they obtain a "no objection" from the New York Fed prior to the transaction closing.

"Right." Silva, to my surprise, had backed me up.

Esther shook her head and looked at me. Her face contorted into a look of objection and disdain. Lily looked equally upset, and both made as if to interject. I didn't care and kept talking: "No, that's a contract!" Esther again tried to interrupt me, but Silva cut her off: "The other party asked for that." He was, again, backing me up.

Here we were, right before meeting the Goldman team, and Esther and Lily were defending Goldman while Silva backed me. By now I expected Esther and Lily to take Goldman's side. I just didn't expect Silva to take mine.

Esther and Lily looked like they weren't about to give up. After some more quick cross-talk, Esther tried again. Looking at me directly, she said, "I don't disagree with you, but arguably they posted us, right? And they notified us. The question is: Did they give us enough time? They don't require our sign-off on it; they just require a posting to us."

I looked at her with what I suspect was a look of, *Why are you pretending not to understand the phrase "and obtain a no objection"?* I was horrified. She was clearly taking Goldman's side—even though she worked for the New York Fed. She was throwing us all under the bus, especially her boss, Michael Silva.

I looked at him. He had a serious, pensive look. Before anyone else could say a word, he replied, "Well, you know, I've seen a lot of these term sheet legal clauses. I usually insisted on them. The one thing I know as a lawyer is that Goldman never got a no objection from me."

You could almost see Esther and Lily deflate as Michael spoke. It was not what they wanted to hear. "Ohhh, okay," said Lily. "You literally have to say 'I do not object.'"

"Yeah," replied Silva.

Esther, sensing how the tide had turned, quickly turned with it, interrupting him to say, "To Carmen's point, they can't ask at the eleventh hour, and you didn't give them what they wanted."

At that moment I thanked my lucky stars that Esther and Lily had acted this out in front of Silva. His confirmation that he had not provided the no objection—and he was the only one who could confirm this, as he was the one who had to do it—spared me from the political and time-consuming exercise of having to go to Johnathon to get in front of whatever Esther and Lily concocted.

Right before our meeting with Goldman, Silva asked me if he could be the one to ask the "no objection" question. Although he phrased his request in the form of a question, he and I both knew I had no choice but to agree and no time to circle back with Johnathon and Connor to discuss. I quickly analyzed the situation and decided this was a battle not worth fighting.

This did not mean I did not see what he had done or felt conflicted and unhappy about it—I did. It was my job to inquire into legal and regulatory matters. I did not report directly to Silva, but he was the senior New York Fed person on the ground, and he wanted to ask the key question. With this request, Michael was interfering with my job, but I had to defer to him. I consoled myself by thinking that, so far, he had exhibited a clear understanding of the seriousness of the question. After all, it technically fell to him to send Goldman the no objection, and he had not done so prior to Goldman closing the transaction. If the enthusiasm he had displayed earlier turned out to be sincere, there was little risk he would fail to push Goldman on this point.

Besides, I thought, he was a lawyer who had worked at the New York Fed long enough to know the potential legal ramifications behind Goldman going around doing deals while misrepresenting whether they had prior approval from the New York Fed. In this particular case, the misrepresentation impacted him directly.

During the meeting the Goldman team tried to talk their way out of the issues. Moses Goldberg, Goldman Sachs's international general counsel, took the lead in explaining the transaction. He tried to explain away the issue of Goldman's contractual requirement to obtain a no objection from the New York Fed prior to closing the transaction by saying. "There has to be some conflict, um, in some of our documents that, our intent was posting, not to seek approval, but just to make sure you were aware of the coming developments that we were seeing."

As he spoke, my eyes shifted to Bruce Acton, another of Goldman's lawyers. I saw Bruce's eyes slowly but steadily widen. Three seconds of silence followed Goldberg's presentation, during which Bruce's right hand quickly traveled up to his mouth in a desperate attempt to stifle a laugh. This did not surprise me. First of all, to a lawyer, the term sheet contained the words "no objection." That required something more than just "posting someone to make sure they are aware of the coming developments that we are seeing."

Second, his "conflicted documents" statement, if true, sounded a lot like admitting there was shoddy drafting on the part of Goldman's legal department. And yes, people make mistakes, and contracts get amended all the time. But to a regulator, the statement raised a red flag. Shoddy drafting can create really big risks for a bank. So when a regulator hears something like that, they start wondering just how many deals are plagued with issues and whether the bank has controls to prevent or correct shoddy drafting before a lawsuit or some other financial issue forces the bank to pay out a whole bunch of money in damages.

I quickly looked at Johnathon. You could read the words, *Really? This is the best explanation you can come up with?* written all over his face. Silva's expression was blank. This, I thought, was the perfect opportunity for him to ask about the "no objection" issue. He chose not to. Instead, he opened the floor to questions from others.

It was after more than an hour of discussion that Silva finally asked the key question in the deferential style in which New York Fed employees were culturally expected to speak to the banks they regulated. "Um, just to button up one point, I know the term sheet called for a notice to your regulator. The written term sheet also called for an expression of no objection—sounds like that dropped out at some point, or ...?"

The Goldman employees looked at each other. After two seconds of silence Goldberg repeated his previous explanation. Then Acton stepped in. He was no longer laughing. His face had become serious, his eyes as hard as two blue chips of ice.

Bruce admitted it was a term sheet condition and insisted it had to do with Goldman's ability to do the deal with Santander as well as Goldman's ability to walk away from the deal—which they wanted to preserve.

He seemed to be implying that we should grammatically modify the sentence in our minds, deleting the words "obtain a no objection from the prudential regulator" from it altogether because Goldman did not intend for the term sheet to say that—even though the transaction documents they signed clearly required it.

I looked at Johnathon and Silva. Johnathon's face made it clear that he was not having it. Silva's face remained serious. Once again, to my surprise, Michael did not challenge Goldman's answers.

I was upset. I thought Michael had deliberately fumbled the question and, by not pushing Goldman's lawyers, seemed to be giving the bank a pass—at the expense of both the Federal Reserve and the New York Fed employees he was dragging along with him into this situation.

Johnathon then stepped in. Instead of pushing Goldman's lawyers, he asked them for copies of documents that the legal and compliance risk team would need to assess Goldman's compliance with the legal requirements that applied to the transaction. I took my cue from

Johnathon, stayed calm, and focused on asking my other questions about the existence of other legally required documentation.

Goldman's answers were not reassuring.

Johnathon and Connor's hunch was correct: the transaction had issues. I knew Connor would not be happy with Goldman when we reported back to him. I wondered what additional issues the next batch of documents would bring.

Before I could go and report back to Connor, however, Silva pulled the team into a quick postmeeting. "Why don't we just have a quick pow-wow right here," he began. We stood in a circle facing each other in the middle of the Goldman regulator floor, in plain view and clear earshot of everyone who had not attended the meeting. The conversation began with a few of us in the risk stripes—including me—expressing legitimate concerns about what we had just heard Goldman say and explaining to the rest of the team why, as experts, we were concerned.

Suddenly one of the Silva's team members jumped in: "I would just say that from a process perspective, I think there's a lot to be said for the thoroughness of the process that they engaged in."

I was shocked. After all, we had barely begun looking into the transaction.

And then another person agreed, suggesting that the New York Fed step in to make sure Goldman did not get upset about how the New York Fed was questioning the transaction. And then he offered the twisted logic behind this: "I think we don't want to discourage Goldman from disclosing these types of transactions in the future, and therefore, maybe, you know, we can include some comment that says don't mistake our inquisitiveness and our desire to understand more about the marketplace in general as a criticism of you as a firm necessarily."

I couldn't believe what I was hearing.

First, Goldman Sachs telling us about this transaction was not a favor. Goldman had told the New York Fed because it contractually had an obligation to obtain our approval in order to do the transaction.

Second, we were the regulator. Part of the job is to be critical of any supervised firm, especially when the firm was misbehaving. To judge from Silva's team, you would think they worked for Goldman Sachs. The tension between the old guard and new, in this case, seemed to come down to the old guard's keen interest in making Goldman happy. Was it fear? Was it laziness? Was it ignorance of the law? Was it vested interest?

Whatever their reasons for this, I wondered whether I—or anyone else—would ever be able to change this harmful state of affairs at the New York Fed.

CHAPTER 17

The Ambush

On my way to see Connor I was making a mental list of the travel preparations I still needed to do for my upcoming visit with Hendrik's family. Luckily we had booked the week-long trip before I was hired, so they had to allow me to take the time off. I was so looking forward to this escape—to be surrounded by people who cared about me. And in a place with no mental manipulation.

But when I arrived at Connor's office, I set aside those pleasant thoughts and focused on what needed to be done. After I recounted how the Santander meeting went, Connor told me he disagreed with Silva and his team. He dismissed their pushback. It was clear to him, as it should have been to everyone else at the New York Fed, that the transaction documents and the procedures Goldman management had followed—and failed to follow—revealed too many issues to ignore. He insisted I present the Santander transaction the following Monday to the legal and compliance risk team. I assumed he wanted to notify the team and secure their support as yet another nod to the political culture, where it seemed nothing could be done without everyone agreeing to it.

During the Monday meetings Connor and his leadership team finally relayed the timeline and parameters we were to use to prepare the documentation to support the legal and compliance annual ratings and annual report.

The annual ratings and the annual report would be formally issued together with the letters communicating the results to the supervised banks at the end of May, just like they had been the previous year. Each one of us was to go to our respective banks and collect data using the same guidelines—SR 08-8. After collecting the data, our team would get together to evaluate the information and compare the banks in a group-wide meeting known as a vetting session. This would be a day-long affair held toward the end of March. We would use the results of this session to rate each of our banks.

I listened to my management with a mixture of relief and horror as they described what we were going to do. Relief, because Johnathon and Connor had been instructing and directing me to gather data using SR 08-8 since I had arrived at the New York Fed. I could use all the work I had already done evaluating Goldman's legal and compliance management and divisions. I could also use all the data samples I had examined: the documents for Kinder Morgan, Capmark, Santander, the UK FSA AML findings, and the audit reports generated by Goldman's internal audit team. All I had to do was ask for and evaluate additional data samples so I could complete the SR 08-8 picture. In the case of legal and compliance, this meant asking for additional copies of policies, procedures, and files generated as a result of employees complying with those policies and procedures.

But my stomach tightened as I thought about all the data I had already gathered. Goldman Sachs would not do well under SR 08-8. My colleagues had also been gathering data for months under Connor's direction using these same guidelines. We had all been comparing notes for months already. Based on those notes, Goldman would rank toward the bottom of the pile. Not the very worst bank—that honor fell to another—but one, maybe two spots above the worst one.

This would not be a problem if the ratings were given out by the legal and compliance risk stripe without input from the SSO team and the business-line specialists. It could, however, turn into a problem if Silva's team would be able to give input and their view did not align with mine. Whether the SSO teams would have an input on the annual ratings remained unclear.

From what I could gather, most of my colleagues had been facing issues with their SSO teams as well, although the issues they were facing fell into slightly different categories. This made sense to me, as each of the SSO teams was being run differently. For example, some of my peers complained that they had to defend—on multiple occasions—the data they gathered and findings they wanted to issue against their assigned bank.

Being questioned once or twice was fine. It was good for another person to check to see whether there were mistakes. After all, the bank itself would try to fight off the finding so it could avoid the time and expense of fixing the issue. The bank was likely to fight hard if the issue also carried with it the possibility of losing access to the Federal Reserve's discount window. However, having to defend a finding internally more than a couple of times was repetitive, cumbersome, and a waste of time.

Other colleagues complained they wanted to gather data in a certain manner—for example, meetings as opposed to documents—but their management was pushing them in the opposite direction. They would be ordered to gather information from documents only or from what other regulators on site at the bank were doing, but not from meetings with bank management. Still others complained, in veiled terms, of racism and sexism.

What could I do with their stories other than compare them to mine? As I listened to them, in my heart I wished those were my issues. Issues like that I could work with. My issues were different.

No one else was being asked to delete gathered evidence or to pretend not to have heard or read things. No one else was being told not to share information with the Federal Reserve Board.

I grew nervous thinking of how the two Mikes and their SSO team would react to the parameters Connor had laid down for my work. I knew they would push back—hard. The SSO team had made it clear they wanted me to use very different data and parameters for the Goldman report.

Johnathon's request to Michael Silva to tell his team to back off had clearly been ignored. Not a week had gone by before they were back to their usual behavior. These were dangerous waters for me to navigate. I was already de facto escalating everything I encountered. I suspected this would continue and intensify as the annual ratings process took center stage. It would fall to Connor to *escalate* the issues I was raising up the chain.

Escalation, yes. In the private sector disagreements such as the ones I was having—and would clearly be having in the coming months—are resolved by a process known as escalation. It works like this: when a disagreement arises, each person disagreeing refers the matter to their manager. Then the two managers get together and discuss. If they in turn disagree, they push the issue further up the chain until, perhaps, it gets to the CEO. In large banks only very few issues get to the CEO level. And the ones that do sometimes go even higher—to the bank's board of directors, the ultimate boss.

The New York Fed worked a little differently. On paper they had all sorts of committees at the top—the Operating Committee (OC in Fedspeak), for example, to which Bill Dudley delegated tasks. Some, confusingly, had the same names as the corresponding committees at the Federal Reserve Board level; others had different names. The names themselves seemed to have changed with the rebranding of the supervision function in 2011, which only added to the confusion. On paper it was all a bit befuddling.

In practice, however, the New York Fed structure was very small—especially at the top—so many of the same people ended up being part of the same committees. I had observed and figured out that the escalation of a legal and compliance risk supervision issue would end up looking something like this: up to Connor O'Sullivan, then up to Sarah Dahlgren, then up to the committees set up by Bill Dudley. Conversely, the escalation of an SSO team issue would look something like this: up to Michael Silva, then up to Steve Manzari and Art Angulo, then up to Sarah Dahlgren, then up to the committees set up by Bill Dudley.

These committees were in between Dudley and Sarah Dahlgren, but the members of these committees included Michael Silva, Sarah Dahlgren, Steve, Art, and the others. Bill was apparently even a member of a few of the committees—though exactly which ones, no one was sure.

In a nutshell: the same people.

On my way back to Goldman I tried my hand at calculating Connor's odds of escalation success: not good. Meanwhile I wondered how on earth I was supposed to navigate the annual ratings mess. As I sat through more overview meetings of Goldman's legal divisions collecting issues with the ease that an open can collects raindrops in a rain forest, I pushed aside feelings of despair and looked forward to my upcoming two-day FISG 100 training course. After completing it I would be one step closer to gaining access to the systems necessary to study and issue findings. Only FISG 200 would remain.

———————

I ARRIVED BRIGHT AND EARLY at the New York Fed for my first day of FISG 100 training. I had looked forward to this for months. Today was the first of two formal training sessions I had been prevented from attending upon arriving at the New York Fed, and I hoped that, after taking the course, I would finally have the tools and information I was missing. I imagined myself working long hours after the course, turning all the issues I had found into documented MRAs and MRIAs and including them in my annual ratings report.

The training took place in a large open conference room with the same navy blue, white, and gray color palette as the other office floors. There were several tables laid out with work materials. Nametags were located in front of each set of binders. Toward the front of the room was a desk and a few easels that held materials. Behind the desk against the wall were writing boards. The back of the room was pretty empty except for a few stacks of chairs.

I found my nametag, dropped my bag and coat in my seat, and wandered back out to grab coffee from the breakfast buffet spread laid out for the trainees just outside the room. Then I took my seat and, while waiting for others to join me at the table, wondered if this was the same room they had used the previous year.

If it was, Connor and Johnathon could have easily fitted me into the training if they had wanted to. There sure were plenty of empty seats to go around.

A few minutes after the first session began, my Blackberry began buzzing. It was Johnathon. I picked it up, answered his question, and gently reminded him that I was in the two-day training session. He knew this already, of course: I had reminded him a couple of days before the course started. I put my Blackberry aside and tried to focus on the training.

But Johnathon refused to go away.

His interruptions popped up at steady intervals throughout the day. As he kept calling with casual questions, I started to think he was interrupting my training on purpose. None of his questions were, objectively speaking, urgent. Yet he insisted that I get right back to him. He even had me step out of the training room and into impromptu phone meetings.

By the end of the day it was clear to me that he was doing this on purpose.

I was not going to be denied, however. I went home that first day and went to bed late rereading the materials so I could "do" the course on my own, so to speak.

The same thing happened on the second day. Balancing Johnathon's constant interruptions and the training was arduous. After the class was over he called one last time. He casually asked me how the training was going and what I thought of it. I wasn't sure how to reply.

With the two-day training course over, I focused on preparing for my upcoming Santander presentation to Connor and my legal and compliance risk colleagues. A few days later Johnathon, the rest of the team, and I gathered in one of the larger conference rooms at the New York Fed for the meeting. For a while we waited for Connor O'Sullivan to arrive.

But he never did.

That morning we were informed that Connor would no longer head the legal and compliance risk team. Barely eight months after taking over the group, he had been promoted to Bill Dudley's chief of staff.

THE NEWS LANDED like an exploding grenade. After a few seconds everyone nervously exchanged glances. As well-seasoned professionals, we all knew this left a gaping leadership hole in our group. We speculated about what it might mean. Personally, I wondered whether Silva had something to do with this. Connor was actually trying to implement the new supervisory structure and insisting that his team use SR 08-8 as the basis of our annual ratings and report. Silva and his team clearly did not like that. And Silva and Dudley went way back.

I kept my musings to myself.

My peers had other theories, however. Some of the veterans in the group pointed to the dismal employee survey results that had come out about three weeks prior as a motivation for the changes. I remembered the survey well: Silva had discussed the results during the SSO meeting, and according to him, the survey had revealed a number of issues, including complaints about lack of clarity under the new supervision framework. Some argued that Connor's promotion would be good for our team. After all, Connor would be in front of Bill Dudley every single day, and who could be better to advocate for the needs and issues facing our team, especially when they escalated up the chain? Conversely, others speculated that this was a bad sign for the New York Fed. Connor was a lawyer, they argued. Bill Dudley was lawyering up. Still others pointed out the common reason for an employee getting reshuffled: FUMU—fuck up, move up.

There was another point of concern to me. Throughout my entire career I have had the sad privilege of watching many companies and banks implode in front of my eyes. Making organizational changes six to nine months after having first made organizational changes was, in my experience, a sign that an organization was in distress and disarray and no meaningful work was getting done. This seemed to fit what I was experiencing at the New York Fed.

I also wondered whether the sudden changes were tied to Greece and Spain looking like they were going to push the European crisis past the tipping point. The noise coming from Europe was intensifying. I shared that last thought with colleagues who had been at the New York Fed during the 2008 financial crisis, but they brushed it off. During the crisis, they told me, the changes came together with a pushback on deadlines for work due; this was not the case now.

We then all headed over to a last-minute town hall, where management gave their spin on the changes to the entire bank supervision function. Curiously enough, Sarah Dahlgren was not present. She had a couple of her lieutenants announce the changes. "These are changes that leadership has been discussing for a little time," claimed one of these representatives, who then presented the changes as a continuation of the transition that began last summer. According to management, some of the changes were focused on "areas where we think we could continue to get even more out of what we started."

The new head of risk and policy, Art Angulo, spoke next. He opened by giving us a long list of all the different positions he had held during his long tenure at the New York Fed. It was impossible to tell the difference between those that were genuinely different and those that were just organizational relabeling. He then announced to the FISG group Connor O'Sullivan's new position as chief of staff to Bill Dudley and that Emma and James Harold would act as interim coheads, taking Connor's place starting the following week.

In other words, Connor would be allowed to drop his hot potato immediately.

Later that day Connor said goodbye, thanked us for teaching him supervision, and apologized for the suddenness of the change. He claimed it really was a last-minute decision. Of his new role as chief of staff, he explained that he would be helping Dudley get out of his office at Liberty Street more and getting him to meet people, especially over in the Maiden Lane building where we worked. The room reacted with silence. Eventually one or two people spoke up, expressing the shock everyone in the room felt. After Connor gave his evaluation on the challenges facing our group, someone spoke up, suggesting that, in his new position, he had "Dudley's ear."

Connor didn't react and, after a few more seconds of silence, adjourned the meeting.

Emma then met with us and informed us that we were to continue our work as per the plans laid out by Connor. This was consistent with the town hall message, which had made it clear that a cross-firm, horizontal analysis comparing the firms with each other was a top priority. She went on to cancel my presentation for the Santander transaction. The day ended with the New York Fed hosting another of its happy hours, which was full of unhappy faces pretending to be happy, stealing occasional glances at their watches, wondering how soon they could leave.

I WENT TO the SSO team meeting the next day curious about how Silva and his team would respond to the latest organizational changes. Silva opened the conversation with: "Yesterday's news was big news." He wasn't gloating, but there was not a shred of surprise, regret, or concern in his demeanor. Someone on his team asked whether the changes meant risk personnel would no longer be working four days out of the week stationed at the bank they supervised. Silva answered that this would not change in the near future. "In Sarah's mind, risk embeds are up for grabs, but that may be revisited by her by the end of the year," he said, meaning that Sarah still hadn't decided whether to move people like me out of Goldman and back to the New York Fed's building.

Another team member raised the question on every business-line specialist's mind: "What does this mean for the SSO teams?"

Michael responded, "Business as usual." However, he also acknowledged that the need for guidance on performance measurement for the business-line specialists was "well known." On the risk side, Michael thought the announced changes would mean better alignment of management and talent. He relayed Sarah's view that there needed to be "a little more management on the risk side." According to her, SSOs needed to get their act together and not put the risk specialists in the middle. I glanced around the room to gauge the other risk stripes' reactions. Knowing smiles all around.

I could not agree more. But I also knew that what management said was one thing and what they would actually do was another.

I went ahead with finalizing preparations for my SR 08-8 document request, the results of which I would use to prepare the annual ratings and report. The request extended to each of the legal and compliance divisions I had been examining. In addition to policies and procedures, we requested more information on specific transactions and clients, including conflicts, Kinder Morgan, and Capmark. Over the previous weeks I had worked with Johnathon to secure the blessing of the two Mikes in the hopes of avoiding problems. I also had a secondary reason for moving forward quickly with the information requests. The trip to visit Hendrik's family was quickly approaching, so having Goldman working on compiling and producing documents the same week I would not be there occupying their time with meetings made sense.

I planned it so the documents would be ready for me to review once I returned from my time off. I sent the request to Goldman, relieved I got it done in time.

Then again, as I should have guessed, I was not completely done. Right before signing off and going on our vacation for a week, Esther and Lily approached me with a last-minute meeting request. They claimed that they wanted to bring me up to speed on a Fed-specific question that arose about Goldman's consumer compliance rating. When the question arose—or why Goldman raised it with them—they did not say. I did know that Esther and Lily were not responsible for covering consumer compliance; they were relationship managers, charged with covering corporate functions.

I took one look at their request and immediately concluded this was an ambush.

In my experience ambushes are common in banking. The frequency varies, but they generally seem to fall into two categories. The ambush happened either when the stakes were high or when people didn't have enough work to keep them busy. How you deal with an ambush depends on your relative position in the team pecking order. Sometimes they truly come from left field. Most of the time, however, you can prepare for them in advance. This usually involves working regularly with the team and managing your manager. It does require some patience and, sometimes, extra work, but the benefits are usually worth it: you have a better chance of surviving if you go into the ambush as a team.

Given that the annual ratings process was starting in earnest, I made an educated guess as to what this ambush might be about: Goldman was making another push to get their rating raised.

Now, any large bank with a regulatory department will have their employees focus on making sure the bank gets the least number of findings and the highest possible annual ratings they can. That is their job. How a bank's regulatory department goes about doing their job very much depends on the individual bank's culture, the type of employees they hire, and how they incentivize and compensate those employees for that job.

In the case of Goldman, Erin O'Brien led this regulatory effort. Goldman had brought her into the firm to lead it, but had not yet made her a partner of the firm. I knew that Erin, Mike Silva, Sarah Dahlgren, and Esther had overlapped for many years at the New York Fed—my colleagues had filled me in. In fact, a few years later Erin would hire Esther to work for Goldman.

So I figured this was going to be one of those all-too-common meetings in which indirect statements and ulterior motives reigned supreme. I insisted that Terry, who was responsible for Goldman Fed consumer compliance, and Telephone Bob, the person tasked with overseeing consumer compliance at Goldman for the Federal Reserve Board, attend the meeting with me. Esther and Lily could not really object to that.

I immediately went about securing their attendance and hoped that all those biweekly and monthly meetings that Bill, Terry, and I had over the past few months would be enough for us to stick together and fight the ambush. As soon as I explained my last-minute meeting request, they agreed to attend. After all the work we had done together, there was not much need to explain; they figured out pretty quickly that Esther and Lily were up to something.

Emboldened, I headed off to face the ambush.

CHAPTER 18

Plowing in the Sea

Lily looked anxious and seemed unhappy to be there. We were sitting in the conference room, waiting for everyone else to join, the tension quietly building on top of our mutual silence. Eventually Terry, Telephone Bob, and Esther joined on the phone.

The meeting began with a dial-in mix-up. Normally such a mix-up would have resulted in a moment of levity. In this case it did not. Telephone Bob, Terry, and I remained silent. This made Lily even more nervous. After clearing up the call-in numbers, Lily nervously opened the meeting.

"Esther and I just wanted to update you, Carmen, to post as an FYI that—this is probably not new information to you who are on the phone—but, um, just to let you know that the, um, so we are all on the same page, that Goldman has inquired about their 'three' consumer compliance rating, which they do from time to time, and they wanted to know a timeline of the review. And so it raised some questions. Who owns the rating?"

The silence coming from Telephone Bob, Terry, and I was absolutely deafening. The question of who owns the rating was, as far as we knew, a settled question. There had been many meetings between Terry, Telephone Bob, and the CFPB about this topic last year; Lily, Esther, Michael Koh, and I had attended quite a few of them. We had agreed on who owned what.

After a pause Lily continued, bringing up an outstanding memorandum of understanding (MOU) from 2008. Even though Lily herself indicated that the Fed had acquired this MOU, apparently Goldman wanted to know who owned the MOU that Lily knew the Fed owned. An MOU that, it seemed to me, Lily, Donna, and Mila were supposed to have been tracking. An MOU they should have transitioned to Johnathon and updated Bob on.

Lily's face clearly reflected an awareness that she was walking on eggshells. She nervously soldiered on: "And, um, as you know CFPB is scheduled to, was scheduled to begin their exam this past Monday, so we just wanted to make sure that we were, we understand that the expectation is, well, we all know actually what their expectation is, but, on our side, as long as this comes together, it's, we own the rating or they do own the rating."

More silence from Terry, Bob, and me. *As long as what comes together?* I wondered.

Lily swallowed hard and kept going: "And this way we can respond to the bank's inquiry as to how their three rating will be reviewed and who will be responsible for doing that." Again, she paused. Again, more silence from us. And again, Lily and Esther's agenda became clearer.

Lily, looking like she wanted to run out of the room, ended with: "So that's where we are. We've posed the question to our legal group, our legal is seeking guidance from board legal, and, we will let you know when we hear a response."

By now I had made a few friends at the New York Fed, and they had been schooling me on the subtleties of Fed-speak. Referring a settled matter to legal for review was Fed-speak for "We are deliberately trying to derail your work."

Telephone Bob, Terry, and I had not had enough time to coordinate prior to the meeting, but it did not matter. After working for months with them, I had a pretty good idea of what they were thinking. At this point the question was not *if* we were going to smack these two down but rather who would take the first swing. From a seniority standpoint, the honor belonged to Bob.

He gladly obliged, with an easy, indirect question to Lily and Esther: "Who in board legal is working on that?" Asking for a specific name may not sound particularly aggressive, but in this world it was a clear signal that we were not going to take this lying down.

After a pause, Lily answered, "That I don't know."

What followed was a systematic, orderly takedown of the smoke screen Esther and Lily were trying to put up to derail our work. I knew that forcing us through their legal inquiry and reenacting meetings where things had already been decided would be a way of not allowing us to move forward with gathering evidence and doing real work.

I tried to throw Esther a bone by suggesting that because she was so new to the team, perhaps Lily and their mutual boss, Michael Koh, had not had the chance to fill her in. Terry and Bob showed no such mercy. In the end they managed to push Lily into confessing what she and Esther were up to and what this meeting was really all about: "Goldman wants to be relieved of their rating."

So, according to Lily, we were having this meeting because Goldman wanted their rating raised.

When I walked out of the meeting about twenty-four minutes later, I felt sick to my stomach. In my experience meetings like these always had consequences. It did not matter that I knew Bob and Terry would back me up. I was headed out on vacation, without access to my New York Fed Blackberry or phone (bank policy), so I would have no chance to get in front of Johnathon and manage whatever narrative Esther and Lily would come up with in my absence.

Later that night, as we waited to board the plane, Hendrik asked me how things had been going at work. "It's tough to say who works for whom," I answered. It seemed to me that doing the job I was hired to do had put that job in jeopardy. And now the actors of this drama were left alone to make up their own lines for a whole week. The plane had not taken off, and I was already dreading my return.

––––––––––

A COUPLE OF DAYS LATER Hendrik and I were eating a snack late one afternoon when his Blackberry buzzed. When he picked up his phone I thought nothing of it: this happened way too often, even when we were on vacation. Assuming it was for him, I looked away and focused on the beautiful mountain view, trying hard to not think about *my* work.

Hendrik asked, "Is her Blackberry not working?" I immediately looked up at him. His face had turned hard and serious, the way it did when—as he liked to say—someone was "messing with my baby." He looked my way: the phone call was for me.

"Always happy to help the Federal Reserve," he announced with fake enthusiasm and handed me the phone.

Johnathon, I remember thinking.

Despite my best efforts, the New York Fed's IT department had failed to update my Blackberry so it would work while I was away on vacation. Office policy mandated employees to only communicate using office-issued equipment. Because the Blackberry would not be working, Johnathon had insisted I give him Hendrik's telephone number just in case an emergency came up.

My heart sank a little bit. Johnathon sounded stressed. He wanted permission to give Hendrik's phone number to Erin O'Brien, who was insisting on speaking to me. Goldman had some questions about the information request I had submitted to them. I agreed to talk to her.

Erin sounded nervous when she called. She wanted to talk about one of the information requests that NYSDFS and I had made from their Investment Management division. As part of my SR 08-8 exam I had requested a set of data from a specific date range that, by law, they had to collect from their clients. The purpose of my exam was to see whether they had collected the data when they were supposed to have collected it and, if so, how complete the record was. A simple exam.

Erin wanted to get out of providing me the data. I told her, "You are required by law to collect the data. Why can't you provide it to me? Is it because you do not have it?"

She said they had it but that it was all hardcopies, so it would take them a while to pull together a spreadsheet.

"You don't have to give it to me in a spreadsheet," I reassured her. "You can just photocopy the files and either give them to me in a printed copy or scan them and email them to me in PDF."

This was not what Erin wanted to hear. "If we do that, we can't disguise the client identities," she said.

I tried not to laugh. All they had to do was black out the names with a marker. After a few minutes of back and forth and much hemming and hawing, I asked her, "Fine. How much more time do you need to put together the files?"

Asking for a time extension is, of course, part of their game. It begins with one item and somehow ends up morphing into most items getting an extension. Long before that call a series of older regulators had regaled me with stories about how banks use all sorts of tricks to buy themselves time. According to them the banks will always try to push back negative information releases to more convenient times of the year—say, just after you have finished issuing the annual rating.

Sometimes the request for more time is legitimate; sometimes it's not. The trick was to give yourself enough time to figure it all out and build the inevitable time delays into your plans. Erin and I agreed on a couple of weeks' more time for the Goldman team. I was to receive whatever data they had by the end of February—about a week or so later than originally planned.

Hendrik and I returned to New York a few days later and moved into our new apartment in downtown Manhattan. It was about a five-minute walk door to door from both Goldman and the New York Fed. As it turned out, I could see both my office at the New York Fed and my office at the Goldman regulator floor from my living room windows. What a view ...

———————

THE DAY AFTER THE MOVE I went straight back to work, braced, I thought, for what was to come. The day began promisingly. I joined other regulators for a meeting with Goldman's lawyers, where we discussed issues surrounding lawsuits filed against Goldman by the Mississippi Public Employees Retirement System[1] and ABP[2] pension funds.

Back at my desk Silva walked over and asked if I had a few minutes to meet. I held my breath as I walked over to his office, wondering whether the other shoe was about to drop. He asked me about the latest on the Santander document review, and I brought him up to speed. He then instructed me to prepare an email to Goldman about Santander. He wanted me to suggest that, in our estimation, "there appears to be a breach" and to make sure I copied Bruce Acton and Erin O'Brien. I told him I would prepare the email and run the draft by Johnathon prior to sending it.

After lunch I made my way to the SSO meeting. After telling us about his one-on-one lunch with Goldman's chief financial officer, Silva informed us that New York Fed senior management had been busy that week with risk and SSO summits, where "a number of the SSOs are very worried that risk stripes go too far down the road doing the work they do." He paused, looking around the room.

His team looked at us, the risk specialists. We, in turn, looked back at them.

Silence reigned. Silva then added, "I am inclined to let them run and watch it play out."

He then turned the conversation to CCar, the Fed's stress tests, which were in full swing. My participation in the Goldman stress tests had been more as a spectator than anything else. This was in part because the stress-test model the Fed had come up with revolved around the bank's balance sheets. The only aspect of the conduct rules the CCar stress-test model seemed to have included was how much money the bank set aside to pay for lawsuits.

The atmosphere in the room changed as soon as the CCar conversation began. Over the next few minutes I watched as the relationship-management business-line specialists came together to defend Goldman against the expert risk specialists. Back and forth the conversation went, each side trading punches like boxers in a ring—but politely.

After someone defended the risk specialists skeptical of Goldman's numbers, Ryan O'Hara said, "We are in no better position to defend our numbers than they are." Michael Koh quickly replied, lamenting, "It feels like we are giving mixed signals to the firms." Risk specialist Patrick complained that for one of its businesses, Goldman had given them a "number without detail or description." Risk specialist Sai pointed out that with respect to their legacy assets, Goldman had responded with "absolute evasiveness and," after eight days of waiting, "did not come back with the information we wanted." He suggested that if Goldman did not come through with the data, he would simply go ahead and issue an MRA on the basis of that alone.

Min Sung, Koh's deputy, with his face twisted in anger, stepped in to defend Goldman, insisting that until we had reviewed the data, "we should not judge" and suggesting that doing so would be discrimination against Goldman.

At this point the risk specialists looked at each other and, after a pause, decided they were not done. Risk specialist Sai continued, telling the room that Goldman had taken a while "to confess they could not give us the information we wanted after repeated requests," adding that Goldman "only wanted to talk about what they had given us," which was, apparently, not relevant for the purposes of the test at hand. After a pause Koh and Sung started talking simultaneously, eventually taking turns vigorously defending Goldman with the incoherence and conviction of passionate people who have no idea what they are talking about.

I held my breath, wondering if they were going to come to blows.

Silva finally stepped in, asking the risk specialists, "Should I put it on Erin's list?" to which risk specialist Sai immediately and decisively replied, in a tone that made it clear the conversation was over as far as he was concerned, "I would request that." Koh and Sung then stepped back in to suggest that it would not be wise to do so, using a tone communicating that they thought the conversation was *not* over. The only thing everyone seemed to agree on was that the Fed's internal process was a mess.

I looked on with mixed feelings. I was glad to know I wasn't the only risk expert facing challenges, but I worried that I might somehow be next on Silva and Koh's list.

As if on cue, Silva brought up Santander. He informed us that he and Esther had presented the transaction to the Fed Policy group. I thought, *Yeah, I'm next.* Silva relayed that the policy group had asked them to put together a list of transactions that could have the same issues identified in SR 07-5, the supervision and regulation letter Connor O'Sullivan had identified as applicable to the Santander transaction. Silva then asked me to talk to the group again a little bit about what SR 07-5 said and whether I had the chance to look at the latest batch of documents.

As I began to respond that I had the documents but still had not had a chance to look at them, Ryan O'Hara erupted, screaming, "There was no violation of 07-5!" His eyes, full of hatred and disgust, fixated on my face.

The room froze. As tense as the CCar conversation had been, no one had raised their voice or deployed it with such heartfelt rage. Everyone turned to look at Ryan. His face was red, contrasting with his white shirt, just as it had back in December when Silva had dragged us to the conference room to settle the fight between Ryan and a couple of other risk specialists.

After a pause Ryan continued, at first in a slightly more civilized tone: "According to most people. Technically it went through the review process."His red face turned again to me, and he screamed: "So it's done!"

The entire room remained silent. All eyes slowly turned to me, as the object of Ryan's aggression. I stared back at him, with what I am sure was an arched eyebrow, and immediately decided this was stinky bait. So I decided to play it cool. After a couple of seconds, during which I sat quietly staring him down, his face grew exponentially redder.

At which point Lily—of all people—jumped in to say, "But she's the expert."

Everyone's face turned to her—including mine, with what I'm sure was a look of complete surprise. She was looking at Ryan and pointing with her pen in my direction. Before I could say anything else, Silva announced with a sad expression that the New York Fed did not want the Santander transaction mentioned in the roll-up, especially as a "you should not have done that."

Glad for the distraction, Silva's team quickly assumed flying-paint formation. They eagerly commiserated with Silva about excluding Santander from the roll-up, declaring it a pity. The risk specialists remained silent.

"Speaking of the roll-up," Koh interjected, he told us he had "looked at the template. It looks a lot like last year's." His face expressed deep unhappiness as he added that the "deck doesn't say anything about the business lines." I quickly glanced around the room. The business specialists looked uncomfortable. The risk specialists all smiled. It seemed like the SSO teams were not going to have a say in the upcoming ratings.

AFTER THE MEETING, back at the New York Fed office, I talked to Johnathon about what I had just witnessed at the SSO meeting. He took it in. The look on his face was a mixture of relief—I wasn't the only one experiencing pushback—but it also lacked surprise. Johnathon reminded me that Silva was new to supervision.

"This is how the Fed works," he said. "I want to make sure that you and I are on the same page with respect to how the Fed works, right? Versus the private sector. I want you to understand the Fed way of doing things."

Johnathon went on to explain—again—that there were two teams: the relationship business-line specialists and the risk specialists. The parameters had never been clearly articulated from the top. As for the teams themselves, each one was being run differently. For example, the JPMorgan Chase SSO had been around for a while. "It's an iron-hand woman. They've already made their determination. They don't care what risk do." According to Johnathon, my colleague was not being given access to the data. "Nada," said Johnathon. At Citi, on the contrary, my colleague was free to do as he pleased—"full rein."

In the case of Silva, he was giving a lot of deference to Koh, who had been around almost eighteen years. The implication was that Silva was a "fish out of water" because he had spent most of his twenty-plus years at the New York Fed in other roles, and Koh was the one who really knew.

We then discussed resourcing. Johnathon confirmed that the rumors going around were true: Sarah and her team had frozen hiring for the risk stripe experts and asked management to justify the positions they had. The implications were that, going forward, they were going to restructure how the team of risk stripe experts was going to be run. I asked him point-blank if that meant we were going to be fired. "No," he said. "Who's going to do the legal and compliance work? Hello!" he said, his face and gestures making clear that no one he had worked with at the New York Fed outside the newly hired legal and compliance risk specialists could do the work.

We then moved on to one of those administrative tasks that every bank employee needs to do and absolutely hates—setting up the mechanism for performance appraisals in the system. Like a lot of banks in the private sector, the first six months at the New York Fed was a probationary period. The bank reserves the right to fire you within the first six months—for no reason. Seasoned bank employees know to keep their mouths shut and tread with great care during those first six months.

Typically, if you survive the probationary period, your first evaluation happens six months after that—a year into your tenure. From a logistical standpoint, assuming I survived the probationary period, my six-month evaluation period began at the end of April. As team leader, Johnathon was in charge of making sure we were set up in the performance appraisal system before April, and he wanted to move forward with setting me up in the system. This was a good sign. He would not have been bothering to do it if the New York Fed was planning to fire me on or before April.

As with everything else at the New York Fed, the performance appraisal process was a shit-show. Johnathon knew it, and he knew that, the second he started explaining how it worked, I would immediately know too. We laughed, and I told him what Silva had said about the performance appraisal process not mattering anyway because what everyone else said was ultimately what counted. At first Johnathon tried to say that wasn't true and then tried to convince me that I should not lose hope, as he would have a say in it as well. He reminded me, in a more serious tone, that there was a bonus in pay—of comparable size to the private sector. I found his slight change in demeanor telling: suddenly I realized this conversation would be about much more than procedures.

"I want to manage your career and expectations," Johnathon said. "There are these opinions that are coming in from Michael Silva's team ..." He seemed to be looking for words. I asked him if he was referring to "the ambush," and he smiled. Then he indirectly confirmed that the initial views from Silva's team would likely play a role in my performance appraisal—and that this would factor in when determining the size of my bonus.

This was an unpleasant surprise. Things do not play out this way in the private sector. Although it's true that there are a lot of games played around with bonuses and that every bank is a bit different, generally the most direct influence on your bonus comes from the people you report to directly. Colleagues in other divisions outside your accountability hierarchy generally have little or no say on the size of your bonus.

Johnathon then dove right in: according to him, although people were very complimentary of my work performance, "you're very transactional, and the relational is the area that you need to be sensitive to. You may not agree with what other people say because of their views. It may be stupid; it may be confrontational, right? But it's up to every one of us to sort of diffuse that and to get to a level where we can have a, what I would call a meaningful dialogue, right?"

I recalled the scenes of "meaningful dialogue" I had witnessed other risk specialists have with these business-line specialists. They were pretty similar to the ones I had been having. These people were not being stupid. And they *were* being confrontational.

I told myself to just breathe, stay calm, and see if I could ferret out specifics. He couldn't pinpoint any. "Part of it is also a personality makeup, right? Are you, you're familiar with Myers-Briggs, right?" Myers-Briggs is a personality test that a mother and daughter developed based on Carl Jung's theories. I was familiar with it, as it was very much in vogue when I was in college. Like all tools, this test could be used for either good or evil, and I was wary of anyone who tried to use it to control me.

"What do you think you are?" Johnathon asked.

Like any self-aware person who has spent a lifetime dealing with manipulative, coercive, and controlling people able to use every trick in the book, alarm bells immediately went off in my mind.

"I know what I am. What do you think I am?" I shot back.

"Listen: it's about how you are perceived," he calmly insisted. I was perceived, he said, as having "sharper elbows" and that I was "sort of

breaking eggs." He then suggested that I work to remediate this perception. He then told me he was making this suggestion because he cared
about me. "You really need to make these changes quickly in order for
you to be successful as part of the team," he said, raising his hand and
pointing as if outside the office. I knew he meant Silva's team. Despite
Johnathon's show of support, Silva's team never stopped trying to obstruct my work—or the work of other regulators.

I wondered whether Johnathon ever had that conversation with
Silva. And if he had, whether he had actually done so to support my
work.

It was as if Silva and his team were putting pressure on Johnathon
to put pressure on me just as I was about to receive a data dump of
documents from Goldman and we were about to begin work on the
annual ratings and report. But Johnathon was supposed to protect me
and my work.

So I decided to push back, openly suggesting that it would be unfair
for me to be fired from that team if I was indeed doing the good job
he had just said I was doing. I remembered all the conversations we
had had in which we both agreed that, from a legal and compliance
standpoint, Goldman was a house on fire. We both had been hired as
experts. We both knew this was true. The legal and compliance risk
leadership knew this was true. Goldman knew it was true—they had
even admitted to it.

Within the legal and compliance team there didn't seem to be any
dissent among the experts.

Then Johnathon stunned me: "I'm here to change sort of the definition of what a good job is, right? There's two parts to it, right? Actually
producing the results, which I think you are very capable of producing
the results, right? But also to be mindful of enfolding people, right?
And diffusing situations, right? And making sure that, um, people feel
like they're heard, irrespective, right?"

He then suggested I needed to be more deferential to Silva's team.

Are you kidding me? I thought. I immediately put on my lawyer armor and walked Johnathon through the facts, step by step, fighting the
feeling of hopelessness clutching at my heart. I was plowing in the sea.
Silva's team had goals fundamentally different from and completely

contrary to our goals as regulators, and unless we did something about it, they were going to win.

I pushed Johnathon to go beyond understanding the conflict: after all, resolving it was above my pay grade. As team leader, it was *his* job to step up and do that. But he had nothing concrete to offer: "Remember, Carmen, the Fed is a totally different creature." And then he offered his parting advice:

"Absorb and defuse."

CHAPTER 19

The Dog and Pony Show

Back at the Goldman regulator floor the following day I finally got a chance to look at the Santander documents—and in the process discovered the documents had issues. This was not surprising. I reported back on what I found to everyone within the Fed. Johnathon and Silva immediately understood the problems and implications, and both wanted to move forward with pressing Goldman.

Michael Koh pushed back, dragging me once again into his office to insist that he could not see the issues I was raising. Once again it was all smoke and mirrors: I would point out the issues, and he would try to talk around them.

The following day Koh came unexpectedly up to my desk. He asked whether I was available to join him and a few others for a meeting with Goldman senior management. I quickly picked up my things and joined the two Mikes, Esther, Lily, and Analisa for the long walk upstairs to the 42nd-floor conference room.

We walked in and introduced ourselves to the Goldman team as they arrived, a few at a time. I had just finished settling down when Silva suddenly jumped up from his seat, beaming. "I know you!" he excitedly exclaimed, heading toward a tall, very fair, blue-eyed man. They shook hands. "Good to see you!" he continued. The man, Sean Gerald O'Reilly, responded in kind, clearly happy to see him.

Sean Gerald O'Reilly—better known as Jerry—had occasionally come up in conversations before this meeting. As was the custom during my time there, whenever someone brought up the name of an ex-president of the New York Fed, like Jerry, the employees immediately fell all over each other to express admiration. Today was no different. I watched as, one by one, Koh, Esther, and Lily greeted Jerry, their faces beaming with admiration.

Jerry had joined the New York Fed in 1968 and spent most of the following twenty-five years there. He was president of the New York Fed from 1985 until the summer of 1993. An *LA Times* article from October 1993 reported that Goldman's then chairman recruited Jerry to join the firm in a special-projects role in the office of the chairman.[1] This flexibility allowed the chairman to deploy Jerry wherever needed. He began working at Goldman on January 3, 1994, a few months after leaving the Fed.[2]

One of Jerry's duties at Goldman was to cochair the Business Standards Committee (BSC).[3] In that role he was charged with making sure that Goldman's BSC recommendations were implemented across the firm. For our purposes, the relevant recommendations for improvements in Goldman's BSC report fell into two buckets: the ones Michael Silva and his team were focusing on and the ones I was focusing on.

Since I had started at the Fed, Silva had spent quite a bit of time on the following issues: "reputational risk management" and "can versus should." Both were discussed in the introductory executive summary overview section of the BSC report.

The only thing I could find that approached a definition for "can versus should" was in the BSC report: "In particular, our approach must be: not just 'can we' undertake a given business activity, but 'should we.'"[4]

I have never heard of a law, rule, or regulation called either "reputational risk management" or "can versus should." Nor had my legal and compliance risk colleagues. Even the New York Fed legal department had not heard of it. Nevertheless, Silva and his team spent countless hours discussing these topics and bringing them up as supervision points during meetings with Goldman.

What I knew and worked on were Federal Reserve Supervision and Regulation letters 07-5, 08-8, and a whole bunch of banking, SEC, Financial Industry Regulatory Authority (FINRA),[5] and other regulatory laws, rules, and regulations defining and regulating issues and topics like conflicts of interest (applicable in the Kinder Morgan–El Paso transaction) and structured products (applicable in the Santander transaction). Unlike Silva and his team, I was focused on two of the BSC report recommendations for improvement—conflicts and structured products—and the inconvenient data trail the paperwork seemed to be pointing to.

Such as Goldman's choice of Jerry to be cochair of the BSC.

Indeed, Jerry's name had a habit of showing up every so often in the press attached to conflicts-of-interest issues. There was the 1997 reveal of his romantic relationship with the president of the Boston Fed, a voting member of the Federal Reserve's Open Market Committee— the committee that, among other things, decides whether to raise or lower US interest rates. While he worked at Goldman. Both the *Boston Globe*[6] and *New York Times* covered[7] the relationship after a retired Federal Reserve governor had alerted the press, concerned about the conflicts-of-interest issues he felt Jerry's relationship with the president of the Boston Fed raised. What the press did not write about—but would be immediately obvious to a lawyer practicing in this area—was of course the potential for improper acquisition and misuse of material, nonpublic information.

According to the *Boston Globe* and the *New York Times*, the relationship had begun in 1995,[8] when she left her husband[9] for Jerry, who was then already working at Goldman in the office of the chairman but was not yet a partner of the firm. The articles point out that in 1996 Jerry was appointed partner at Goldman. The couple eventually married, and she retired from her position as president of the Boston Fed in 2007.

Then there was that April 2009 *New York Times* article that revealed Goldman's conflicts of interest during the 2008 financial crisis.[10] Jerry and then New York Fed president Timothy Geithner were, according to the *Times*, "close, speaking frequently and sometimes lunching together at Goldman headquarters.[11]

What the articles only hinted at but my colleagues filled in was that during the 2008 crisis, Jerry used his clout over Tim Geithner, then president of the New York Fed, to get Goldman employees access to

AIG's books under the pretense that Goldman was going to lend AIG money to help them stay afloat.

What was actually happening was that AIG owed Goldman so much money that if they failed to pay Goldman what it owed, the bank would go bankrupt. So Goldman wanted to get into AIG's books to see if there was any way they could get paid. When Tim Geithner let them in and Goldman realized they were never going to get paid, they turned around and pushed him to throw AIG under the bus to save the bank—while pretending to the press and the world that the whole thing was not really a bailout.

I could go on, but you get the picture.

One of the rules included in SR 08-8 is that the board of directors and senior management are required to set and promote a culture of compliance with the law. As a regulator, from a conduct-rules perspective, Jerry seemed to lack the credibility to hold the role of BSC cochair tasked with implementing their firm-wide conflicts-of-interest and structured-products program.

IAN JONES HAD WALKED into the conference room right before Jerry with nary a second look from the SSO team. He promptly opened the meeting by introducing himself as the other chair of the BSC and informed us that this presentation was an update on Goldman's progress in implementing the BSC report's recommendations.

It was obvious from his body language that Jones did not enjoy being upstaged by Jerry. He rectified that situation by reminding the audience of his importance: "I unfortunately have a hard stop at ten o'clock because I have a meeting with Lloyd"—that is, the CEO of Goldman.

He then informed us that twenty-one of the thirty-nine recommendations had been fully implemented, with another eleven to be completed by the end of the first quarter. In his mellifluous voice he calmly proceeded to take his best shot at pulling off the "fall on our sword" maneuver: "The remaining seven which fall into structured products and client relationships and training, that's the bulk of the work that we think will take *at least* until the end of the second quarter, and it'll probably stretch into the third quarter before we can get them done. We are not disappointed by that. We set out with an ambition to get things done by the end of the second quarter of 2012, but the work that needs to be done there, is, you know, it's an ambitious undertaking."

Notwithstanding the smooth delivery, I was not impressed. Maybe because I had seen so many other members of Goldman's senior management try to pull the "fall on your sword" argument on topics that matter from a legal standpoint, with the classic "we are working on it" move to try to avoid a finding. The bottom line was that structured products in general—and Santander in particular—fell under old laws, rules, and regulations that had applied for a very long time. This was covered by both SEC rules and SR 07-5 under the Fed—which applied to Goldman at least since 2008, when they became a bank holding company supervised by the Fed.

Based on my previous work at big banks, I had a pretty good idea of how long it took to implement a project like this. Spoiler alert: it was way less time than Jones claimed, provided the bank was doing it in earnest and not stalling or treating it as a cost-of-doing business move. He should at least have pretended to be disappointed at failing to meet the time frame.

Jones continued with the presentation, focusing mostly on Silva's favorite topics. Occasionally he veered into my territory. Like when he ventured his thoughts on regulation: "What that entails is also a huge—ha-ha—and time-consuming unpleasant project that we deal with, and boy, oh boy ..." Speaking condescendingly about regulation being something funny, time consuming, and unpleasant to a regulator is not the kind of behavior that inspires confidence in management— and was not helpful to Goldman's SR 08-8 data-point scorecard.

In his defense, he was not the only one who did it. Just the latest.

Jones then assured us Goldman had spent a lot of time on their efforts around conflicts of interest, "really intently focusing on getting the execution of those recommendations correct." I remember thinking that this was not the impression we got when we met with Rachel and her team.

At this point Jerry interrupted Jones and, in his growly voice, told us, "I just wanna emphasize that in all of these initiatives, there is now in place or there will shortly be in place *extensive* documentation, and if you or some of your people wanna do, uh, you know, uh, an exercise, just *pick out* something and, and ask us about, telling us—ha-ha—putting up a dog and pony show on the documentation side, it's really, uh, it's very impressive, very impressive."

I thought that referring to work on legal and compliance policies and procedures as a "dog and pony show" was a little condescending, but I was more interested in his main point: he and Jones both claimed that Goldman had extensive documentation for conflicts. *Really?* I remember thinking. I had already asked Goldman for this "extensive documentation" that Jerry and Ian were claiming they had implemented. Extensive does not mean relevant. I had a hunch that the extensive documentation Jerry was discussing would not look good under the microscope.

I glanced at my SSO colleagues. They were attentively taking it in, smiling. I caught a couple of them throwing quick glances my way. This was music to their ears. I could feel my stomach clenching.

It was at this point, about thirty minutes into the meeting, that I unexpectedly got a full-frontal view of what was going on between Goldman and the New York Fed at the most senior levels.

Jerry again interrupted the presentation, looked straight at Silva with a troubled expression, and said, "One of the things I would like, Michael Silva, that's frustrating to me here, as you may recall, one of the things we did in this transparency thing, is that we created this modified balance sheet. In case you've forgotten, I've got a copy of it right there." Jerry handed the paper over to Silva and continued. "We obviously introduced this to the SEC and—that's their turf—but *that* balance sheet, whether it's for Goldman Sachs or JPMorgan or whomever, contains *much* more valuable information that's relevant to systemic risk issues than the mandated GAAP balance sheets, which frankly don't tell you much at all. And I wish the hell there was some way, not just for *us* but for the industry, that this approach—not as a substitute to the GAAP balance sheet—but as a *supplement*. Just glance at it. The information there is *so much more important* than the traditional GAAP balance sheets, and I get very frustrated about that. Maybe you can pull a rabbit out of a hat."

Jerry laughed softly. Silva laughed too and, looking straight at Jerry, said, "Maybe more of an elephant out of a hat." The two men, looking at each other, continued to laugh.

"But I certainly agree this is a much more useful format, absolutely," Silva added.

The two men kept looking at each other, smiling and nodding. The rest of the room watched the exchange in complete silence.

It's really difficult to convey the range of emotions that competed for my attention as I witnessed this exchange. Did I just see Goldman Sachs give orders to Michael Silva? Did I just see Michael Silva willingly accept them, without question or pushback? This is not supposed to be happening! Why is this happening?

Was this just another "fake work" regulatory project to keep the New York Fed busy with pretend work along the lines of "reputational risk management" or "can versus should" to dissuade them from doing actual work? It certainly seemed that way, but I could not tell for sure. I was there to supervise conduct rules, not numbers.

I quickly analyzed the scene from multiple angles. That Goldman would want to try to use the New York Fed to get to the SEC made perfect sense: banks will do what they can to get their way. But the fact that Silva was so willing to go along and not push back made no sense. I discreetly looked around to see how others in the team were reacting.

Everyone was focused on Jerry and Silva, wearing expressions that suggested they had seen this before and thought it was normal. I imagined that any big bank executive who had ever tried to pull this off—and failed—would watch this scene with a mixture of fury and envy.

For a second I considered jumping in and saying something. But I quickly dismissed the idea as a waste of time; it would be far more productive to bide my time and let my work speak for itself.

Silva held the document tightly. After a long pause Jones moved on to the "can versus should" question. He explained that Goldman had set up a tracking mechanism and that compliance would monitor it: "in this regard you will see something called conditional approval. Conditional approval is a very rigorous standard that we've adopted in the most important committees that are charged with approving transactions. The committee would tell a team that they are fine to go ahead with this transaction provided that you satisfy four or five conditions. If they fail to satisfy any of them, any one or all of them, then they cannot go ahead."

Interesting: they were not legally required to set up such a tracking mechanism—which is precisely why they had done so.

Of course Goldman was willing to set up and show off to regulators compliance programs, such as this conditional approval, that are not legally required to be in place. This meant that regulators could not issue findings, fines, or enforcement actions against them if the so-called compliance programs were not in order. I was not the only regulator supervising Goldman to notice the pattern. On several occasions I had discussed this with colleagues at the New York Fed, the FDIC, and NYSDFS.

These regulators were collectively blown away by the cynicism behind Goldman's show of doing a good job on things that did not matter. It made their refusal to even try to do anything on issues that did matter that much worse. On a different level it was demoralizing.

Adding insult to injury, Jerry reinforced his message to the SSO team by adding, "The net result of this often will *not* be a decision on our part that says the conditions weren't met. Therefore, there is a documentation of *denial* to proceed with the transaction. What often happens because of this conditional approval is these things die a natural death. They just *go away!* Because, uh, there is a recognition by the client, or the team, or above that this thought just isn't going to happen."

So the cochair of Goldman Sachs's BSC was trying to get the New York Fed to accept that illegal or shady transactions just die a natural death. That they just fade away. This was priceless. But Jerry wasn't done.

"One of the problems that Michael touched on a minute ago is that we're struggling to find the best ways to, kind of, *monitor* this 'can versus should' philosophy. Like Michael says [it's], you know, a judgment standard, not a rule set. So it's hard to capture in nice, neat, little buckets what fits into what bucket. I wish I could think of a way that we could have a bucket that says *dies natural death*."

The crowd laughed, happily going along. I remember looking on in silence, watching Jerry performing for his adoring audience, feeling grateful his eyes never seemed to wander down to my side of the table.

Jerry continued, "I just want to impress as strongly as I can that getting our arms around the beast is impossible. But make no mistake: things have changed! And one of the most powerful manifestations of that change is this conditional approval document."

"Well said," Jones interjected while looking at Jerry, and then he continued with his presentation. Toward the end of the meeting Silva eagerly thanked the presenters: "We appreciate the effort very much. Clearly a tremendous amount of work." He then turned to the rest of his team and asked if there were any questions.

Koh turned the conversation back to the "can we versus should" conditional approval process. "Jerry, I was gonna ask," he began, "the case studies that you mentioned you have that you and your team have worked on: is it possible for us to see them? We're just curious in terms of—"

Jerry interrupted him: "Sure!" quickly adding that he would schedule a follow-up meeting for the team to look deeper into the conditional approval process. The groupies beamed. Jerry smiled right back.

After the meeting wrapped up, somehow I managed to keep it together on the long walk back to the Goldman regulator floor. I even chatted with Esther along the way.

Inside I was horrified.

The rest of the day dragged on for me. Unable to concentrate on typing up my meeting minutes, I watched as the SSO team moved around the floor. Koh, Lily, and Esther seemed in good spirits. Word of the meeting was spreading. My digestive issues intensified. I told myself to stop fretting and focused my attention on actual, tangible work—of which I had plenty.

THE FOLLOWING WEEK the Goldman regulator floor was abuzz. The CCar presentation had been pushed through to management. Meanwhile I watched the nonverbal cues and movements on the floor. Some of the risk specialists on the numbers side were not happy with some of the business-line specialists. You could feel the tension between them. I thought about what was to come for me with the annual report and fought back a sense of dread.

I found out through the grapevine that Emma had gone on extended medical leave. As a result, leadership of the legal and compliance risk team was changing yet again. Supervision of my team would now be shared among Johnathon, Riley, and Judy Adelson—three very different people. More experienced colleagues told me that the three of them did not get along. *Great! Just what we needed!* I thought—right as the annual review process was kicking into high gear.

The two Mikes led the next roll-up meeting for the SSO team. Silva introduced the meeting by pointing out that the process of producing the annual report was "unique"—perceptions and opinions mattered, and consensus was key. He told us, the "new" risk specialists, that we would not be able to understand the process until we experienced it fully. Koh then told us that he wanted us to fill out a deck. As he circulated it, Silva jumped in, "That's sort of the crux of the matter at this moment. I need very honest feedback from the risk specialists. Can you deliver that format? We talked to Art about it."

Art was the new management layer Sarah had placed between herself and the risk stripes when the management reshuffle took place a few weeks ago. "He said 'yes, you can,' but apparently he didn't tell *you*," Silva laughed uneasily.

No, he did not, I thought.

I glanced through the template. My first reaction was: *How am I supposed to fit SR 08-8 into this?* It seemed the SSO team was not thinking of doing the review along the lines of the SR 08-8 but had something altogether different in mind. The risk stripes quickly jumped in with questions. One asked how much supporting evidence they were expecting. Another pointed out that they had been trained to use last year's report as the baseline and to only add to it if there was any significant change.

Koh struggled to provide satisfactory answers because he was starting from the premise that "given the new structure, we don't want to do things the way they were done in the past." Silence reigned.

Silva weighed in, "I do want to say, especially to the risk specialists, that you're being asked to assign ratings based on not as much work as you probably would've liked. I just want you to make sure you understand that I was specifically indoctrinated, specifically trained that you guys, your job is to give me your best view. If I have questions about that view, I will ask those questions, but once I sign that report, I own it, not you."

Totally incorrect, I thought. *What a sham.* While my management wanted me to assign ratings based on work I had been doing since November, the SSO team wanted me to assign ratings based on something altogether different they just came up with. Silva wanted to take responsibility for the ratings away from the risk specialists. And they were deliberately giving us orders as if they had the power to do so.

Someone asked about the timeline and due dates, and Koh indicated that these were not firmed up yet. In turn, he then asked whether the risk stripes had received their templates yet. Apparently only one had; my group had still not circulated any form for us to fill out, and the same was true for most of the other risk stripes. Koh confirmed this was because a lot of the forms we would be expected to complete had not been finalized. Differing views, he said, had "held up the rollout of the framework."

As Koh moved to close the meeting, he made it clear how things would work at the Goldman team: "Obviously risk is not in a position to be able to bring it all together because there's a lot of other context that obviously the onsite team is gonna have better perspective on, to kind of weigh the different factors, and that's when we need to do that all together."

There it was again: Koh was saying that the SSO team would have the last word on the annual report—brazenly going against what Connor, Johnathon, and everyone else in my management had said. Forget SR 08-8, they were saying. Forget all our evidence and findings against Goldman.

They would take it from here.

CHAPTER 20

Sarah Dahlgren

In hindsight people's motivations can be so clear, so ... predictable. But when you're in the thick of it, dealing with the minute-by-minute landmines of a gaslighting campaign by seasoned veterans, immediate explanations for surprise moves can sometimes elude you.

This was the case when, toward the end of the day, Silva walked over to my desk, sat down, and told me he was eager to move forward with emailing Goldman about the Santander transaction. Somehow he seemed different. Really trying to be nice, as if he were on my side. I brushed the thought away. Silva told me he had reviewed the draft email I had prepared earlier informing Goldman that, upon review, we believed the "no objection" requirement was part of the final agreement. That email asked Goldman how they would manage the legal and reputational risk that arose as a result of them ignoring this requirement. Silva wanted me to send the email. He also instructed me to follow up with Johnathon about how to move forward looking into Goldman's Chinese wall and insider-trading issues. He was being proactive on regulatory issues for once. Something must have happened.

And indeed it had. The next day I opened the door to the Goldman regulator floor and knew instantly that something big had happened. As I walked to my desk everyone looked at me, as if gauging my mood, debating whether to approach me. Very strange. I kept walking toward my desk.

As I put my things down Lily got up from her desk and made her way to Esther's office, shutting the door behind her. Almost simultaneously

Donna did the same, only she went into Mila's office. Not long after, Sung and Michael Koh retreated into their offices, shutting their doors.

I sat down, wondering what the hell was going on. A few seconds later Evan walked over to my desk.

"Congratulations! You must be so happy! I know how hard you have been working on this," he said as a genuine smile spread across his face.

"What do you mean?"

"Didn't you see what happened? Judge Leo Strine issued his opinion on the Kinder Morgan–El Paso deal. It's all over the news."

As he spoke, Analisa and a few of the other NYSDFS and FDIC regulators I worked with walked over.

I turned to my computer and looked up the opinion. Scanning through it, I quickly realized the judge had dropped the regulatory equivalent of a nuclear bomb over the SSO team, the business-line specialists, and every Goldman employee who had spoken to us about their conflicts policies and procedures and the Kinder Morgan–El Paso transaction. Judge Strine observed that "on top of [other conflicts-of-interest problems], the lead Goldman banker advising El Paso [Steve Daniels] did not disclose that he personally owned approximately $340,000 of stock in Kinder Morgan."[1]

Hammering the point home, the judge added in a footnote, from one of the testimony transcripts: "Q. Would [the fact that Daniel had a personal financial stake in Kinder Morgan] matter to you? A. It might. Q. Why? . . . A. It would just be one more piece of information for the potential for conflict. That is not between two divisions, but between one person's brain."[2]

One by one the faces of James, Bruce, Rachel, Jerry, and every other Goldman employee whose statements were now exposed as lies came to mind: "Although it is true that measures were taken to cabin Goldman's conflict . . . *those efforts were not effective*" (emphasis added). Strine continued, "Interestingly, the record suggests that it was Goldman's close clients in El Paso management who suspected at times that Goldman was not honoring the Chinese wall and who decided that Goldman be walled off from merger discussions and negotiations."

Strine concluded, "The record suggests that there were questionable aspects to Goldman's valuation of the spin-off and its continued revision downward that could be seen as suspicious in light of Goldman's huge financial interest in Kinder Morgan." As I kept reading I figured out why Morgan Stanley had been upset all those months ago.

In order to give the appearance of having dealt with a part of its conflict, Goldman directed El Paso to hire Morgan Stanley as their main adviser—but Goldman did not stop acting as El Paso's adviser. In fact, Goldman made sure El Paso signed an advisory contract with Morgan Stanley whereby Morgan Stanley only got paid if the deal Goldman had put together went through.[3]

In other words, if Morgan Stanley got El Paso and its shareholders a higher offer than the one Kinder Morgan was making, it would have to do so for free. I thought back to the moment Rachel told us that Morgan Stanley had been brought in to advise El Paso and that no one had come to top Kinder Morgan's offer. According to her and Goldman, this was evidence the offer was fair and the conflicts had been dealt with.

Now we knew why no one had topped the offer.

Goldman's behavior ensured that El Paso and its shareholders, which included pension funds, were trapped into their offer and got the least amount of money for their investment. Goldman knew this at the time and did not tell us. They had, arguably, lied and misrepresented the situation to regulators. There are a number of laws, rules, and regulations that make that a punishable offense.

Judge Strine did not block the deal from going forward, but he did indirectly caution the parties to settle the matter. "After full discovery," he wrote, "it would hardly be unprecedented for additional troubling information to emerge, given the suspicious instances of non-disclosure that have already been surfaced."[4]

I looked up at Evan with a smile. The other regulators came forward with their congratulations. I stood up, and we chatted for a bit. For a brief moment I glanced down the hall at the other risk specialists. Many of them were looking back at me, smiling.

Soon enough Erin O'Brien called, her voice cracking with panic. She said Goldman was "very nervous" about handing over the document request and wanted more time. She also insisted that Goldman be allowed to schedule a meeting with the regulators to walk us through the documents.

I forwarded the Strine opinion to Johnathon and alerted him to Goldman's request. He instructed me to allow them a few more days and work with Silva on scheduling the meeting. We could use Strine's legal opinion to support the annual report.

That night I went to bed thanking my lucky stars. Maybe I'd be able to draft the MRIA and MRA regulatory findings and push Goldman to clean up their conflicts issues after all.

I ARRIVED AT the New York Fed offices for my Monday meetings with one priority in mind: the annual report. I sat down in the conference room with my colleagues and waited for answers. Riley, Judy, and Johnathon—our three team leaders—were there, sitting side by side. Riley spoke first: we needed to hand in a first draft of our report in seven days.

He then outlined what the template would look like and what his expectations were with respect to supporting evidence. Next Johnathon outlined his vision for the template and supporting evidence— which was completely different from Riley's. Finally Judy stepped in, with yet another completely different—and irreconcilable—message.

They never argued directly with each other. They never raised their voices. They simply spoke to us as if the other two were not present. This went on in different variations throughout the morning meetings—and would repeat itself for the next couple of months. All of us risk specialists watched in stunned silence.

The following day, in the middle of the SSO meeting, Donna asked whether Esther and Lily would be doing a review of the El Paso transaction as well as Santander. I looked up from my minutes, searching for a reaction from the two Mikes. Koh closed his eyes for a second and, in his usual monotone voice, announced, "Yes, working in concert with others." I quickly glanced at Esther and Lily. They were smiling. Mila then asked for an update on Santander. Silva told the team about the email I had sent at his request.

As I began work on completing the SSO team slides, Mila and Donna told me they would be completing the slide covering the Litton consent order. Naturally, they were the only ones who could: for months they had been covering the order and withholding information from Johnathon, Bob, Terry, and me about what Goldman was doing to clean up their mortgage servicer issues.

Two days later the legal and compliance risk template finally arrived. I took one look at it and went into shock. To complete this template properly would mean transcribing the entire body of daily supervision work I had been doing for the past four months. There was no way I could do that in five days. My mind came up with maybe ten different ways they could have given this template to us months earlier. I made my way to the New York Fed to discuss it with Johnathon.

Johnathon agreed the template made no sense—for all sorts of practical and conceptual reasons. He instructed me to not answer the questions directly; instead, I was to write for each category, on a clean slate. Again we went around in circles over closing the MRAs and MRIAs. I still had no access to the systems, as I had not completed the FISG 200 mandatory training course. Any systems work would need to wait until April.

He shrugged. *Oh well,* his demeanor said. Closing the old MRIAs and MRAs issued against Goldman was not his priority.

At the end of our meeting Johnathon told me that I had been selected to represent the New York Fed at a conference in Washington, DC. They would cover all the expenses. "Don't tell anyone else," he warned. According to him, very few people had been approved to go.

I spent the next four and a half days, which included the weekend, working overtime to complete the template in time for the deadline. *I would get it done,* I told myself.

The day before the template was due Goldman finally released the answers to our examination requests. For the conflicts portion they had put together a stack of printed binders. I distributed them one by one around the office, beginning with Silva. I went back to my desk, ignored the chronic pain radiating from my stomach, and scanned the binder.

About fifteen minutes in, I already knew that Judge Strine's warning—"After full discovery, it would hardly be unprecedented for additional troubling information to emerge, given the suspicious instances of non-disclosure that have already been surfaced"[5]—was on the money. Erin's panic was justified—the regulatory findings wrote themselves. The clinical precision with which Goldman had selected and arranged the teams, cynically interpreting the law, was absolutely breathtaking. They also refused to answer a number of important questions, including providing a conflicts policy for GS Bank, the division headed by Jerry O'Reilly. In due course we would find out they did not do so because they did not have one.

I had little time to dig deeper. Uncovering additional issues would have to wait. I had a draft report to hand in, and the clock was ticking.

Despite the pressures of producing the report, we were still expected to show up for meetings. So it was that I found myself at yet another SSO team meeting. Greece and CCar dominated the conversation. To be honest, I barely paid attention; my mind was on the report. I sent what I had been able to cram in by the deadline. Exhausted, I went home.

THE FOLLOWING DAY Goldman employee Greg Smith resigned with a flame-throwing op-ed in the New York Times, dealing a blow to the bank's stock.[6] In the op-ed he claimed Goldman employees referred to clients as "'muppets,' sometimes over internal email" and spoke callously about "ripping their clients off,"[7] among other colorful expressions.

I could smell the panic from the moment I walked into the Goldman lobby. The regulator floor was buzzing too. Regulators gathered around, throwing out scenarios describing how Goldman would deploy damage-control measures. Everyone looked at Silva and Koh as they walked in and out of the Goldman regulator floor, trying to read from their body language what Goldman might be telling them.

I tore myself away for another meeting with Mila and Donna to go over the roll-up slides for the Investment Management division. Absorb and defuse, I reminded myself as I walked into Mila's office. Donna's face showed concern. She told me that they had gone to a meeting with the business heads of one of Goldman's asset management divisions. Lambert, the head of compliance, was at the meeting and "spoke on behalf of the business when he shouldn't have."

I remembered him well. He was the compliance head who had told us way back in December that he did not think Goldman needed to comply with the consumer laws due to their individual clients' wealth. My mind flashed back to the moment when Donna had asked for but refused to hear my feedback about him.

I looked at her, then at Mila, trying to figure out what to make of their concern. By the looks on their faces, this seemed like a big deal to them. I wrote down their feedback and asked them why they thought it was such a serious matter. Donna answered, "This was indicative of less independence because he started to answer on behalf of the business." I nodded seriously and took notes.

Absorb and defuse, I kept repeating like a mantra.

Shortly after this meeting I found out that the first draft of my report had been rejected. So had the first drafts of everyone on Johnathon's team. Apparently he had given us the wrong instructions. So it was that all five of us got stuck for the second weekend in a row madly rewriting the reports from scratch by Monday.

I arrived at the New York Fed exhausted and ran straight into four livid colleagues. We compared notes with the other team. According to them, yes, this was not unusual. Riley had won the turf wars, so his team did not get screwed—ours did.

"That's why I always wait until the last-possible minute to begin doing anything," one of them said.

"They are going to tell you what they want you to write anyway. Even if you disagree," warned one of the veterans.

"Have they not heard what 'escalation' means?" I remember asking.

The veteran employee looked back at me with a serious face and an arched eyebrow, as if to say, *You've been here long enough to know the answer to your own question.* This was a culture in which senior management knew enough to avoid dirtying their hands with sticky evidence. "Right," I said.

That day I had lunch again with Paul Lin. "This place is crazy," he began as we settled into one of the random burger places not far from the New York Fed.

"I know what you mean," I answered. This time I really thought I did.

"I'm counting down the days until I vest in my pension, then I'm gone," he said. Pensions in the New York Fed vested after five years.

He had about two years to go. He had visibly aged over the past couple of months. It wasn't hard to imagine why. "How are you?" he asked. I filled him in. We bonded over our misery.

A FEW DAYS LATER, after taking care of some SSO team housekeeping matters, Silva jumped straight into the topic everyone on his team wanted to talk about that week: what had Goldman told him about Greg Smith? Apparently Goldman had immediately tasked a senior employee with handling the matter. The firm had conducted a search of their email database and found no use of the word "muppets" in it, though the use of the phrase "ripping [client's] face off" was common. A few SSO team members laughed. *That sounds plausible. Shoddy paperwork seems an integral part of their culture,* I remember thinking. Michael added that the CEO, Lloyd Blankfein, had given him the classic "there's no possible basis for this" line. In the end Goldman told Silva that they felt there wasn't a lot they could do.

"I've been talking to the SEC," he added and then briefly brought up El Paso, updating the team on the ongoing efforts to land a date for Goldman's damage-control meeting with the regulators.

Suddenly Koh got up, his eyes focused on the door of the conference room. He moved aside just as Sarah Dahlgren walked in. I had no idea she would be joining the meeting. What had been an ordinary SSO meeting suddenly turned into a chance to hear from the head of the entire supervision team at the New York Fed.

I wondered why she had come.

Sarah took Michael Koh's seat as she greeted the room. After everyone had settled down, she assumed her power pose—both arms on the table, fists closed—and began, "Celebrating mistakes is important." She pointed to the CCar process as an example of a mistake to be celebrated. Kevin Stiroh, one of her direct reports, had implemented it. New York Fed employees who had participated in the CCar process agreed it had been a disaster. As she spoke, I was reminded of the first time I had seen her, back in November at a town hall.

We had gathered for the town hall meeting in a windowless, auditorium-style room at the New York Fed. The lights were dimmed, and a television-quality video had come up on the screen. Sarah's face, alone on the screen, had come into view. Quickly, methodically, almost robotically, she had recited, "FRBNY, OC, CCar, MRIA." The camera suddenly cut away. A New York Fed senior manager came on, exclaiming words of praise for Sarah. After a few seconds the camera again cut away, back to her face. She continued, in a calm, serious tone: "MRIA, RAP, roll-up, IO, ITRAK." A second cut. Another senior manager was now on camera, praising Sarah. I can't remember the order in which she rattled off the fifty or so acronyms then in use in the New York Fed. Nor do I remember the exact words of praise management heaped on her. They were empty platitudes. What I do remember is the audience's reaction.

The same one as today: silence.

After talking about CCar, Sarah then voiced her concerns. "We are not comforted by the things we are reading in the newspapers. What does a big oil shock look like?" she wondered out loud. "We have the US fiscal situation to go through. We could be back to where we were last time in 2008" as a result of the events in Europe.

As for the Greg Smith op-ed, well, those are the "hardest ones to predict," adding, after a pause, that a lot of what Smith had said reminded her of the Bankers Trust days. "There were signs, but the institutions did not recognize them." The mention of Bankers Trust sent a shiver of silent discomfort through the more experienced staff sitting in the room.

Bankers Trust was an investment and commercial bank brought down in 1999 by two separate scandals.[8] Multiple clients accused the bank of misleading customers about risky derivative products. A Procter & Gamble lawsuit ferreted out tape recordings made by the bank showing the sales force making fun of the clients. Earnings plummeted. Separately, New York State auditors began looking at the bank's unclaimed funds accounts, which snowballed into a joint investigation by the FBI, the US Attorney's Office, and the Federal Reserve and resulted in the bank pleading guilty to criminal charges.

I wondered to what extent Sarah was comparing what we were seeing in Goldman with what they saw in Bankers Trust.

"Is the Board of Directors attuned to this situation?" Sarah asked
the SSO team. The team looked at each other, signaling they did not
know. Silva jumped in, relaying his conversation with Goldman senior
management. It included no mention of Bankers Trust.

Sarah then took some questions. One of the business-line specialists asked what she expected of them. She urged them to "talk about
the cross-firm perspective. Build it into your discussions."

Another team member asked for her thoughts on making banks less
complex. Calling it a tough question, she indicated that "the challenge
is that everything we ask costs money and may have unintended consequences, such as, a change in business model."

Silva then asked Sarah whether she could help "manage expectations regarding what we can actually achieve given the infrastructure
and time frame."

Sarah agreed with him: "There will be just too much to do."

He then added, looking at Sarah, "We expect you to tell us what we
can't do. We will push back on what we can't do."

Koh then brought the conversation back to CCar, the Fed's stress
tests. He complained that, given the length of the process, it could not
be the standard unless that became the new primary way of supervision
going forward. He segued right into pointing out that both Goldman
and Morgan Stanley were nontraditional bank holding companies, and
as a result, "some things are just not going to fit."

Sarah, looking around the room, then said, "It bothers me that we
give the banks an answer where there is not a lot of back and forth between us and the firm. None of the firms should have been surprised
what the results [of the CCar tests] will be, and this time they were."

I was not there to supervise numbers, but I thought of all the legal
and compliance issues I had been flagging. I had heard from colleagues
already that the New York Fed supervision teams had a tendency to
allow banks too much time and space to object to findings.

Sarah's words made it clear that the deferential attitude was clearly
coming from the top.

Another team member then asked about staffing turnover. Sarah looked around the room. She was clearly unhappy as she informed us that "turnover is actually much lower than we have projected." She meant she was unhappy with the fact that New York Fed employees were not finding jobs in the private sector and leaving. Her statement, delivered with a serious look and eyes that swept across the room, reminded me of my interview with Connor all those months ago, when he had indicated that the Fed was looking to push out the problematic examiners, business-line specialists, and relationship managers.

That may very well have been true at the time, but the members of the SSO team were not leaving.

An uncomfortable silence fell across the room. By now I had been part of enough gossip sessions to know that not only were the problematic employees not taking the hint, but they were also advocating that instead of bringing in people from the private sector, they should get incentivized to stay on with raises.

I could not see any of the relationship managers or business-line specialists working for Silva being hired into banks by anyone I had worked for previously. They did not seem to have the attitude and skills necessary to thrive in the banking private sector, where strict deadlines, long hours, and "produce or die" cultures reigned supreme.

The risk specialists—sure. The relationship managers and business-line specialists? No.

Ryan O'Hara then jumped in and asked her, "Has the re-org lived up to your expectations?"

Sarah answered with a question to the room: "How much better do you feel about your knowledge of Goldman and how the information from the risk stripes comes in?" Silence reigned. I quickly glanced around the room, especially at the other risk specialists.

Things seemed to have flipped. Apparently we were there to help the business-line specialists, not the other way around, as our management had repeatedly told us.

Sarah Dahlgren then left the room. No one said a word.

The big boss had spoken.

CHAPTER 21

The Annual Ratings Report

I woke up sick and swollen the morning of the all-important vetting session. My bouts of irritable bowel syndrome were getting progressively worse. But there was no way I was missing work. The legal and compliance vetting session was the meeting where the whole team discussed and agreed upon the banks' ratings for the year. All legal and compliance risk specialists would attend this all-day meeting to ensure there was consensus on the ratings assigned to these institutions. I had to be there: this was the job. I put on a more forgiving outfit to accommodate my distended belly and hurried off to work.

The large conference room had one long table in the middle. To one side was another table decked out with a full breakfast buffet. Occasionally food service personnel would come in to replenish it and, in due course, serve a full lunch spread, followed by coffee, cookies, and cake.

The room was filled to capacity. I grabbed a seat toward the middle and looked around, making eye contact and waving hello to everyone I knew. As I looked around, I noticed a man I did not know looking at me a little too intently. He got up from his chair and made his way toward me.

Out of nowhere Johnathon appeared and asked me to come with him to grab some coffee.

As we waited in line, he leaned over slightly and gestured discreetly toward the man I had noticed earlier: "Do you see that man over there?"

"Yes," I answered. "Who is he?"

Johnathon said he was from the legal department and that he wanted to ask me about the Santander transaction. I could imagine why. Spain's economic situation was deteriorating. If nothing else, it was prudent for the New York Fed to assume wrist-slapping position vis-à-vis Goldman just in case things blew up and splattered across the Atlantic and questions were raised about the New York Fed's behavior.

"I don't want you to talk to him," Johnathon said.

"Why?" I asked.

"For your protection," he answered.

My protection? I thought. *Or, do you mean, Goldman's protection? Perhaps yours?*

I exhaled and gave Johnathon an incredulous look. This was an unacceptable request on multiple levels. On one hand, the lawyer could legitimately accuse me of obstruction if I refused to answer his questions. On the other hand, being ambushed by a lawyer I had never met, whose job and agenda I had no prior knowledge of, about a complicated matter without the files on hand, when I was sick and had prepared for a completely different meeting—that was not a position I wanted to be in.

Even if Johnathon were right, the circumstances made it impossible for me to avoid the man. All Johnathon had given me to work with was "for my protection." *From what? Getting fired?* I thought. So I could either get fired by the legal department for obstructing their investigation or by the legal and compliance risk department for aiding it. I decided that if things came to a head, I wasn't going to obstruct.

Judy Adelson began the vetting session by telling everyone we were not leaving the room that day until our work was finished. One by one, each risk specialist would present the proposed contents of their bank's report. Riley and his assistant had laid out a series of white boards facing the attendees. He was to capture the main points in the white board, with his assistant designated as the official note taker. Next they announced the order of presentations. I was hoping to be first or second, given how sick I was feeling. *Maybe if I volunteered to be first I could go home early?* I thought. Alas, no. My report was to be the last. *Why?* I wondered.

The wait was long and stressful. And sure enough, during one of the coffee breaks the lawyer approached me and said that he wanted to question me about the Santander transaction. He quickly informed me that failing to answer questions would constitute obstruction.

I followed him to one of the sofas in the waiting area outside the conference room. On the way I mentioned Johnathon's request that I not speak with him. He brushed it aside, saying he would "take care of it."

We were just getting started when Johnathon walked up to us. The lawyer and I both got up from the sofa. The two men walked right up to each other purposefully. They looked and moved as if they were about to come to blows. I stepped aside and held my breath, silently praying it would not come to that.

It did not—but only just. Johnathon looked at me as if I had betrayed him. I looked back at him and shrugged, as he was the one who put me in this situation. He walked away sullenly. I stayed behind and answered the lawyer's questions. It turned out that he was trying to gauge whether the Fed should send a letter to Goldman about the Santander transaction.

And Johnathon had not wanted me to talk to him.

BACK INSIDE the conference room my turn to present finally arrived. Everyone leaned forward. Animosity filled the air like bad car air freshener. It was clear this was the main event. It is hard to overstate how divisive Goldman is within the New York Fed. No other bank elicits such a visceral, polarized, even emotional response.

There seemed to be only two camps—for or against Goldman. No one raised their voice or was impolite. It was all in the gestures, body language, and indirect statements. A few people I did not know looked around anxiously. I heard one softly say, "Where is Mila?" Another responded, "She wasn't feeling well. I guess she is not coming."

Now I knew why my report had been pushed to the end. Unbeknownst to me, someone had invited Mila to be present—even though she was no longer a legal and compliance risk specialist and hadn't been since the previous July. I quickly connected the dots. She had my job at the beginning of last year, which was probably the excuse for inviting her. Having said that, no one else who had been rotated out of legal and compliance at any of the other banks had been invited to the meeting.

I remembered all the times she and Donna, her direct report, had obstructed my work. I quickly concluded that whatever the reason for inviting her, it would not have been good for me—or my report.

I got up and took a deep breath. I remember seeing my colleagues, who gave me encouraging looks. For those of us tasked with the day-to-day supervision of the too-big-to-fail banks, Goldman was not a po-larizing topic at all. We all pretty much agreed that from a legal and compliance standpoint, it belonged toward the bottom of the list.

I presented my report. Occasionally I looked up and was careful to only look at my colleagues as I spoke. The mountain of evidence I had gathered included Judge Strine's opinion and the string of scandals printed by the press—including, but not limited to, Litton, Capmark, the upcoming Gupta trial for insider trading, and new lawsuits filed by pension funds against Goldman. I also reported how Morgan Stan-ley won an award for outstanding policies and procedures in order to help dismiss the notion that I had gathered evidence biased against Goldman.

After my presentation it was time for Terry to present on the con-sumer compliance work he and I had been doing. He was shy by nature and very brief. He simply said that given the ongoing Litton consent order and MOUs as well as the open consumer-related MRAs, he was recommending the rating for his section remain the same and not be raised until the problems were fixed. I agreed and added that the SR 08-8 problems we had seen with respect to conflicts extended to con-sumer compliance. Again there was not much of a discussion and no pushback. To this room full of lawyers, the facts were the facts.

Johnathon jumped in to contribute his view on Goldman's AML is-sues. Unexpectedly the woman who had informed the room Mila was sick, whom I had never met before and would never see again, abruptly cut him off. "There are no AML issues at Goldman," she declared, star-ing down Johnathon from across the other side of the table.

The room went quiet. Johnathon tensed up. For a moment I thought he was going to go head to head with her. After a few seconds he held back and chose not to.

I finished my report by proposing a ratings downgrade for Goldman. The debate did not last long. The group approved it unanimously.

This may not sound like much. Objectively speaking, it wasn't. If you ask me, with the exception of one component, all the other components of Goldman's rating should have been downgraded, some by two notches. Still, in the face of a mismanaged legal and compliance risk function plus the well-orchestrated, months-long obstruction campaign implemented by the SSO team, the lone downgrade felt like a small victory.

Judy declared the proceedings a success. "From now on, we own the reports, not you," she announced to the risk specialists who had prepared them. That was a strange thing to say: Weren't we all on the same team? Was she intimating that the team leaders had final say on ratings?

Then she referred to Goldman. In an attempt to get ahead of the criticism, she said something along the following lines of: "I know lowering one component of one bank rating doesn't look like we did much. I have been doing this for many years. Believe me, that's more than we usually do."

I went home, exhausted and glad the day was over. I was off the following day—just as I was every other Friday. I made a mental note to call the doctor first thing in the morning.

WHEN I WAS BACK at Goldman the following week Silva relayed that during his meeting with David Vinair, the Goldman executive had complained about the opacity of the CCar process. Silva took pride in announcing that he had raised Vinair's complaints with New York Fed senior management, telling them, "There is no point in meeting with GS if you are not going to be transparent."

Ryan O'Hara added fuel to the fire by relaying Goldman's complaints about being issued three MRAs at the end of a two-year horizontal review. "They did not take it well," he said, his eyes full of fear, his face bright red. "They were shocked they got an MRA. They seem to have unrealistic expectations regarding what an MRA is." I looked at him, surprised to hear that it had taken two years between the time the New York Fed discovered an issue at Goldman and the moment they told Goldman to fix it.

More problematic was Ryan O'Hara's concern that Goldman didn't like being issued MRAs. It dawned on me then that the situation was dire. I already had a sense that the New York Fed employees on Michael Silva's team were in bed with Goldman Sachs. But that wasn't the only issue.

Now it was clear that they were, in fact, *afraid* of Goldman Sachs.

The day after the SSO team meeting it was my turn to report the results of the legal and compliance all-day vetting session to Silva and Koh. As a precaution, I did so in the presence of Johnathon, Riley, and Judy Adelson, who had offered to accompany me. I was nervous, so I began the meeting by acknowledging this and pointing to the fact this was my first time. "This is my first time too," Silva answered, which helped break the ice a bit. I went ahead with my report, explaining our rationale and providing our conclusions.

The Goldman rating, despite all the efforts from the SSO team, had not been raised. In addition, one of the components had been downgraded.

The two Mikes reacted to my report with silence. Silva had better facial control than Koh, whose look communicated his intense displeasure. After thanking me for the report and some other polite forgettable conversation, I left the room.

Protocol required that I then join my other risk colleagues in communicating the results to the rest of the SSO team. I sat at my usual spot at the table in the fishbowl conference room. Once again my presentation was met by a mix of silent, fearful, and angry faces. This was not what they wanted to hear. Even though I was prepared for this, it still made for a very uncomfortable meeting.

The following week brought more scandals for Goldman—this seemed routine by now. The *New York Times* published a couple of op-eds revealing that Goldman had what turned out to be a 16 percent stake in the biggest sex trafficking forum for underage girls in the United States.[1] Erin O'Brien quickly organized a damage-control meeting. I joined Silva, a few SSO team members, and other regulators inside a windowless conference room, where a group of Goldman executives explained their plans for divesting themselves of their investment stake.

More importantly, they spent close to an hour carefully and systematically walking us through the very thorough process they had followed when initially deciding to make the investment, the same way they had done for the Santander transaction. The process seemed to be focused on determining whether the investment would be profitable for Goldman, not the nature of the company they were investing in or the legality of its business.

Their presentation seemed to suggest that because Goldman followed this process, there was nothing they could do differently—and, by extension, nothing the regulators could fault them for. True to Goldman's culture, the executives doubled-down on their actions and defended the firm. There were no apologies.

I listened intently and noticed that their very thorough process left out a due-diligence investigation that might have revealed that the underlying investment could be tied to illegal activities. Had they known about this, as a bank they would have an obligation to avoid entering into the investment. Banker's Trust is a reminder that banks can be convicted of committing crimes too—and that such convictions can have consequences.

At the end of their presentation the Goldman executives, oblivious to the hole in their logic and looking quite satisfied, asked if we had any questions. And I did have one. I addressed the Goldman team directly.

"You just spent an hour explaining that if you had to do *this* investment all over again, you would follow the same process and do it in *exactly* the same way, correct?" I ended by alluding to the lack of due diligence.

The smug smile on every Goldman executive's face at the beginning of my question was gone by the end of it. As the blind spot came into view, they went quiet and averted their gaze. I kept my head up and looked at each of them in turn.

Surely enough, the other regulators started asking questions too. When the meeting finally ended, to my surprise, Silva leaned over and said, "That was very well put." I wondered if I had finally encountered the limit to how far he was willing to go to protect Goldman.

———————

I SPENT THE FIRST FEW DAYS of that month taking part in FISG 200, the multiday IT systems training course. At the end of it I would finally be granted access to the New York Fed systems, where the official supervision books and records of the bank were kept for posterity.

Having access meant I could do things like view old examination reports and write and upload new MRIAs and MRAs. At last it was physically possible for me to begin uploading into the New York Fed systems the work I had been doing. It was also possible for me to see the existing MRAs and MRIAs against Goldman and determine whether they had fixed the problems.

As I began poking around the database after the training, I realized it was a mess. Some things—like typos—seemed accidental. Others smelled like something else altogether. It was not lost on me that I would not be five months behind in uploading my work if I had been allowed to take the course earlier—like everybody else when they began working at the New York Fed. I made a mental note after the course to consult with Johnathon as to how to go about fixing my backlog issue. Given the messy, incomplete training and dysfunctional workplace culture, there would be a lot more to it than just sitting and writing.

Meanwhile I focused on the two matters Johnathon and the SSO team flagged as priorities. The first was putting together the information request to send to Goldman so we could close their existing MRIAs and MRAs—provided Goldman had done the required work. The second was preparing our questions for the upcoming El Paso damage-control meeting with Goldman. I spent the next couple of weeks mostly in a conference room on the Goldman regulator floor, working together with Analisa.

We began by analyzing the big binder of documents Goldman produced for us. We waded through the shoddy drafting and grammatical errors and quickly discovered that the bank had failed to provide some of the evidence we specifically requested—for example, conflicts poli⁻ cies and procedures that were in place on or before November 1, 2011. Also missing were the Kinder Morgan–El Paso–related board meeting minutes they had claimed they had in their possession when we met with them in December.

These were not insignificant oversights on Goldman's part. Our request had made it clear we were conducting a point-in-time exam. There were two ways to look at this: they were either withholding documentation or were not providing it because it did not exist.

A close reading of the material they did provide was written in doublespeak for business selection, not conflicts of interest. For Goldman, business selection revolved around figuring out how to make the most money. This often involved simultaneously participating in as many sides of a deal as possible. This approach is the opposite of conflicts-of-interest regulations. These regulations revolve around a firm and its employees only representing one party in a deal so as to act in the client's best interest.

It appeared that Goldman had labeled its business selection procedures to also cover their conflicts of interest.

We also discovered that, over the objections of Goldman's compliance department, the legal department had approved the reassignment into the El Paso team of an employee who had historically worked for Kinder Morgan. Unsurprisingly, the CABS system records were shoddy. Tons of information was missing or just plain incorrect. This turned out to be consistent with an internal audit. Goldman's internal audit team had conducted a check of sixty-four transactions and found sixty-seven issues.

Still, Goldman's team had not issued a failed rating on account of the fact that Goldman would have done the transactions anyway.

Analisa and I were a bit surprised when we realized that one of the Kinder Morgan–El Paso Goldman employees was also involved in Goldman's sex trafficking–related investment. We were even more surprised when evaluating the procedures Goldman provided for their private banking division, which informed Goldman employees that "e-mails or other written communications should not be used for vetting conflicts."

Basically, if you don't write it down, you can't get caught. You also can't prove if a conflicts check was actually done. Bottom line was that the more Analisa and I read, the worse things looked at Goldman.

Analisa and I soldiered on. We were in the conference room dissecting a particular batch of documents when there was a knock on the door. We looked up and saw Evan, smiling and waving through the glass wall. He quickly opened the door and asked us what we were doing. "Preparing our questions for the conflicts meeting," we answered.

"Oh, I see," he said, adding something like, "I was just curious. You guys have been sitting here for so long. Don't work too hard!" he cautioned, smiling, and left the room. Analisa and I looked at each other. We weren't working too hard; we were just doing our job.

A bit later there was another knock on the door. This time it was Koh. He also wanted to know what we were doing. "Let me know if you need anything," he said to us when we replied. Analisa and I exchanged a look and went back to work.

Sometime after that interruption Silva knocked on the door. He came in and sat down. He knew we were working on the conflicts questions and wanted to know about our progress. So we brought him up to speed.

Fear crept into his eyes as we explained that Goldman had failed to produce the conflicts-of-interest policies that were in place as of November 1—the policies in use during the Kinder Morgan–El Paso transaction. Instead, Goldman admitted that some divisions did not have conflicts-of-interest policies prior to December 2011. They provided copies of the still-incomplete set of policies they had created as of that date.

We showed him the binder and walked him through it, flipping the pages, explaining how the documents provided by Goldman were drafted in doublespeak and focused on business selection, not conflicts of interest. Silva looked at the binder like a toddler might look at a piece of food they don't want to eat. He made no attempt to touch it. Instead, he looked at both of us and offered his assistance should we want to ask Goldman any follow-up questions.

We quickly took him up on the offer, stating we would be sending him our follow-up questions for approval prior to sending them on to

Goldman. He got up and, after telling us to "keep up the good work," walked out of the conference room.

After that, he stopped by nearly every day to check on our progress.

One day not long after, I took a break from the conference room to check my email. Riley's assistant had finally finished transcribing the notes from the legal and compliance vetting session and circulated them to the team. I opened the document—and my jaw dropped.

The meeting minutes had barely anything to do with the vetting session.

It was as if the assistant hadn't been in the room and had come up with meeting minutes based on what other people who had not been in the room had told her they believed the legal and compliance risk specialists had said during the meeting. On top of that, she had inserted notes on Wells Fargo, a bank that was supposed to be supervised by John C. Williams and the Federal Reserve Bank of San Francisco. The notes made it seem as if our New York Fed team had been supervising Wells Fargo.

I looked at my other emails in that chain. Amy Kim, the risk specialist covering another of the too-big-to-fail banks, was so upset about the minutes that she circulated a redline of her portion of the minutes. Riley's assistant replied-all to say that no one was to touch her meeting minutes. Amy Kim was then reprimanded.

I talked to some of my other colleagues. They were enraged. So was I.

How could this have happened? Was this a listening issue or a reading comprehension issue? Or was it something more sinister? During the vetting session Riley had set up big white boards. He had carefully written down highlights of what we had said, as we said it, in clearly legible handwriting. The assistant was physically present and, the few times I glanced at her, looked like she was writing. She had plenty of time to copy what the board said—even if she did not understand what she had heard. She also had copies of the reports we had prepared and had used during our presentations. The boards were left up for twice as long as it would have taken her to write the content down.

At least one statement she had written in the meeting minutes was a flat-out lie—literally the *opposite* of what the risk specialist had said and written down in their report.

———————

AT THE MONDAY MORNING MEETING Riley, Johnathon, and Judy Adelson walked the legal and compliance risk specialists through the vetting session minutes and the consolidated report they had in turn prepared based on that. That report was also barely recognizable: the team leaders had stripped out a lot of the content, including the most important points. Someone asked why Wells Fargo was part of the report. Riley, Johnathon, and Judy's confusing, convoluted reply amounted to the New York Fed's management neither trusting nor deeming John C. Williams at the San Francisco Fed capable of supervising Wells Fargo. Exactly why, they would not say, but the body language, facial expressions, and nodding heads all around from the veterans made it pretty clear this was not a controversial assessment within the New York Fed. We then all took turns complaining about what was incorrect and incomplete about our respective sections. Management reminded us that Riley's assistant was the official note taker. She sat there with the same fixed smile I remembered from the vetting session.

We then all witnessed management pushing Amy to say that her redline of the meeting minutes had been incorrect. She fought back. I remember looking at her with encouragement. But as the back and forth continued, her face morphed from confident and determined to confused and ashamed. In the end she looked down and was silent— the gaslighting had worked.

As I spoke with other colleagues and other New York Fed employees after the meeting, similar stories poured in. The phantom thread that ran through the stories was the underlying assumption that those who had been there for a while had paid the price and focused on the benefits of staying put.

Those benefits were considerable: twenty days of vacation plus federal holidays, every other Friday off, and two pension plans—a 401(k) with matching, plus an additional defined-benefits pension plan that would pay your full salary. And don't forget the generous six-figure salary and five-figure bonus that was comparable to what you would receive at a private-sector bank outside the sales jobs areas. All that for a nine-to-five job—a true rarity in banking outside the secretarial and menial jobs. Plus, the freedom to add a second job on the side if you were willing to work and use your free time for it—of which you had plenty, as no one was expected to do much in the way of real or meaningful work. All you had to do was adapt to the Fed way of doing things.

Some indicated they had been trapped into their circumstances—bills to pay, mouths to feed, difficulty in finding other jobs, fear of unemployment, humiliation at leaving the New York Fed, and so on. Others told themselves they had been tricked, and by the time they realized what was happening, they had already paid the price, so they would stick it out and get what they could out of the New York Fed until their pensions vested and they could call it a day. Maybe take a parting shot or two on the way out by way of clearing their conscience—without endangering their pensions.

I asked myself if I was being primed to fall into that trap.

CHAPTER 22

Look in the Dictionary

Erin O'Brien wanted to know what the Fed was thinking. Though she started our weekly one-on-one meeting with some housekeeping items, she was visibly nervous. Finally, after circling around it for a few minutes, she asked me what we had in mind for the upcoming El Paso damage-control meeting—or, in not so many words, what was the New York Fed going to ask Goldman about the El Paso transaction.

Other than letting her know we were planning to ask questions, I told her little of consequence. This made her unhappy, but there was nothing she could do. She informed me the CFPB had finished doing their exam and were handing in their report. "That's great!" I remember saying—and deliberately left it at that. She looked back at me, trying to decide what I meant. After the meeting I took the unusual step of giving myself a very tiny pat on the back. It was rare for me to muster enough control to leave someone guessing. Maybe I was finally learning!

Soon after the meeting the final batch of Goldman documents arrived. The delay meant that Analisa and I had just enough time to pore through it. As we expected, Goldman was unable to provide the missing documents we had requested. We also discovered that in setting up the teams, Goldman had assigned to the El Paso team three employees who had previously done work for Kinder Morgan. But the showstopper was the El Paso team seating chart.

Goldman seemed to have built a conflicts-of-interest Chinese wall that actually made it *easier* for the two opposing teams to communicate with each other, not the other way around. For example, two individuals from the Investment Banking division—one assigned to El Paso, the other to Kinder Morgan—were stationed on the seventh floor. They were not sitting next to each other, but they could easily see each other across the floor. Nothing stopped them from walking into each other's offices for a casual, telephone-free, email-free exchange of information. Sitting even closer together were employees assigned to opposing teams working out of the eleventh floor of their Houston office.

Yet another question to ask.

The morning of the conflicts damage-control meeting I made it into the office as early as I could. This would be the first time I would lead the question session at a meeting with Goldman. I was a bit nervous but ready to go.

Analisa arrived looking feverish. To her immense credit she was there, and despite being obviously under the weather, she had a smile on her face. I thanked her for coming in sick. "I wouldn't have missed this for the world," she said. Johnathon was sick too—so sick he literally could not speak. He emailed he would call in.

I was sitting at my desk about to go over my questions when Silva walked over. "Do you have a minute?" he asked.

"Sure" I replied and followed him into his office. He sat down and looked at me.

"I'm sorry, but I am afraid you will not be able to ask any questions during the meeting."

I was shocked. "Why?" I asked.

"Well," he began, "any questions could cause Goldman to waive its privilege with respect to the Kinder Morgan transaction." He was referring to Goldman's confidentiality privilege.

Confused, I protested. "I don't understand. What privilege? The trial is over. Every regulator will be present, including the SEC. Besides, our questions are not just about Kinder Morgan—they are about their conflicts-of-interest program."

Silva asked, "Have you run your questions by Johnathon?" I told him that I had. "Did Johnathon get a chance to see *all* of them?"

I was not obligated to run *any* of my questions by Johnathon—or anyone else beforehand. No one was. That was not part of the protocol. As part of my training Johnathon had reviewed my proposed questions back in November, and after a while he stopped, deeming it unnecessary to continue. He had simply asked me to work with Analisa in putting the questions together for the conflicts meeting.

Nonetheless, I had run the first batch of thirty or so questions we had put together by him the previous week as a precautionary measure. In fact, at the end of the meeting I had offered to meet with him again to discuss the next batch of questions. Johnathon had declined, again deeming it unnecessary.

"Johnathon did not see them all," I told Michael Silva, "I offered to discuss all of them with him, but he declined."

Michael Silva was blatantly attempting to obstruct my work. He knew it, and his guilty face reflected that. I pushed back and eventually got him to agree that I could ask the questions pertaining to the conflicts-of-interest policies and procedures. He forbade me to ask questions about the Kinder Morgan–El Paso transaction.

He then instructed me to put together an email and circulate my questions to the New York Fed team prior to the meeting, but I was to leave out the other regulators from my email. With Johnathon out sick and literally unable to speak, I could not escalate or bring him in to push back.

I had no choice but to agree. I had barely an hour to put the email together.

Fuming, I went back to my desk and began typing up the questions. Analisa walked over to my desk. I told her about my conversation with Silva and suggested that because she did not work for the New York Fed, she was free to ask the questions I was now unable to ask.

"We can't ask them," said Analisa.

"Why?" I asked.

She said if Silva said no, they had no choice but to comply.

"What?" I asked.

She silently looked back at me. I checked the time—it was running out. "I'll tell you later," she said. I finished my email and made my way with Silva and a few SSO team members and other regulators to the conference room.

Goldman's senior management team was in full force that day. Leading the proceedings was David Solomon—then cohead of the

Investment Banking division at Goldman and, as of April 20, 2018, Goldman's sole president and chief operating officer. Joining him were Jeffrey Date (Goldman's general counsel), Alan Cohen (then Goldman's global chief compliance officer and, as of 2018, with the SEC), and Rachel Epstein (head of the Business Selection and Conflicts group).

Solomon opened with a presentation, a sales pitch filled with misrepresentations: "We've long believed that the best way to maintain ... and the best way to perform for those clients is to be extremely transparent with them on issues that may have real or perceived impact on the advice that we give to them, and that transparency has always been essential. We believe that we are a leader and continue to lead our industry in terms of our transparency."

I wasn't there to listen to a sales marketing pitch; I was there to ask why Goldman had systemic problems managing their conflicts. From what I had gleaned, they seemed to have a leading position because of how they improperly use inside information to get ahead—at everyone else's expense.

"So with regards to the other 2011 approach by KMI [Kinder Morgan] to El Paso, El Paso asked that we act as their adviser on the matter. As you know, we accepted subject to adopting certain safeguards which Rachel will describe in more detail when we talk about our conflicts process. These safeguards were discussed with El Paso's management, the board, and outside counsel."

I had asked for the meeting minutes of the discussions Solomon was referring to. Rachel had told us months ago they had them. And before this meeting Goldman had already admitted that they did *not* have them.

He closed by acknowledging that in failing to disclose to El Paso Steve Daniels's direct and indirect investments in Kinder Morgan entities, "we missed something that was significant on our part." Steve Daniels had been Goldman's lead investment banker assigned to cover El Paso in the transaction.

I thought back to the El Paso seating charts and team assignments, wondering if this was also significant information Goldman had failed to disclose. I felt a pang of anger as I remembered Silva ordering me to not ask questions about the El Paso transaction.

Rachel presented next. She insisted Goldman had followed its conflicts policies and procedures—the ones in place during the El Paso transaction: "In our judgment as it relates to El Paso, and I think David [Solomon] alluded to this, we actually think that the conflicts policies and procedures were followed and that the decision to accept the mandate was properly vetted and elevated."

I had reviewed those conflicts policies and procedures she was alluding to—the ones written in doublespeak that seemed to have more to do with business selection than conflicts. I was looking forward to asking questions about them.

First, I watched as the SEC team grilled Goldman on the El Paso transaction.

About forty-six minutes in, the SEC stepped aside. It was our turn.

Analisa and I had agreed before the meeting that I would begin by asking questions about their general conflicts policy and then drill down to the conflicts documents for each of Goldman's divisions. After announcing to the room—mostly for the benefit of the SEC—that we had reviewed Goldman's conflicts policies and procedures, I began by asking Rachel what I thought was an easy question: "What is a policy?"

After two seconds of silence, Rachel answered, "I'm sorry?"

I asked her again: "What is a policy?"

"It is what we, what we use it for is a mechanism by which we communicate to our team our expectation about their behavior and how they bring things with potential conflicts," she replied.

"What is the difference between a policy and a procedure?" I asked.

"A procedure, frankly, I think of it in the context of how we ... what procedures do they need to do and how do they follow it for purposes of bringing things to our attention as well as in terms of the mechanism we use to make sure that people are doing it so we tell them what they need to bring to us, when they need to bring it to us, and how they need to bring it to us," she said.

One of the purposes of a firm-wide policy is to educate the entire workforce, no matter their job function. Definitions and explanations of basic concepts matter because they help employees know what to be on the lookout for.

Having looked at their documents and not found much in the way of basic explanations, I decided to ask Rachel, "Do you have in the policies a definition of a conflict of interest, what that is, and what that means?"

Rachel: "No."

There it was. No definition of conflicts of interest. If you don't even define what a conflict is, how do your employees—not just your business people, but your legal people, your audit people, and your compliance people—know what to look for?

Having confirmed this, I decided to move on to another component of a typical conflicts policy—a discussion of the types of conflicts the firm and their employees could face. For example, personal conflicts, conflicts between the employee and the firm, between the employee and a client of the firm, and conflicts between clients of the firm. Simple.

"Do you have any document—we didn't find any that we discussed—do you have any document that talks about specific types of conflicts of interest that there could be?" I asked.

She said, "Yeah, we have lots of trading rules—"

"But it's not discussed in the policy," I interjected.

"No," she admitted.

"Okay," I replied.

She then went on to defend the fact that they don't have a definition of conflicts in much the same way she did all those months ago. After some cross-talk, Jeffrey Date, the general counsel, stepped in to say that their definition of the term is like what you might find "in the dictionary"—implying I should just look it up.

One by one—Alan Cohen, Jeffrey Date, and Rachel—took turns displaying their inability to articulate a definition of conflicts that came anywhere close to something like one would find in a dictionary. I looked at each one in turn as they spoke. I was not smiling.

At this point the SEC, horrified at what they were hearing, stepped in and tried to get clarification. Panicked, Rachel, Jeffrey, Alan, and David Solomon started talking all over each other.

Eventually David Solomon took over. He did not even try to define conflicts. Instead, he tried to explain how their "policy" works: "So what the banker has to determine, which is in the policy, is that there is an activity ... so if there is an activity, they know they have to come discuss it."

Having heard enough, I decided to move on and ask about another element that big, complex banks supervised by the New York Fed typically discuss in their conflicts policy: conflicts management. The policy would explain to employees that some conflicts can be managed and some cannot. For example, a conflicted employee could be removed from a team. The firm putting the interest of one particular client ahead of another client is an example of a conflict that typically cannot be managed. Another example is when, during a securities issuance, a firm allocates the securities in its own best interest rather than those of the client whose securities the firm is issuing. Putting the interests of the firm ahead of those of its client is often not a manageable conflict.

"Moving on to the next thing that we were looking for and we were hoping to see in the policy discussion, and we didn't see it, and we were wondering if you had it elsewhere. Um, do you have examples of conflicts that may or may not be manageable?" I asked, looking from Rachel to David Solomon, then to Jeffrey, and finally Alan.

Four seconds of silence gripped the room. Rachel began, "Wh— what?" I looked at her. After two more seconds of silence, she continued, "You mean, do we, do we tell people here are the things we can—"

David Solomon interjected, looking at me with a troubled expression: "What does it mean, what does it mean for a conflict to be manageable? What does that mean for a conflict to be manageable?"

At this point I explained to them the difference between a policy and a procedure from an SR 08-8 standpoint. I told them that when we examined the documents, we were looking for certain topics to be reflected in their conflicts documents, and we didn't find them anywhere.

Rachel replied that Goldman felt it was better to analyze things on a case-by-case basis and "make sure that senior people are focused on them and that senior people in the firm are making decisions about whether or not, because these are not legal judgments, right? These are about commercial judgments. They're about reputational risk."

At this point the collage of laws, rules, and regulations applicable to conflicts flashed through my mind. These were definitely legal judgments. Competing for my mind's attention was the thought that she believed the same senior people in this room who could not define conflicts of interest should be the ones in charge of analyzing conflicts situations on a case-by-case basis.

David Solomon interrupted her to address me directly: "But to your question specifically, Carmen, we don't think about conflicts as either manageable or not manageable. You go back to Jeffrey's definition of what a conflict is, okay."

He then took a shot at defining conflicts: "A conflict is a perception, okay, of something that could affect the advice you're giving, the judgment, etcetera. Our, our job is with our clients is to discuss those things and to work collectively with them to decide whether or not those perceptions inhibit us from" advising them.

I looked straight at him as he spoke, thinking a conflict is *not* a perception. Again, I was not smiling.

Looking increasingly frustrated, David Solomon continued with his view on managing conflicts: "It's not a question of what you can manage and what you can't. It's a question of, with your clients collaboratively, what their judgment is, what their counsel's judgment is, what their board's judgment is with transparency, as to how they think it affects what we're doing, and a combination of our judgment around all those issues."

Remember, the whole reason we were having this meeting—the Kinder Morgan–El Paso transaction—was that Goldman's lack of transparency with respect to conflicts had landed them in hot water.

As if oblivious to that fact, David Solomon actually brought El Paso up as an example.

How can the client think anything if you don't tell them you have a conflict? If you hide your conflicts from them, how can they make a correct assessment?

One by one I continued to bring up elements typically discussed in a conflicts policy and then continued to receive similar responses from Goldman's senior management. First silence, followed by cross-talk, followed by an inability to point to a conflicts program document— and, in one instance, any other firm document—that addressed the policy element. The atmosphere in the room became increasingly tense. Goldman senior management stared at me, anger and hatred dancing in their eyes. I wasn't fazed. After all, I have been in worse situations than this. Much worse.

Analisa and I then moved on from the more general firm-wide conflicts documents to the divisional documents. We had asked for the documents in place prior to December 1, 2011. The ones that would have been in use during the El Paso transaction. The ones the BSC report mentioned Goldman would be reviewing and presumably upgrading. The ones Jerry had referred to as "extensive" a couple of months before.

"Considering that Goldman Sachs Bank USA became an official bank on November 28, 2008," Analisa asked, "when we actually requested the documentation and the policies surrounding conflicts of interest for the bank, the memo was dated December 5 of 2011. Can you confirm that prior to this, um, memo that the bank did not have an applicable conflicts-of-interest policy, procedures, and risk assessments" before then?

Panic and cross-talk ensued. No one from senior management wanted to touch that hot potato. In the end they were unable to produce documents for the bank dated earlier than December 5, 2011, because they did not exist.

"As a response to our document request we note that at the end of 2011 the Investment Management division, um, did not have policies, procedures, or risk assessments, um, in terms of conflicts of interest. Um, so we wanted to know: What is the expected roll-out date?" I asked.

Again I looked at Goldman senior management. Three seconds of silence enveloped the room. Panic was written all over their faces.

Eventually Erin spoke up, "I'm sorry—can you ask that question again?"

This was followed by more cross-talk from Goldman senior management.

Finally, Rachel said, "We'll come back" to you.

In other words, they didn't know. The MRAs and MRIAs were writing themselves.

I pressed on. I had enough questions to fill up the allotted time, and I wanted to get them all in.

About twenty-five minutes or so before we were scheduled to end the meeting, just as I was about to start asking questions about audit testing, Silva interrupted me: "Um, the rest of the questions, if we are down to this level of specificity, I wonder if, given the wide number of people here, the most efficient way to proceed might be just to submit them in writing and let them respond."

To which Erin replied, "If we're going to answer and [are] able to answer the questions, I'd rather do that, Mike."

"We want to be mindful of your time," Michael Silva replied.

"I know, I know, but I think that it's helpful," said Erin, signaling we should continue "to try and get through."

By the time Analisa and I were done, it was clear that Goldman did not have a firm-wide conflicts-of-interest policy or program and that senior management in the room did not meet the expectations the New York Fed laid out for them in SR 08-8. Before we left the room the SEC jumped in to indicate that they would be following up with their own document requests and a possible exam.

After the meeting Silva went alone into a back room in the direction the Goldman team had left. Analisa and I waited for him. A few minutes later he walked out, looking like he had been reprimanded. He informed me that someone was upset about my questions.

"Who? Why?" I asked. He refused to answer. He then requested that the questionnaire detailing the remaining questions we had agreed to send to Goldman be sent to him instead so he could forward it to the legal department for "approval."

After the meeting I caught up with Analisa and the regulators from other agencies. I was trying to understand why she had not proceeded to ask our other questions. I asked them just how independent their work was from the New York Fed. According to them, they were definitely encouraged to follow the New York Fed's lead. At least at Goldman there seemed to be consequences if they didn't. They pointed to how, earlier that year, the New York Fed had pressured the FDIC into firing one of its new FDIC examiners because Goldman had not liked the employee's line of questioning.

Looking back, that's when I knew. My fate had likely just been decided in that back room.

CHAPTER 23

We Made a Deal

I left the office that day furious and depressed, my tummy so swollen that I hardly dared to eat. I grabbed my bag and headed out to the airport to catch a flight. Yes, in the midst of all this craziness, I still had a life I had to live—and I made sure to live it. Hendrik and I were traveling to a friend's wedding that weekend. On the way to the airport I caught up with him on the phone, relaying how upset I was at Silva's behavior.

After my flight I got off the plane still unhappy and barged into the arrivals hall, head down, avoiding any incoming feet. I walked right past Hendrik, who had to run after me, calling my name. I looked up, happily surprised to see him. We had not planned for him to pick me up at the airport. I dropped my bag and moved in to hug him. But he stepped away, his hands behind his back.

"What's wrong?" I asked.

He smiled nervously and got down on one knee. In his left hand were a bunch of flowers. In his right, an engagement ring.

We spent the weekend celebrating our engagement and our friend's wedding—and not thinking about my job.

Upon my return I was sitting at my desk when the phone rang. "Congratulations on successfully completing your probationary period!" the woman from human resources happily announced.

"Thank you" I replied. I could not bring myself to say more than that. I had survived the New York Fed's probationary period. In six months management would evaluate my performance.

During our one-on-one meeting Erin O'Brien asked me, in a polite but annoyed tone, why we had not asked more questions during the conflicts meeting. She said Goldman had gone to great lengths to secure everyone's attendance—which had proven quite a challenge. I relayed Silva's concern that Goldman might waive its confidentiality privilege.

"What do you mean waiving our privilege? Every regulatory agency was there," she said, looking mystified, holding her pen in front of her mouth.

I looked back at her and agreed: "When Michael told me that, I thought perhaps the request was coming from Goldman."

"No," she answered, simultaneously looking away.

If the request did not come from Goldman, who had it come from? Was it Silva's decision to obstruct our regulatory work? Or was someone else at Goldman telling him what to do? I wondered at what point the bullying ended and the collusion began.

Meanwhile Silva's SSO team was working on producing the next draft of the annual ratings report, consolidating the proposed risk ratings into one draft. The final report was to be sent to Goldman the first week of June at the latest. Prior to that it would be presented to Sarah Dahlgren, New York Fed senior management, and the Operating Committee, whose membership was never made clear to us.

Silva informed us during his weekly meeting that he was thinking of "pulling out" the reputational risk bullet from the draft report. "It can't get any worse. I don't know what else to say. I have not received support for telling GS that they need to take into consideration their reputational risk. So the bullet will be removed because we don't have supervisory guidance around it." He claimed the Operating Committee was telling him to take the bullet out of the report. He asked his team what they thought. The SSO team members looked at each other. One by one they took turns voicing their support, flying paint with their boss in perfect formation.

Later that day Silva stopped by my desk to tell me that the legal department was still looking at my conflicts-of-interest questions. His words were polite; his body language was another matter. He gave me a hard look that lasted a little too long. I chose to ignore it and replied,

"Well, it hasn't been two weeks yet. I know how busy those lawyers are. Do you think they will be ready by Thursday?" I was thinking of my upcoming weekly meeting with Erin O'Brien.

"I don't know," he answered and walked away.

Not long thereafter Mila called me into her office. I walked in and sat across from her. She began by telling me she wanted to discuss the legal and compliance section of the proposed annual report. She wanted my buy-in to make some adjustments. In other words, she was asking for my permission to change my section in the report.

"Why?" I asked her.

She looked at me. Her eyes widened, her face expressed deep discomfort. She turned her head slightly to the right, looked down at the papers in front of her, and played with one of the corners. "We made a deal with Goldman last year that we would raise their rating," she said.

I had of course figured this out a long time ago. Still, hearing a recently promoted New York Fed business-line specialist who had spent months interfering with my work say it out loud made my stomach turn.

"I see. Based on what evidence?" I asked. She said she wasn't there when the deal was made, so she could not really say. I said that the evidence I had seen did not support raising the ratings. I also informed her that I would have to run her request by Johnathon, Terry, and Bob.

I walked out of Mila's office and eventually made my way to Analisa. I asked her if she knew about the deal. She responded she did not and suggested we talk to her boss. We walked into his office and asked him point-blank. Her boss looked down and answered yes. He then told us that Silva and Koh had made that deal with Goldman last year.

I went home that day completely bloated. Finally, I made an appointment with the doctor.

———————

DURING MY NEXT one-on-one meeting with Erin O'Brien she brought up El Paso and conflicts-of-interest matters again. I told her they should expect more questions in the coming days. She then asked what we thought of what we had reviewed so far. I told her that there seemed to be consensus building around the fact that Goldman's conflicts-of-interest program had a lot of problems.

"Such as?" she asked.

As an example, I pointed to the fact that Morgan Stanley and Barclays had managed to put together comprehensive and coherent policies and procedures that met legal requirements as well as SR 08-8 standards. I had reviewed both and also had knowledge of the programs put in place at the other banks I had previously worked in. The first step in holding employees accountable is a clear articulation of policies and procedures, but Goldman seemed to be struggling with that.

"So what?" she answered, adding, "We do things differently."

"You are now a bank. You should start properly papering your program just like your peers do," I replied. She stared at me, her face hard with repressed fury. I looked straight back at her. We stared at each other for what seemed like a minute.

She then changed the topic to address other matters on our agenda. After a few minutes she picked up the papers in front of her with both hands, knocking them slightly against the table as she attempted to straighten them, and said to me in parting, as she looked away, "I'm sure I'll be seeing you again soon."

Sometime after this meeting Michael Silva stopped by my desk. He informed me the conflicts and El Paso questions were still with the legal department. According to him, they were evaluating whether the proposed follow-up questions regarding the El Paso transaction had a clear basis in law or established regulatory standards. He said he expected to have feedback from them this week.

Once again his words were polite, but his face had a hard look and his body assumed a menacing stance. Nothing approaching physical contact—we were, after all, in an open-plan office—but it was unmistakably threatening. I felt the hairs on the back of my neck stand up. I understood perfectly what he was trying to convey. The questions were never going to be sent to Goldman. *You are going to have to do better than that to intimidate me,* I thought.

I looked straight at him and said, "I don't really need the answers to the El Paso questions to move forward with issuing MRIAs and MRAs on the other parts of the conflicts-of-interest program—the policies, procedures, the IT systems, and risk assessments." The evidence from the disclosed documents was plentiful and spoke for itself. He looked back at me silently, his bright blue eyes filled with uncertainty. I then added that I had updated Johnathon on the situation and he agreed that the evidence we already had on hand was sufficient to begin papering the MRIAs and MRAs.

In fact, he had instructed me to begin working on the paperwork.

I spent my flex Friday visiting the gastroenterologist. After evaluating me, he scheduled me for a full endoscopy under anesthesia. The first available date was the following Friday. I called Hendrik. He quickly cleared his calendar. I spent the weekend weighing how quickly I could get myself another job.

During the weekly SSO meeting Silva reported on the presentation of the annual report to Sarah Dahlgren. "The meeting with Sarah went well," he said, adding that she "always suspected Goldman is the best-run firm in the New York portfolio." I looked at him, then down, trying to hide my shock. Koh went on to report that "all of the ratings kind of remain the same." *Did he mean Goldman's or all of the other banks?* I wondered. Koh did not clarify.

The conversation then turned to the presentation of the annual report to New York Fed senior management. Silva indicated he "will present the high-level points and then open it up to the floor" for questions. After a brief discussion about the possible questions that might come up in this next presentation round, Koh concluded, "I don't mean to trivialize the vetting sessions. It is very adversarial."

The two Mikes led the presentation of the annual report to senior management. The group took in the issues I had raised in my report with no questions and zero pushback. After the meeting Silva's SSO team made it clear that they were surprised there had been no pushback on the conflicts findings.

Still, there was one more presentation of the report to go—to the Operating Committee. Anything could happen.

That next Friday I went into the endoscopy worried about how I would react to the anesthesia and what the doctor would find. I had been under full anesthesia once before, and my body had not handled the aftermath well. In the end, however, it went well, but the doctor's report was as bad as I feared: my stomach lining was entirely gone. Stress and anxiety were the culprits.

While I was recovering from the procedure Silva and the SSO team presented the report to the Operating Committee. I had been invited but was unable to attend the presentation because I was still recovering.

WHEN I DID RETURN to work, a slightly out-of-breath Evan approached me and Analisa. He informed me that during the presentation to the Operating Committee Mila had interrupted Silva's presentation, jumping in to say that Goldman did indeed have a conflicts-of-interest policy. Evan had participated in most of the conflicts meetings and said Mila's claim horrified him. He urged me to step in and fight back before the SSO team went ahead and further edited my content in the report.

Analisa and I looked at each other, shaking our heads. I slowly made my way back to my desk and, through spasms of pain, typed up an email and sent it to Silva, Koh, Mila, and Johnathon. In the email I confirmed that Goldman Sachs did not have a firm-wide conflicts-of-interest policy, that we were working on an MRIA as well as other MRAs related to this topic, and that I was happy to provide them with extensive documentation to support these conclusions.

A few hours later Johnathon sent me a brief email, copying only Silva. He claimed that the conflicts-of-interest due diligence was not complete and that all the stakeholders had yet to review and vet my initial findings. Then he went on to inform me that "it's premature to represent that legal and compliance is working on issuing an MRIA as well as other MRAs." Johnathon ended by saying, "Let's try not to front-run the supervisory process."

If a lot of that sounds like news to you—it's because it was. This was New York Fed doublespeak for "back off." I read his reply again, made a note of it, but did not answer. I just kept going to work and doing my job.

Two days later, at 11:32 P.M., Silva sent me a much longer and hysterical email. His angry and desperate message began by asking how I could claim that we were working on issuing MRIAs and MRAs when Johnathon said in his email that due diligence was not completed. He then proceeded to hector me about the process and labeled my work "troubling." He insisted that Goldman's BSC report could double as a firm-wide conflicts-of-interest policy. But that was wrong. The report did not include the elements of a conflicts-of-interest policy—the ones we had discussed with Goldman during our last conflicts meeting. For example, it did not even define what a conflict of interest was.

Based on this misrepresentation, he concluded that "the existence of the written Goldman Sachs conflicts-of-interest materials that I have discussed, which are easily available, combined with the absence of clearly established Federal Reserve standards in this area have caused me to raise serious questions in my mind as to your judgment in reaching and communicating conclusions without a sound basis in the supervisory process." After his signature he helpfully added a link to the BSC report.

Misrepresentations and lies—the cornerstone of Silva's gaslighting process. It was clear that he wanted me to *do* something, but what that was he would not put in writing. What was it? Was Silva asking me to drop the examination? Was he asking me to produce a fake report? Was he asking me to lie by saying he was right? Or all three?

One thing was certain: this was Silva's opening move—creating a paper trail for my HR file. It was also clear that I'd need to spend most of the coming week drafting detailed responses and figuring out the ideal time to send them, which, in theory, would be soon after Silva revealed his true intentions.

As soon as I was back in the office I stopped by Analisa's desk. I showed her the emails and asked her what she thought was going on with Silva. She looked at me for a few seconds in silence, as if considering her answer.

"I think they want you to stop working on the conflicts exam," she said.

According to Analisa, her boss had spoken to Silva to ask him if the conflicts examination was going to end up anywhere. "He does not want me to spin my wheels," I remember her saying.

"Why don't they just tell me that's what they want?" I asked her.

"They would be obstructing the examination. That is not allowed. They are hoping you will figure it out on your own."

I then suggested we talk to her boss—not that I did not believe her, but I wanted to hear it from yet another person. Eventually we made our way to his office. Her boss promptly confirmed all this was true: Silva and his team wanted me to stop looking into conflicts-of-interest issues at Goldman.

I wondered whether I would be able to get one of the two Mikes to articulate this directly.

CHAPTER 24

I Didn't Start the Fire

Anxiety permeated that week's SSO team meeting. Silva led his team through an extensive hand-wringing session about the European crisis. This culminated in a detailed discussion about Spain in general and Santander in particular. I will never forget the look of sheer panic on Esther's face as she struggled to go over the Santander transaction, insisting that Goldman had done "extensive due diligence" and had "relied on the belief that Spanish banks were in okay shape" when they did the transaction.

She looked at me for support as she spoke and, in the end, asked for my input. I looked back at her and, in turn, at the rest of the group and deliberately chose to remain silent. After a few seconds risk specialist Sai jumped in to say that the deterioration of other Spanish regional banks would affect Santander but that it would not disappear.

After the group calmed down, Silva made a seemingly casual reference to the Federal Reserve Supervision and Regulation (SR) letters. Stealing a glance at me as he spoke, he announced to the group that he had "never read, referred to, or even seen an SR letter." I had no idea why he said that, but had I been him, I would have been embarrassed to admit I had never read the instructions the Federal Reserve Board puts out outlining what bank examiners will look for when supervising banks.

I put my head down and wrote his statement in my meeting minutes. He then debriefed the team on the annual report's vetting session. He indicated a couple of corrections had been made to the report. Which corrections he did not say.

He then told the team that he had debriefed Goldman. "Although it's not in the report, I did point out that the Federal Reserve would prefer that they did not do El Paso and they did not do Santander." I stole a glance around the room. Most people were nodding in approval.

Mila waded in, asking, "What about the mismatch in the deck content versus the letter content?" By which she meant that the supporting evidence for the supervisory letter—the input and ratings I had provided in the slide deck and other documents—did not match what Silva's team was going to tell Goldman in the annual report letter.

I looked at her and quickly thought back to our meeting, when she had asked for my buy-in to change the documentation. She had to keep the deal Silva made with Goldman, it seemed. They just wouldn't quit.

Probably sensing the landmine, Koh decided to ignore her question. He went into one of his monologues, which, after much meandering, ended with him saying they were planning to deliver the annual report letter to Goldman on Thursday.

Ryan O'Hara asked, "Let's say the Operating Committee doesn't reach a consensus by Thursday—"

Silva interrupted him, categorically stating that he "didn't intend to respond [to] or interact with the Operating Committee anymore."

Toward the end of that day I was sitting with Analisa going over the entire record of meeting minutes and documents related to Goldman—from the beginning. She was helping me compare notes and collect data points for my email responses to Johnathon and Silva. And then Michael Koh came up to us and asked me to come with him— Silva wanted to see me.

Before he had finished speaking I knew what this was going to be about.

I managed to make a quick stop at my desk to turn on the recorder. After months of recording almost every important meeting, it had become second nature. Koh and I then stood outside Michael Silva's office, waiting for him to wrap up a meeting with another risk specialist. I quickly glanced around the floor. The sun was beginning to set. I noticed that many people were actively packing up for the day and getting ready to go home.

I looked at Koh and tried to catch his eye. He refused to look at me. *This is going to be ugly,* I remember thinking. I prayed there would still be people working on the floor by the time I was done. I did not want to be alone with these two.

We walked in and sat down at the table next to Silva's desk. He sat in front of me, on my right. After loudly closing the door behind us, Koh took a seat in front of me to my left.

Leaning over in a menacing way, Silva began the meeting. "Carmen, you have to come off of the view that Goldman doesn't have any kind of conflicts-of-interest policy. The lawyers don't find it credible. We, we, can say they, they have to improve it, maybe they have to improve it a lot, but we're losing credibility saying they, they don't have one at all."

I waited.

"Um, the only way I'm gonna make progress in terms of improving their policy or following up on El Paso is if I bring along everyone who has to be brought along. Follow the process. And credibility is, is key to that."

Enough: I had to reply. I began by explaining the evidence I had gathered and how I came to my conclusions. My eyes alternated between Koh's and Silva's: their gazes were both chilling, in slightly different ways. Koh's eyes were empty and glazed, as if he forgot to bring his soul with him into the meeting.

Michael Silva looked like he did not have a soul at all. Occasionally his eyes would flash, as if something far more dark and sinister had been stirred within. The contrast between their eyes and the polite tone of their voices heightened the terror. What made this meeting so scary was not the menacing, intimidating body postures, though there were plenty of those.

What made the meeting truly terrifying was their eyes.

In the middle of my first detailed explanation of the evidence I had collected substantiating my views, Silva interrupted me to gaslight the proceedings. He claimed Johnathon had told him that Barclays's and Morgan Stanley's policies were not "recognized standards" and that Johnathon told him that Goldman did have some semblance of a policy.

I told him that I had discussed this topic at length with Johnathon. He had agreed with me that they did not have a policy. Clearly the two Mikes were expecting me to "get their point" and "go their way." When I stuck to the truth, their body language became even more menacing.

Silva then interrupted me to drop an outright lie, claiming that he did not have the Barclays policy. I quickly retorted, "I'm happy to provide it *again*. It's okay." I had personally given him a copy of both Barclays's and Morgan Stanley's policies when we had been going over the Goldman binders.

And still Silva kept pushing.

"Carmen I don't, I don't understand why the fixation. I'm gonna lose this entire case because of a fixation on whether they do or don't have a policy. Why can't we just say that Goldman, that they have a policy, but they have to dramatically improve it."

I would not give in. I was not going to lie on the record, nor was I going to protect the bank I was hired to regulate. Silva kept trying.

"You have to stop saying they don't have a policy. You have to stop disagreeing with the lawyers."

Which lawyers was I disagreeing with? What case was he referring to? Silva never said—and I didn't ask. It wasn't necessary.

"Can't we say they have a policy, it's right there on the public website, it says conflicts-of-interest policy, but then talk about all the ways in which it's deficient?"

Silva was referring to the BSC report, which is *not* a conflicts-of-interest policy. He was lying. And he was asking me to lie.

Then he tried a different tack. "What's the point of this point-in-time thing?" he asked menacingly, implying he did not understand the purpose of a point-in-time bank examination. Now we were getting to the desperate pleas, it seemed.

Though he remained mostly silent, Koh jumped in a couple of times. As if the obvious requests to lie from his boss were not clear, he tried to "clarify."

"My understanding is Goldman does have procedures, policies and procedures," Koh said. "I don't know what actually transpired under the time that they didn't have it so, you know, but I think, but I think sometimes when we're gonna issue an MRA it suddenly, you know, haha, it *clarifies*, you know, the misunderstandings, etcetera. And I think, the other point is, you know, I mean, everyone, not only you guys, but everyone always are enhancing their policies, right? That's the expectation, right? And I think that my understanding is that what existed and obviously as part of the BSC process they were revamping all policies and procedures, but they should've had something at that point in time, and they shared with you apparently, then you're saying that it did not, he did not violate the policy that was in force at that time, right?"

He was referring to Steve Daniels, whom Goldman senior management had defended during the conflicts damage-control meeting as not having violated any existing conflicts policies. I confirmed that he had not, because there was no policy in place to violate.

To that, Koh replied, "My understanding is that there is a policy. I think last year when the business lines and risk, legal and compliance risk did, they did a horizontal analysis across all the firms, and came up—"

More lies.

I interrupted him: I'd heard enough. Yet again I pushed back with a list of facts and technical arguments. Unlike previous meetings, in this one I did most of the talking.

There were a few telltale signs that this meeting was not just about what was being said. First, Silva and Koh relentlessly insisted that I had to say Goldman had a policy. That they did not, was—after all these months and all those meetings and all those documents—an established fact; indeed, it was a fact that no regulator inside the New York Fed who had participated in the process had previously disputed as being anything other than a fact. Neither had NYSDFS nor the FDIC regulators.

Even Goldman Sachs had admitted on multiple occasions that they did not have what we were asking for.

Second, the timing of this meeting: just as the annual reports were being finalized. Third, Silva and Koh's refusal to accept any solution I proposed to their perceived problems. For example, I offered to go back to my legal and compliance risk stripe and ask them to hold another meeting exclusively on the topic of conflicts-of-interest policy. In that meeting we would have every legal and compliance risk examiner at the other peer banks bring their respective bank's conflicts-of-interest policy. We would then go through each of them. But Silva's response was, "No. I am going to lose this entire case because of a fixation on whether or not they have a policy. Why can't you just say they have a policy but need to improve it? There is just too much out there. They have these procedures. That is a policy."

What that "case" was he was referring about, I never knew. I had no idea there was a case to begin with.

Because the meeting was clearly a trap to force me to lie, I had to come up with my own strategy. I decided then that my goal for that meeting was to get one of the two Mikes to state in plain English that they wanted me to drop the examination. This would be, of course, obstruction.

I knew it wouldn't be easy. Both of them were seasoned regulators. They were no Mila. Still, I pressed on, hoping for an opening, straining to see a crack. A few times I thought I was close. For instance, when Silva said,

> You also have to understand how the process works at the bank and the roles within the process. I lost the Santander transaction in large part because I insisted that it was fraudulent, which they insisted was patently absurd and as a result of that I didn't get taken seriously. I see the same thing happening now because I am insisting there is no policy at all which they say is patently absurd. There may be a terrible policy. It may have to be improved a lot, but I cannot say there is no policy, especially when they say their policy was above peer.

He never said who "they" were—it wasn't necessary. It clearly wasn't the New York Fed.

In the end that was as close as I got. To their credit, the two Mikes did not break down and articulate in plain English their desire for me to drop the examination. In that sense, during that meeting I failed.

But by not giving in to the pressure to lie, in a different way I succeeded.

Toward the end of the meeting I attempted to "absorb and defuse," Johnathon-style, agreeing to work with them while simultaneously offering to put together the draft of the supervision letter. This might have worked if I had managed to somehow add a poker face to my limited skill set. Alas, I didn't.

In the legal world it is a truth universally acknowledged that whoever controls the drafting of a document controls its content. And once that content is circulated, say, using email, it creates evidence in the New York Fed's computer systems. As Silva, himself a lawyer, quickly put two and two together. His eyes flashed ominously in recognition. After a second or so of silence, he dismissed me with, "All right. Thanks for coming in."

When I asked him what I should tell Johnathon about this meeting, Silva quickly replied, "Nothing. He and I are talking."

I spent nearly forty-three minutes in that meeting covered in goosebumps, my stomach churning. When I listen to the recording now, what most surprises me is that I managed to keep my cool through it all. All credit goes to my guardian angel.

I walked out of the meeting shaking and headed toward the bathroom. On my way there I gratefully noticed I was not alone on the floor. I took a detour and told Analisa about the meeting. Though she believed me, she was still astounded that Silva and Koh had asked me to lie in the annual report.

THAT NIGHT I TOOK the whole file home with me: the clock was ticking. The window to answer Johnathon and Silva's emails would quickly close. Now that I knew what they were up to, it was critical that I answer and use my emails to escalate the issue further up the chain.

I worked through the night and the following days reviewing everything, lining up my facts and dates. My failure to get the two Mikes to say in plain English that they wanted me to create a fake report made answering the emails that much harder. One by one, I sent out my responses—and forwarded them in turn to Riley and Judy, the other legal and compliance team leaders. I requested a meeting to discuss the issue the following Monday.

I also suggested this be added to the agenda items for our Monday meetings with the legal and compliance risk team. After all, they had unanimously voted in favor of the conflicts finding that Silva wanted to change. I never received a direct response from any of them.

Eventually I received an email that was sent to the entire legal and compliance team indicating that the Monday meetings were canceled for that week. This was not the first time meetings were canceled—Johnathon, Riley, and Judy were not getting along. That was followed by another email from Johnathon, moving up my weekly meeting with him from Thursday to Wednesday. This was not unusual either. But still ...

On Wednesday, May 23, I got up from my desk at Goldman to go to my weekly catch-up meeting with Johnathon at the New York Fed. On the way out I ran into Delilah, the secretary. She looked at me meaningfully and said to me, "It's always the good ones." I looked back at her, smiled, thanked her, and left.

I walked into the New York Fed offices at 4 P.M. and immediately ran into Johnathon. We greeted each other in the hallway and he casually directed me to one of the small conference rooms close to the floor exit. As we approached, I noticed through the door a figure sitting inside the conference room. I could not see his face—but I didn't need to.

In the blink of an eye I told Johnathon I needed to make a quick pit stop in the bathroom, which was conveniently located very close to the conference room. I went in and turned on the recorder.

I walked into the conference room and was greeted by Silva's joyful face. He quickly introduced me to the man sitting next to him—Michael Reynolds, from Human Resources. "Nice to meet you," I said and took a seat right in front of Silva. I placed the recorder on top of the table, right in front of me and in plain view of his face. I stole a quick glance at Johnathon, who took a seat to my left. He looked straight down at an invisible spot on the table.

Silva, eyes beaming with pleasure, promptly began: "Carmen, I am here to tell you you've been released from the bank."

"Okay," I said.

He made it clear this was what human resources call a "for cause" firing, which meant that he went on to list a series of reasons for firing me. The recording is a bit muddied in places (the device is not top notch, and the acoustics in the room were awful), but it's clear enough he does just that.

"We've lost confidence in your ability to allow your work to be adequately supervised. We've lost confidence in your ability to not jump to supervisory conclusions without being listened to, and we've lost confidence in your ability to not substitute your own judgment for the judgment of anybody else."

"Could you tell me what evidence you're basing this on?" I asked.

After two seconds of stunned silence, Silva responded, "This isn't about debating the decision, Carmen. The decision has been made."

He then informed me that Michael Reynolds from Human Resources was there to tell me what would happen next, adding in closing, eyes twinkling with pleasure, "And, um, we wish you well."

"Thank you," I said.

During the whole time we were there Johnathon looked down at the table. He never said a word.

At that point Silva and Johnathon got up and left the room. Reynolds then asked me if I had any questions. I asked him what I should say when people ask me what happened. He tried to deflect the question. I pressed him for an answer. He looked straight at me, with the same condescension that I had seen in James Muller's eyes all those months ago in the first conflicts-of-interest meeting, and he said to me, "You should be truthful."

I looked at him and smiled.

Another HR employee greeted me as I walked out of the conference room. Her job was to collect my electronic equipment, escort me around the floor so I could grab whatever personal items I had, and then escort me out of the premises. This all took about ten minutes. I had spent too little time there to have accumulated much. I asked her about my things at Goldman. She indicated the secretary would pack them up in a box and send them to my apartment.

She escorted me all the way to the entrance of the building. On the way down to the lobby she insisted I take the black car the New York Fed had arranged for me. I politely declined, pointing out that the walk home was only about five minutes.

I exited the building and immediately ran into Reynolds and a member of the Fed's senior management team. They were standing immediately outside the exit barricade chatting. He gestured in my direction. Both men looked at me, threw back their heads, and smiled.

I looked straight back at them and took the phone out of my purse, making sure the USB device with forty-two hours of recordings dangled in plain view of their faces.

I smiled back at them and walked home.

CHAPTER 25

Let This Cup Pass from Me

I walked into my apartment, dropped my things on the table, grabbed a glass of water and a doctor-approved baby food packet, and sat alone on my couch to think things through.

I began much like a lawyer would—making a dispassionate assessment of the situation.

A lawyer goes to work for the New York Fed. She is assigned to supervise a bank, verifying whether said bank is complying with the law. In the process the lawyer discovers that numerous laws, rules, and regulations are being violated and disregarded. And not just by the bank the lawyer supervises—but also by some of her fellow New York Fed regulators.

The laws, rules, and regulations being violated have a purpose: to guarantee the proper functioning of the US banks *and* the US monetary system. Taxpayers pay a lot of money to supervisors to make sure they work in the taxpayers' best interest to protect the financial system and ensure banks are complying with said laws.

Instead of working to ensure these laws, rules, and regulations were being equally and equitably enforced against the banks they supervised, those New York Fed regulators, it seemed, were busy breaking the law and helping a supervised bank break the law, rigging the system and playing favorites.

Their actions are a direct threat to the integrity and stability of the US financial system—or, in Fed-speak, a threat to their "safety and soundness."

Something needed to be done—for the sake of the country and for the sake of the worldwide financial system, of which the United States is a critical component. The US legal system is set up in such a way that only a person directly harmed can take advantage of that system—no one else can do it. The US legal system does not have a separate constitutional court like some civil law jurisdictions do, where indirect victims can bring public interest cases.

I had been fired for refusing to go along with their behavior. I had been harmed. I could try to do something about it.

Next, I took stock of my "assets."

First up: I had evidence.

That evidence could be used in a legal proceeding to try to convince a judge to put aside the US common law convention that he who controls the process usually wins and instead focus on the underlying facts and evidence to get at the truth. This would signal that the US legal system could be trusted to step in with transparency and enforcement, ensuring that billions of people around the world who directly and indirectly use the US banking system could continue to safely rely upon it.

Second: I had my brain, which, although small, had a pretty good track record of punching above its weight due to its willingness to work hard.

I then turned to my "liabilities."

First and second: I was a woman with limited financial resources. As a seasoned American-trained lawyer, I was well aware that the US court system is a forum for men of means to settle their differences instead of turning to guns. The general population turns to the courts in the hopes it's something more than that. And sometimes it is—just enough times to keep hope alive. But I knew better and was under no such illusions. This was unlikely to be one of those times. Having said that, this was a fight against the Federal Reserve. No billionaire in the world had enough money to take them on.

Third was my longstanding aversion to real-life drama. To move forward I would need to be able and willing to withstand the strain that the highly personalized and adversarial US legal process would cause.

Beneath the surface there was a lot at stake, but on the surface the lawsuit would look like a simple, personal grievance—something akin to: "I was wrongfully fired for refusing to lie on the record." Then again, a lifetime of not caring what other people thought was a huge plus.

I did not know what to do.

A few hours later I looked up from the sofa and into Hendrik's eyes as he paced in our small living room. There were no smiles. He was *livid*.

"We are suing! These people are more evil than I thought. They need to be stopped!" Words to that effect kept pouring out of his mouth. "We need to meet with Samuel, Xander, and Yates!" His eyes were full of rage.

I immediately realized that he and I had switched positions. He had warned me against taking the job at the New York Fed. He believed it was broken beyond repair. I had ignored his warning and taken the job anyway, believing that, although the system wasn't perfect, trying to fix it was worth a try.

He thought that if we sued, we were going to win. He believed that, in cases such as this, justice in general and the legal system in particular were there to make things right and fair. But I knew the US legal system would do no such thing because its place and purpose in US society was different from what he imagined.

Although we were both lawyers, we did not come from the same legal world. The world of law is divided into two camps: civil law and common law. Common law is law made by judges. A case is brought to court, and the judge's decision becomes the law and remains the law until another judge, usually in a more powerful position, decides something different. Great Britain and some of its former colonies, including the United States, base their legal systems on common law. About one-third of the world's population currently lives under this legal system.

I had both studied and practiced law in the United States—a common law jurisdiction. About half my lawyer friends practiced common law—most in the United States. All of that experience had given me a pretty clear picture of how things worked in US courts. In practical terms, in the United States the underlying assumption that governs how the legal system operates is that whoever controls the process wins. Two things are key to controlling the process: money and access to the judge assigned to the case. Facts and evidence are of tertiary consideration.

Hendrik studied law in the Netherlands—a civil law country. Civil law is written in a code of law. When a case is brought to court, judges don't make the law—they apply the law to the facts. A judge's decision does not change the code of law. Most of the world's countries and two-thirds of the world's population live under this legal system.

Like Hendrik—and unlike most US lawyers—I too had studied and practiced law in a civil law jurisdiction. The other half of my lawyer friends practiced civil law. Quite a few were litigators. Hendrik's father was a judge. All that experience and all those friends had given me a pretty clear picture of how things worked in civil law courts. In practical terms, in civil law courts the underlying assumption that governs how the legal system operates is that whoever can prove the facts wins, and whoever cannot prove the facts usually loses. To prove the facts, you need one thing: evidence.

Now, I would be the first to tell you the legal world is nuanced and complex. For the purposes of our story, we will not go into those nuances and complexities because we don't need to.

From Hendrik's perspective, as he stood in our living room and looked at me, the USB recorder, the stack of notebooks filled with hundreds of pages of my meticulous meeting minutes, and the countless other pages of documents piled up on the table, accumulated through countless hours of working from home—we had what it took to win.

I looked at him silently, pondering how to deliver certain unpleasant truths about how the US legal system worked.

I stayed up long after he had gone to sleep. Sitting in our living room looking out of the window, I mentally checked in on the five stages of grief and quickly concluded I was still in the first one: denial.

Not about being fired or how that had effectively derailed my career. Those were logistical problems that would, I was sure, resolve themselves eventually. Work again I would. Doing what, I did not know.

What I was in denial about was knowing what I was going to do with my situation. Although I told Hendrik I didn't know, it was inevitable.

I was going to sue the Fed.

———————

BUT FIRST I NEEDED to find a new job. For most people the first step after getting fired is filing for unemployment benefits, which in the United States in general and New York in particular can be both a time-sensitive and time-consuming process. One of the consequences of being fired for cause was that I was not entitled to unemployment benefits. As a result, I went straight into emailing and texting my friends and some lawyers.

At the top of the list were Samuel, Xander, Yates, Wilson, the Gen-X Network, and those friends who had warned me not to take the job. Next up were emails to friends who had encouraged me to take the job. I sat and looked through job postings as I waited for everyone to get back to me. As they did, I set up a bunch of appointments. Next I tended to my social calendar. Finally, I made arrangements to increase the amount of time my fiancé and I spent with our trainer at the gym.

I began the conversations with Samuel, Xander, and Yates by telling each of them they had been right. None of them were surprised. Each in their own style then asked me pretty much the same question: "What evidence did you gather?" In their eyes, whether or not to sue was not up for discussion. They understood the limits of the US legal system but believed there were some things that were too important to brush aside without a fight.

After listening to my detailed answer, each one asked pretty much the same follow-up: "Do you have the evidence with you?" I went on to explain what I had—and what had been left at the New York Fed and Goldman Sachs. To my surprise they all responded by peppering me with questions about exactly what I had left behind. Although their tone remained calm, I could detect a hint of concern in their voices. The reason for their concern was initially lost on me—I was too upset to think it through.

Finally, they all went on to say they would be going into research mode to pin down the rules that applied to my situation—the "applicable legal statutes"—and proceed to activate their networks. In the meantime I was to occupy myself with organizing the evidence I had into chronological order and writing down a detailed chronology of the events.

"Do you have the evidence with you?" Paul Lin asked over lunch. He was squarely on team "sue the Fed" and was grilling me about the evidence. *Here we go again,* I thought. I gave him the same answer as I had the others. I grabbed my burger and was about to take a bite—against my doctor's advice—when, looking at me with a serious face, he said, "You don't understand," adding words to the effect of: "if you don't have it with you, it won't be there" in the future. His face morphed into a sad look. "Trust me, I know," he said, reminding me that he worked in technology and that, prior to meeting me all those years ago, he had worked at Goldman Sachs. I put my burger down without taking that bite. I wasn't hungry anymore.

Also joining team "sue the Fed" were former colleagues from the banking sector. To this competitive, loyal, hardworking group, prone to obsess about professional sports in their free time, my story had the foul smell of a doping scandal.

The Gen-X Network and Wilson were apoplectic. Their reactions were not suitable for print. Once they calmed down, "Give me your résumé" was immediately followed by "You have to sue!" Those who were lawyers went into research mode as well.

The saddest conversations were with those who had encouraged me to take the job. It is way easier for me to swallow my pride—it has, after all, no calories—than it is to watch the scales fall from people's eyes. To my surprise their sadness quickly turned to anger, and anger led to the disturbingly familiar refrain of "You have to sue."

Hendrik's family found the whole thing mindboggling. His was a serious family with a strong moral compass and a profound awareness of the bigger picture: they immediately grasped the gravity of the situation. Living in Europe also meant their reactions factored in what this all meant not just for the US financial system but also for European banks, the Euro, their savings, their pensions, their jobs, and their ability to pay their bills. As I shared my story, they quietly embraced me as one of their own.

As the days turned into weeks, Samuel, Xander, Yates, Wilson, the lawyers from Gen-X Network, and former colleagues (the Allies, as I called them from now on) began reporting back. A clearer legal picture of both my options and the gravity of the situation emerged.

As I expected, exposing corruption at the New York Fed would be a difficult and time-consuming race against the clock. The rules dictated that only an employee directly harmed by the New York Fed's actions had the ability to sue them and, in doing so, blow the whistle. The rules forbade me from representing myself in court. Before filing a lawsuit, I needed to reach out to the New York Fed and make a good-faith effort to try to settle the matter out of court. Only if that failed could I proceed to file a lawsuit. All this had to be done, as per the law, within a limited amount of time. In theory, if I won the lawsuit, I would be entitled to get my job back plus back pay.

As for the gravity of the situation, the Allies backed up their enraged reactions with a bunch of legal statutes. In the process they provided the vocabulary to explain what this all meant. To their legal ears the stories about deleting evidence sounded an awful lot like destruction of books and records as well as evidence tampering. The stories about changing my findings sounded like fabrication of false evidence. The stories about how the SSO team advocated for Goldman sounded like collusion.

There are a bunch of laws on the books that make all this behavior illegal. And all these shenanigans would remain hidden from the public unless I sued and exposed them.

As the picture became clearer I moved from denial to anger. Every night, for many months that would eventually turn into years, I would sneak out of our bed and sit in our living room. Looking out the window—sometimes at Goldman, sometimes at the New York Fed, sometimes at the new World Trade Center being built under floodlights in the darkness of the night—I would think and pray and endure the battle royal raging inside me. To sue or not to sue, that was the question.

I was not new to prayer. I prayed regularly since I was a little girl. I learned how to from the nuns at my school. Whenever I have faced

difficult decisions in life, I have always debated decisions from all sides
and turned to prayer and books for guidance. It was no different this
time.

On one hand, I thought, *Let this cup pass from me. Are you kidding me?
I have been through enough. I'm not a litigator. This is not a fight someone like me can win. I hate conflict! My intestinal system can't handle this
stress!*

On the other hand, I thought, *This cup is not passing from you. Deal
with it.*

Eventually I would wipe away my tears and go back to bed. The passage of time has not dulled my memory of how agonizing this decision
was. I am wiping tears away as I type this.

Situations continued to arise that annoyed me and made it impossible for me to dismiss, ignore, or explain away what I had endured.
It felt like I was being needled from all sides. For instance, I opened
my credit card statement one day and discovered that the New York
Fed had not canceled my reservation for the conference in DC after
they fired me. The New York Fed had given the hotel my credit card
number instead of the New York Fed's account number, and now the
hotel was coming after me for the room charges. Or when I read in the
newspapers that regulators had approved the El Paso transaction—the
day after I was fired.

Then the Libor interest rate manipulation scandal erupted. Libor—short for London interbank offer rate—was the most widely
used short-term interest rate in the world. US consumers know it as
the benchmark interest rate most often used when determining their
credit card, car, and mortgage loan interest rates. It turns out that
some traders working inside a few banks were involved in manipulating the rate. Congress jumped in to investigate what US regulators
knew about the manipulation and since when did they know it.[1] This
led to the publication of internal New York Fed emails that seemed to
point to various New York Fed employees, some of whom appeared to
have been "in the know" since as early as 2007. As I read them,[2] I discovered Silva's name was in the mix. Then I read about Erin O'Brien's
promotion to partner at Goldman Sachs. And then about how Goldman disgorged its fee for El Paso to settle the matter. Members of the

SSO team kept trying to reach out to me. So did my old colleagues from risk. Not knowing friend from foe, I stayed away from both.

At night my mindset began moving from anger to bargaining and depression. *On one hand*, I thought, *How do I know that it has to be me? I am a results-oriented person. Plowing in the sea is a perfectly valid lifestyle choice that I respect and occasionally admire other people making. But it's just not me. If I am going to do this, I need a lawyer. Actually, I need several lawyers. I also need a job that pays the bills. Plus, I need a viable plan. I will make an honest effort at putting all this in place—but I am not going to flog a dead horse. The second this horse looks like it's dead, I am walking out!* On the other hand, I would end my prayers every night by begging this cup to pass from me.

I finally reached out to the Allies and asked for help in finding a lawyer willing and able to represent me. This was music to their ears. Those conversations resulted in a near-instant activation of their considerable network of lawyers, regulators, and banking and compliance professionals. A steady stream of appointments soon followed.

There were two types of lawyers who could represent me. A lawyer with a track record of representing plaintiffs against the New York Fed or a lawyer who wanted to take the case and was working for a law firm willing and able to let the lawyer take on the case.

Finding lawyers who wanted to take on the case turned out to be surprisingly easy. The vast majority turned out to be Gen-Xers, with a few Baby Boomers sprinkled in. I talked with them, and they reviewed the evidence and would come back, insisting that what I had was incredibly compelling. They would then present the case within their law firms for approval—and hit the brick wall of denial.

Most law firms were afraid of alienating Goldman Sachs and the New York Fed. They could make much more money representing *them* than they would ever make representing *me*, especially as the unique statute applicable to my case likely would have capped the monetary damages at back pay. This meant there would be no windfall of punitive damages. For a few it was not a matter of alienating them—it was simply a matter of not being able to afford to take on the case. They had either too much work that would pay way more than this case or not enough work and needed to focus on finding cases that had a high chance of success and would pay soon. The recession had made it harder for many law firms to take risks.

Still, every meeting yielded more contacts that were easy to follow-up on. The membership of the Allies grew steadily—ever more people felt compelled to help. Eventually we were able to find a lawyer—a partner at a small firm who had previously represented other former New York Fed employees with grievances against the bank.

In between meetings with lawyers I scrambled to clean up my résumé and look for a job. The firing had stamped a scarlet letter on me and effectively ended my career as a legal and compliance professional in banking and finance. It would be hard to convince a bank to hire me, given the New York Fed's power, extensive network, and damage-control mechanisms. Still, I promised to try, so I did, and eventually I found a consulting job making training videos at a big, complex bank supervised by the New York Fed. It was many levels below what I had previously done and paid less than half of my total compensation package at the New York Fed. But I was happy to get out of the house and have the daily reality check and routine of a job to anchor my daily schedule.

Besides, my meeting with the two Mikes had triggered PTSD. I had become afraid of going to meetings. There was only one way I knew of overcoming this, and that was to fill up my calendar with meetings. This job would do just that. Eventually I would get over the fear, but I must confess, it took well over a year.

Finally, a day job would help pay for the legal bills. My financial resources were too limited for me to sit at home just doing this.

Whistleblowing against the New York Fed is something you have to pay for the privilege to do, not something you get paid to do.

CHAPTER 26

Carmen's Way of Doing Things

Run down the time clock. Delay, delay, delay.

According to my lawyer, the New York Fed's strategy was to run down the clock so that I, the plaintiff, either agreed to settle for a very little amount of money or failed to file a lawsuit. This strategy was not unique to the New York Fed. A lot of business entities do this too. And he was right. When he called the New York Fed a couple of times to open the lines of communication, they ignored him. Then he sent them a letter and someone was finally assigned to pay attention and respond. The next steps would be a meeting where my lawyer would make an initial demand—as customary, a monetary ask.

This part was tricky: I was not suing for money. But because this was part of the process, we needed to come up with a number. There is actually a formula of sorts—a combination of judge-made case law plus actuarial and employment statistics. The lawyer explained that it was important for the number to be reasonable. For example, when the case went to court, the New York Fed lawyers would try to discredit the plaintiff as disgruntled and looking to make a quick buck, and they would try to argue the supervision function was a public service function so they had a duty to taxpayers to not waste money. To try to counter that perception I needed to build a positive, reasonable track record by presenting a reasonable number. That part was easy: I was not suing for money.

The law only requires that I make a good-faith attempt to settle before filing a lawsuit and that I do so in a way that, if questioned, can be proven in court. It does not require that I follow the New York Fed's way of doing things. After a number of meetings with the Allies and the lawyer, we agreed on what the group thought was a reasonable, cost-conscious, and sensible plan.

My lawyer would reach out to the New York Fed by phone and in writing and relay to them the various attempts I had already made at opening the lines of communication, where I asked for my job back and even offered to return documents in my possession, which they had ignored. The lawyer would then explain my position and that I had a lot of written evidence to support my allegations. The lawyer would not disclose the existence of the tapes. This was done to address concerns some of the Allies raised that the New York Fed would falsely accuse me of blackmail if we mentioned their existence. My first demand would be to again ask for my job back. If the New York Fed had accepted that offer, I would have gone back to work and the lawsuit would have never happened.

The lawyer made it clear to me—not that he had to—that there was zero chance they would give me my job back. I knew that. So did the Allies. Which is *exactly* why it was my first demand.

If the New York Fed rejected my request for my job back and pushed me for a monetary ask, only then would the lawyer make them a monetary offer. At that point it would be up to them to decide whether they wanted to settle this without a lawsuit. If they accepted the offer, in practical terms I would have to accept it, sign a confidentiality agreement, and never talk about what I had witnessed. If they refused my monetary ask, I could end settlement negotiations. Having made multiple documented efforts to try to settle the matter, I had the necessary proof to move forward with filing a lawsuit.

The settlement number, chosen in consultation with the lawyer and the Allies, was in the multi-million-dollar range. The biggest factors pushing the number up were that, at forty, I was relatively young and highly paid—retirement age is sixty-seven—and they had fired me in such a way as to make it really difficult for me to make up the difference between what they paid me and what I would make working after they fired me.

I could not lie in job interviews. Not only because as a lawyer I was subject to ethics rules but also because jobs like the ones I had were positions of trust subject to background checks. In the legal and compliance job market, seven and a half months at a job—especially at the New York Fed—was a huge red flag. Anyone interviewing me would inevitably ask what happened. This meant that I had to disclose what happened. This created an enormous barrier to getting a job offer.

What to some looks like an employee not willing to violate the law to others looks like an employee predisposed to insubordination. Why take a chance with a candidate who has a story when there were thousands of other jobless, experienced people without a story in the market looking for a job? Even if the hiring manager believed me, there was the matter of how to avoid upsetting the New York Fed and how to avoid employing me in a position where the appearance of a grudge could compromise a bank directly or indirectly regulated by the New York Fed or the Federal Reserve.

All this translated into a lifelong series of much more junior jobs than I previously had in supporting functions of lesser importance and lower pay.

My lawyer and most of the Allies agreed that it was in the New York Fed's best interest to settle the case and to do so quickly. The evidence was compelling. The lawyer was pretty confident, based on his experience settling other cases with them, that the New York Fed would settle and that the settlement number would be high. Most of the Allies were pretty sure they would *not* settle. Their reasons for this were varied, but for most it had to do with how the New York Fed perceived someone like me.

Off went the lawyer. All we could do was wait.

After some back and forth the New York Fed signaled they were not going to settle.

Having satisfied the legal standard, I was free to sue.

THE ENSUING MONTHS triggered the implementation of phase two. Using the court proceedings to whistleblow had numerous advantages and provided us the opportunity to give the system a chance to work.

It was also consistent with my status as a lawyer looking to remain in good standing and a member of the bar.

Planning a lawsuit is like planning a battle. You have to game out all possible scenarios, moves, and countermoves. This needs to be done for the legal moves as well as for the personal moves, calibrating how each decision will impact everyone around you, from family to friends. Doing all this while holding down a full-time consulting job was difficult and exhausting.

During the day I remained focused on what needed to be done, but at night I continued to agonize over the decision. Sitting in my living room late at night I moved back and forth between anger and depression. I kept trying to convince myself that there had been and would be others who would have a higher chance of success than I did. But having worked at the New York Fed, I knew the chances that someone had shown up before me or would join soon after me who had or would experience the same things and had or would have the presence of mind to systematically gather evidence were remote. I realized it was better if this were exposed sooner rather than later. These were problems best addressed in good economic times—before the next financial crisis.

Though they may have destroyed my professional future, I was not going to allow these people to destroy my personal life. As we planned the lawsuit, Hendrik and I took some time off to get married. I walked down the aisle in a light blue dress *knowing* the man I was about to marry *was* the man I wished to marry. Our experience with the New York Fed had revealed our true colors and strengthened the bond between us.

Back in New York we had to make a final decision on which of the lawyers who were willing and able to file the case would represent me in court. Then we needed to figure out how to use the complaint to try to convince the judge to look at the evidence. We had to determine which precautionary measures, if any, we needed to take to preserve the evidence in anticipation of what the New York Fed might do in retaliation. Lastly, we needed to decide how to work with the media at the same time the lawsuit was filed so the whistleblowing would not be in vain.

The lawyer who had helped us in the settlement process wanted to continue with the case. So did other lawyers who had continued to trickle through the door in response to the search the Allies and I had done earlier. In the end they each studied the case, made their own assessment in terms of whether it was worth it for them to take the chance, and offered pretty similar contingency terms. Each believed the case was excellent, so taking the risk was worth it. They all understood why filing the complaint was so important.

In the legal world contingency means that the lawyer takes on the cost and the risk of taking the case in exchange for a lot of the money that ends up being awarded. This of course assumes the lawyer wins the case and later on convinces the appeals court judge to keep the award high enough. This process usually takes years because the other side usually appeals, arguing the money the jury awarded was too much. For litigation lawyers it's like rolling the dice. They know they end up losing many of the cases that do not settle, but all they need to be set for life is one case in which the jury awards a lot of money and the appeals court agrees to keep the award high enough.

For a plaintiff like me, what this meant was that, if there was any money, most of it would go to the lawyers and the IRS. As a lawyer, even though I was not a litigator, I knew all this going in. Which is to say, from a self-interest standpoint, the economically rational decision at this point would have been not to sue. The only reason for me to move forward was to shine a light. And so I did.

In the end the decision came down to this: I chose the lawyer who had been a whistleblower herself. This being a common law jurisdiction, I knew that controlling the process was key. I also knew this was something I had no ability to do. All I could do was signal to the judge that this was a serious matter—not a petty personal grievance. Hiring a lawyer who herself had stood up in the past was the clearest signal I could think of.

We solved the riddle of how to use the complaint to try to convince the judge to look at the evidence by appending written evidence to the complaint. This is a move I remembered learning in law school and hearing it recommended for use in situations in which the plaintiff doesn't have a lot of money to go through the process but has a really good case based on the facts and evidence. It had the added benefit of putting all the submitted evidence on the public record and in front of the judge. This would permit the judge to review it—*if* the judge was willing to do so. In the US common law system the judge doesn't have to. A civil law court is of course very different—evidence is key.

As for precautionary measures, we held back the tapes. We knew the New York Fed would work with the media to ensure that baseless accusations would be printed in various news outlets, trying to paint me as a disgruntled employee, a conspiracy theorist, and a minority out to make a quick buck. The tapes would allow me to respond to this easily anticipated countermove by the New York Fed. And so much more.

Finally, I decided to work with the media to put the story out there at the same time the lawsuit was filed. This was a strategic decision for both credibility and my physical safety. My time at the New York Fed had given me a unique window into what made them tick. The media training session I had attended, the conversations with colleagues, and the research reported back by the Allies all added up to this: one of the very few things that scares them is the media.

In fact, the Fed worked hard to have a deep bench of reporters working in the most important media outlets. They would collaborate with these reporters on stories, sometimes on background, other times pretty openly, hoping to influence what news was reported and how. This is not unusual: many government agencies and big private companies do this too.

Luckily the vast majority of the reporters who work at the news outlets are not on the New York Fed's trusted list. Also lucky for me was the fact that most of those news outlets were willing to put themselves on the line for the sake of free speech and the public's interest. The trick was to figure out who could be trusted. The process was long and complicated, full of nerve-wracking meetings. I will never forget my conversations with the 60 *Minutes* producers. Their questions and increasingly shocked faces were my first window into how the average person who was not an expert in banking was likely to react.

In the end some outlets—like *60 Minutes*—fell by the wayside due to timing and logistical issues. Eventually we chose to work with two different outlets—the *New York Times* and ProPublica, who partnered with the *Washington Post*. Working with them was stressful and scary. I had never worked with reporters in a situation such as this one, and I was afraid I would fail. I put a lot of pressure on myself to get it right. I made myself do it because I had a hunch that the New York Fed and Goldman would try to silence me, and I wanted to do the best I could to make sure the issues I was raising would not be buried.

As we got closer to the day of filing, I continued to struggle emotionally with whether to do it at all.

Not long before the filing we invited some of the Allies over for a dinner at our tiny apartment. We ate, and I fretted and worried. Their presence and words of encouragement gave me courage. One of them gave me a poem to keep in my purse, advising me to read it whenever I felt my strength flagging.

The final stage of grief—resignation and acceptance—came a few days before filing the lawsuit. Hendrik and I were relaxing at home in a bubble bath. And then he became quiet. I looked at him. He was looking up at the ceiling, his eyes lost in thought. "You know," he began, "on the morning of your eighty-second birthday I do not want to hear you complaining about how you should have sued the Fed. If you start going on about 'Darling, I *really wish* I had sued the Fed because of this and that,' I am going to get up and walk out." He added, with a deadly serious face and a wag of his finger, "I don't want to hear it. She who burns her ass must sit on her blisters."

So I decided to file the lawsuit.

FINALLY THE DAY ARRIVED. I barely slept the night before and was really nervous that morning. I could barely concentrate at work. I was sitting at my computer early in the afternoon when I received word from my lawyer the lawsuit had been filed. Not long after, the story hit the airwaves. I will never forget sitting there, looking at Google as the stories hit. *It's done. No turning back now*, I remember thinking. I put my head down and did my best to hide my tears. After a few minutes I got up to look for my boss. It was time to tell him. To his credit, he handled it beautifully.

That night I went home, and my husband and I opened a bottle of champagne. He did not want to. Being from a civil law jurisdiction, he was convinced we would win—he suggested we celebrate then. But I knew the victory lay in the filing. I would have no control over the process. So did many of the common law lawyers I had spoken to over the past year. Many of them emailed me soon after the filing, congratulating me for getting the story out.

After the filing many overlapping events happened in quick succession.

The court assigned the case to a judge. The judge turned out to be Ronnie Abrams. We did a quick Google search and discovered that Barack Obama appointed her as an Article 3 judge—legal-speak for a lifetime position.

Once the lawsuit was assigned to the judge and less than twenty-four hours after it was filed, the New York Fed—represented by Tom Baxter and David Gross—filed a request in court asking Judge Abrams to remove most of the lawsuit from the public eye, put me under a gag order, and to rule that any trial would be conducted in secret.

In an attempt to intimidate me, they also falsely accused me of engaging in criminal behavior—the theft of the evidence my attorneys during the settlement process had told the New York Fed lawyers on multiple occasions I possessed, had offered to return, and had indicated I would use to prove they had wrongfully fired me.

Judge Abrams held an emergency telephone hearing, granted the gag order, and ordered an in-person emergency hearing to decide on the New York Fed's other requests.

What the gag order meant was that I could not talk to anyone about the case. Not even the press. In fact, neither I nor anyone in our working team could even tell the press I was under a gag order from Judge Abrams. Still, the media kept reaching out, trying to get me to sit down and talk with them.

At some point Hendrik told me the complaint had been temporarily removed from the docket—until one of the news outlets picked that up and posted it on their website. He had taken over Google news duties so I could focus on keeping my wits about me.

Our new apartment was in a building where employees from both the New York Fed and Goldman lived. The building's management had told us just that before we had moved in. Not long after the lawsuit was filed I stepped out of my apartment with Hendrik. I saw a few men who looked like ex-military types heading straight toward me. I knew both the New York Fed and Goldman have their own private security forces and that Silva used to be in the military. They looked uncertain, as if they were having a hard time believing it was me. I was not wearing makeup or heels, which meant I looked way younger and tinier than usual.

Inexplicably, my mind, instead of telling me to run, started trying to figure out why those men were even there in the first place and who had sent them. Then their faces morphed into looks of recognition and their eyes moved to take in Hendrik. They seemed taken aback that I had stepped out with someone who looked like a bodyguard. Hendrik and I had been working extra hard with our trainer in the run-up to filing the lawsuit, and we were both really fit. It was at this point that I noticed my husband-cum–security guard was on it.

He grabbed my hand and forced me to run. It was too late to turn back, so we ran across the street just as the light changed, somehow managing to avoid the oncoming traffic. After we were safely across the street I looked back and noticed the men were stuck on the other side, the relentless New York City traffic holding them back. Hendrik tugged at my hand, and we kept running toward the Goldman building. Eventually we took a few turns and used the construction around the World Trade Center and the mass of tourists to blend in.

Numerous odd incidents like this occurred over the ensuing days. The Allies and the lawyer had prepared us for this, but I had never really believed my actions would lead to me feeling physically unsafe. I tried very hard not to become overly paranoid. Still, as the unnerving incidents mounted, I began to take lots of cabs instead of the subway and a different route to work every day for a few weeks. I did my best to never be alone. I found myself looking over my shoulder constantly. Eventually I got used to it and just ignored it. I took inspiration from my husband's family history and decided to not even try to disguise myself. Like his grandfather, the Great One, I had nothing to be ashamed of.

I went on with my life. Let the chips fall where they may.

————————

AT WORK REACTIONS EVOLVED as time passed. Most people were amazed to discover I worked there. Starting the afternoon we filed the case, I noticed coworkers staring at me. By the following day their numbers grew. People I had never seen started casually walking by my desk.

The most surreal moment came when I made my way to the cafeteria to grab lunch. I walked in as I had countless times, grabbed my tray, and headed to the salad bar, focused on figuring out what to eat. The normal chatter literally stopped. Complete silence reigned. I looked up and around. Everyone was staring at me.

This continued for a while. At one point a group of coworkers had gathered at the closest printer to my desk and stared a little too long. That was a turning point. I had been scheduled to move on to a new project working out of a different floor before the lawsuit was filed, so I asked my boss if it was possible for me to move earlier. I explained that my presence was causing disruptions and that this was not good for the bank. I also wanted to come to work every day and have a normal life. He agreed.

Eventually people at work found ways to show their support without being disruptive. A smile here, a thumbs-up there. A kind word or an invitation to coffee or a happy hour. A sense of normalcy finally reigned in my day job.

Not so in my life outside work.

CHAPTER 27

Gagged by the Judge

Judge Ronnie Abrams had a conflict of interest with the New York Fed.

It turned out she had worked with one of the New York Fed's lawyers a few years earlier. Because she had this conflict of interest, she disclosed it to lawyers on both sides.

And then she decided not to recuse herself—she would still preside over my case.

Judges in both common law and civil law jurisdictions have ethics rules that apply to them. Under both systems, if a judge has a conflict, they need to disclose it. Once they do that, they can recuse themselves. In the United States there is a lot of case law that addresses a judge's power, which is considerable. There are a lot of US legal court cases decided by judges that, all added up, arguably make it pretty clear it is almost impossible to force a judge to recuse him or herself. A judge can disclose the judge has a conflict—and the judge can then decide that the conflict is irrelevant and can go on to preside over the case anyway.

Which is exactly what Judge Ronnie Abrams did in this case.

Hendrik could not understand how it was possible for Judge Abrams to decide on her own conflict. His father was a judge. He came from one of those civil law jurisdictions where if a judge has a conflict, there is immediately a separate court proceeding presided over by another judge who rules on the conflict. This happens even before the case is heard. Fairness matters in that system ... and so do facts, evidence, and getting to the truth. Then again, the place and purpose of courts in civil law jurisdictions is different from the United States.

During the in-person hearing Judge Abrams went on to make two decisions. First, she announced that she would allow the lawsuit to remain in the public eye and ruled that any trial would be public. With the press publishing the lawsuit, the cat was out of the bag anyway.

The second decision: she did not lift the gag order.

Because I was not able to attend the hearing due to work, I heard about all this from my lawyer. She then explained how she had tried to get clarity from Judge Abrams, as it seemed she was trying to simultaneously keep the gag order in place but claim she was lifting it. I had heard that logic before—at Goldman and the New York Fed.

After consulting with the Allies about this, we all reached the conclusion that Judge Abrams's ruling was structured like a trap. If I spoke about anything new—and neither "anything" nor "new" were clearly defined—I could be dragged back into court and she could take measures to punish me for doing so. In practical terms the gag order had not been lifted.

Eventually other former New York Fed employees got wind of the case and started reaching out. Among those who contacted us were former legal and compliance risk specialists and even a few risk specialists who had worked with me at Goldman under Silva's SSO team. Some came through my lawyer, others directly to me. Also reaching out were employees from other regulatory agencies on the Goldman regulator floor. Some offered to testify on my behalf in depositions when the time came—despite their fear of retaliation. I was happy—the additional evidence they would provide would strengthen my case. The media, unaware that Judge Abrams had not really lifted the gag order, kept trying to get me to sit down and talk with them.

The Allies kept a steady stream of reports and information coming in. Many were dismayed Judge Abrams had not recused herself and believed it was a sign of things to come. They suggested it was time to reach out to Congress, so we did. But we were not successful in getting any traction: we were told we would need to wait until after Janet Yellen was confirmed as the new head of the Federal Reserve.

In due course we received the New York Fed's motion requesting Judge Abrams to dismiss the case. We expected this procedural motion. I thought the case hinged on the result.

If Judge Abrams did not dismiss the case, the next big step in the process would be discovery. Discovery was something both the New York Fed and Goldman most definitely did not want. In the United States discovery—*if* you get there—is like an all-you-can-eat buffet. I would get to ask for and go through all of their emails, documents, telephone records—anything and everything I could get my hands on that could help me prove my case. This covered anyone and anything that could directly or indirectly be connected to it.

In my situation, because I was stationed at Goldman and had used their systems, this meant Goldman emails, documents, and telephone records as well. Because the New York Fed is a small place, that meant pretty much everyone would be fair game. If in the process of discovery I found new things—say, hypothetically, sexist or racist emails directed at me—I could amend the complaint to add even more allegations to my lawsuit. All the relevant evidence would make its way into the public record.

I wanted discovery very much indeed. I was certain it would only build upon the strong evidence I already had. The New York Fed, of course, did not want the case to get to that stage. It was in their best interest to not only block and prevent me from obtaining new evidence but also to deny me the opportunity to present the evidence I already had.

In due course we sent our response asking Judge Abrams to not dismiss the case.

Judge Abrams sent the parties a questionnaire. Among the many questions there were two that jumped out. The first one: Was there any evidence held by any of the parties that could bring about the settlement of the case? And the second one: Were there any additional parties that could be brought to the lawsuit? After much back and forth, my attorney responded by disclosing the existence of the recordings and indicating that Goldman could be brought in as an additional party to the lawsuit. The rationale for potentially adding Goldman to the lawsuit had to do with how much evidence would emerge tying Goldman to my firing. The answers became a matter of public record.

When the New York Fed found out about the recordings they sent a letter to my attorney threatening me with criminal sanctions. They appeared to be trying to use the threat of criminal prosecution to gain advantage in this lawsuit. Of course, this was ridiculous: when it comes to recordings, New York is a one-party consent state. I also had a legal duty to preserve evidence. The New York Fed lawyers seemed to have forgotten that they had a duty under the New York legal ethics rules not to threaten me with criminal action. The judge then decided to hold a hearing before issuing a decision on their motion to dismiss the case, and a date was set.

The night before the hearing my attorney called with an update. Judge Ronnie Abrams had called the parties to a private emergency telephone meeting to disclose yet *another* conflict: the judge's husband—a white-collar crime lawyer and partner at a big New York law firm—was one of Goldman's lawyers.

This is an astounding detail, one that should clearly have come up months earlier, arguably when we first filed the complaint. After all, the complaint made clear that I had been supervising Goldman Sachs. At the very least, Judge Abrams should have disclosed her Goldman conflict when we had first informed her months before in writing that Goldman could be brought in as a party to the lawsuit.

Again the judge chose *not* to recuse herself.

Instead she made an unorthodox request—if "someone" felt she should recuse herself, they should anonymously "slip" a motion "under her door."

I hung up the phone and looked at Hendrik. He could not wrap his head around how any of this was possible. Where he came from, a judge who failed to disclose a conflict would be fired. I had to explain that things did not work that way in the US legal system, that here it was really up to the judge to recuse herself. As we reached out to various Allies, their stunned, silent reactions said it all.

We moved to request additional information on the judge's conflict via a letter that makes it to the public docket—a necessary step in obtaining enough information to file a recusal motion—before Judge Abrams issued her ruling on the motion to dismiss. The *Wall Street Journal* got wind of the letter and published a story on her conflicts with Goldman.

Judge Abrams never sent us the additional information.

Instead, a few days after the *Wall Street Journal* article she granted the New York Fed's request and dismissed the case.

———————————

HENDRIK STOOD in our living room, a devastated look on his face, struggling to come to terms with this chain of events. I wrapped my arms around him—I knew I was not the one causing him pain, but I felt such empathy for his. He didn't cry. Instead, his face transformed into a look of quiet pride.

As the weekend progressed, I watched various members of my husband's family react to the latest updates in similar ways. His mother's initial uncomprehending "Really?" quickly morphed into satisfaction as she connected the dots. The rest of the family reacted in similar fashion, adding to it a scholarly take. I quietly listened as they considered how this case could be used in lessons to new judges. Hendrik's family seemed to agree that this was not the America they thought they knew. The US legal system had not only failed me; it had also failed the country. The lawyers in Hendrik's family thought my lawsuit would make a great case study on the differences between the two legal systems.

But Judge Abrams's dismissal had a big silver lining: the gag order was no longer in place.

It was time for my recordings to see the light of day.

So it was that from late April until September we worked furiously with ProPublica and *This American Life*, day and night, under incredible stress and great secrecy, so the story would not leak before we were ready. The journalists successfully sought out additional sources with personal knowledge of the events to corroborate my story, including individuals who had been present at various meetings.

Hendrik and his family were proud and supportive. We explained to them that until the program aired, I would continue to be unable to visit them. I would need to work long hours helping the reporters understand the thousands of pages and hours of recordings. The evidence was very technical. The long hours would come on top of my full-time job, which I could not afford to give up. "No problem" was their reaction. We often talked over video conference. The Allies and our friends were supportive as well. Hendrik attended by himself the family weddings and gatherings that I could not.

Before I recorded my interview the journalists said they would be reaching out to the New York Fed and Goldman for comment. We explained to them that based on how they had handled the case, the New York Fed would likely reach out to Judge Ronnie Abrams and request another gag order. They would probably also ask Judge Abrams to block the program from airing. We also explained that the gap of time between the New York Fed reaching out to Judge Abrams and the judge's response was likely to be short. It thus became imperative that I record my radio interview and the program be ready to air before the New York Fed and Goldman found out.

On the way to the recording studio the journalist told me that Esther Abramson had joined Goldman Sachs as an employee; Erin O'Brien had hired her. "Makes sense," I said, adding that she and Erin had worked together at the New York Fed for a long time.

The recording process was long and painful. There was a lot I was asked to comment on that I had delayed processing on a personal level, preferring to stay focused on moving the ball forward and solving the problems that came along, which is something I have a habit of doing. There were also a lot of questions I simply could not answer until the legal process was formally over. This complicated matters, for I had to balance thinking like a lawyer and censoring myself with being genuine.

Soon after I finished recording my part, the reporters told the New York Fed and Goldman they were releasing the tapes. I held my breath and waited for their reaction. Sure enough, as we expected, the New York Fed quickly sent a letter to Judge Abrams requesting a gag order. They also asked the journalists to turn over the recordings. My attorney received a copy of the letter and forwarded it. The clock was ticking.

The program aired before Judge Ronnie Abrams and the New York Fed could stop it.

To achieve this, the story ended up being released earlier than originally planned. My husband and I listened to it on our laptop as soon as
it came out. We sat on our bed and held hands throughout. We listened
to it again later that night. My lawyer and a few of the Allies came over
for dinner in a show of support. I offered to cook, determined to stay
grounded and continue with my life as normal.

Once the story aired, I was floored by the response. My phone would
not stop ringing, and I could not access my email for long stretches
of time—it simply crashed. My Twitter, Facebook, and LinkedIn accounts were flooded with requests and messages of support. The press
reached out for additional comments. Invitations and offers of all sorts,
from interviews to book offers, poured in.

The media reactions to the broadcast were swift and fierce, capped
by a much-repeated remark by Michael Lewis that this was "the Ray
Rice video for the financial sector."[1] Ray Rice, an NFL player, had been
arrested after an altercation with his fiancée in an Atlantic City elevator in February of 2014. Initially his lawyer tried to brush it off as
a minor incident and the NFL stepped up to defend Rice. The subsequent release by the media of two videotapes showing Rice knocking
his fiancée unconscious and dragging her out of the elevator eventually
led to his suspension and release from the team.[2]

Goldman quickly announced that they were going to review their
conflicts procedures. Multiple current and former New York Fed employees as well as employees of other regulatory agencies began reaching out to reporters with their own stories, like the London Whale[3] and
Fed Board Leaks.[4]

To everyone who reached out, offering to help, I asked the same
thing: please help push for a congressional hearing. I had not set out to
prove the US legal system could not be relied upon to step in and intervene when they should, but it seemed to me that my experience had
done just that. Online petitions were circulated, and someone called to
tell me that twenty thousand people had signed one of them.

One day in October, while I was on a break from work, I received
the news that the US Senate would hold a hearing on improving financial institution supervision at the Federal Reserve. Bill Dudley would

be testifying. My elation was tempered somewhat when, a few days later, I was informed that I would not be invited to testify at the hearing and that Congress would not subpoena my evidence. Still, I wasn't going to let that stop me from attending the hearing.

So I booked a night at that hotel I was supposed to have stayed at as a New York Fed employee a couple of years prior and made my way to Washington, DC.

———————

AT THE CONGRESSIONAL HEARING I watched closely as Dudley shifted uncomfortably when he heard the senators say that I had done "a service" by bringing this issue to light. His behavior throughout the hearing astonished me. When he outlined his view on supervision, he claimed, "We all need to know the rules and follow the same rulebook." I couldn't help but immediately hone in on the word *rulebook*. Why not *laws and regulations*? Why rulebook? What rulebook was he talking about?

When Dudley stated, "Supervision must be effective, which means being tough on banks that demonstrate illegal, unsafe, or unsound practices," I thought back to the times when Michael Silva's team asked me to delete evidence or, after hearing Goldman say something incriminating, had told me that I "did not hear that."

When he commented, "I think that the Federal Reserve employees at the Bank of New York that I have worked with for six years act in the public interest," I thought back to all the times Michael Silva's team kept all but saying how important it was to protect Goldman. And then I remembered Dudley had been a Goldman executive prior to joining the New York Fed. Was "public interest" doublespeak for "Goldman's interests"?

Dudley barely mentioned my case. When he did, he merely repeated the Fed's misrepresentation of the facts: "The issues raised in those tapes that were on the NPR story, Banco Santander, conflicts of interest, were fully vetted by us. The record shows that we fully vetted those issues. We did not—we did not repress them." I thought back to Silva and his team flying paint, systematically suppressing Goldman's issues in perfect formation.

Too bad I was not testifying—there was no way for me to counter what I thought were Bill Dudley's blatant lies and misrepresentations.

The senators appeared dismayed that Dudley did not stay after his testimony to hear the testimony of the assembled experts called to testify from academia and think tanks; his speedy departure came off as pompous and incredibly tone-deaf. After the hearing was over, as one of the senators shook my hand and thanked me for my service, I thought that if his departure had surprised them, then Congress had a *lot* to learn about the New York Fed—they did not know the half of it.

AFTER THE PROGRAM AIRED, people at my work started acting differently. I realized that my ability to effectively contribute to the project I was working on was diminished. I was the most junior person on the project. It was important for my work to be challenged and questioned, as I was not an expert. But people stopped doing that. This was not good—not for me and not for the bank.

I discussed this with Hendrik and my friends. They tried to make me realize that my life would never be the same. At first I did not want to accept this. As the days progressed and the events of deference multiplied, I came to realize that I needed to come to terms with this. I took a short sabbatical from work, hoping that after a few months, when things died down, I could return.

During that time we decided to file the appeal. Hendrik's belief in the US legal system was diminished, but we decided to give it one more chance to prove its worth. A further appeal to the Supreme Court was highly likely to be denied. Besides, we could not afford the expense.

In the next few months we worked on the appeal, and I met with a lot of media representatives. People approached me, interested in doing more stories. As I considered the options, I realized that the depth and complexity of both the problem and the remaining material required a lot of exhausting background work. The only format that seemed to offer sufficient space to illuminate the full scope and complexity of the problem would be a book. This was something I had never done before and wasn't even sure I wanted to do.

After much discussion with Hendrik and the Allies I made the very difficult decision to not return to my day job at the bank. I tricked myself into taking that step by telling myself it would only be for a little while, that I would somehow find my way back.

Deep in my heart, however, I knew that part of my life was gone forever.

I looked ahead at my life and knew that somehow I would need to find an anchor that would keep me afloat. Perhaps I could find other projects to keep me going as I mourned what I had lost and figured out what to do next. So I returned to the private practice of law. With a friend I started a candle-making company. I kept up my Dutch lessons and my workouts. Little by little, with the passage of time, I began feeling stronger.

Although I was no longer part of that world, I could not help keeping up with the news. The experience had eroded my trust in the government's ability to supervise the financial system and protect the savings of American taxpayers. And the news that filtered in was sad but not surprising.

A few months after the congressional hearing Bill Dudley, still president of the New York Fed, promoted Sarah Dahlgren to be his senior adviser and began a search for her replacement as head of supervision. Sarah remained Bill Dudley's adviser for a few months, then joined McKinsey Consulting as a partner in January of 2016. Her McKinsey biography highlighted her New York Fed experience managing "a staff of more than seven hundred people and a budget of over two hundred fifty million."[5] I wondered if it was enough to improve the nutrition of the millions of children who fell into poverty after the 2008 financial crisis.

Bill Dudley eventually appointed Kevin Stiroh, the economist who had led the failed CCar stress-test process while I was working there, as head of supervision. *FUMU*, I thought—a tradition at the New York Fed.

Janet Yellen, then president of the Federal Reserve, responded to the congressional hearings by leading the fight *against* change at the Fed. She refused to hand over important documents[6] to Congress in the case of the Fed Board Leaks[7] and continued to advocate in Congress for less oversight, less accountability, and less transparency over the Fed.[8]

The appeals court—as I expected—eventually upheld Judge Abrams's decision. In their short ruling the judges refused to sign their names.

A few days after the decision the *New York Times* announced that the NYSDFS had fined Goldman $50 million for conflicts-of-interest violations, a rounding error on a billion-dollar balance sheet.[9] Furthermore, ex-employees of Goldman and the New York Fed had agreed to plead guilty to criminal charges for their part in exchanging, over the period of three months, confidential information that enabled Goldman to profit, with Goldman eventually paying a fine of $36.3 million.[10] And yet my lawsuit had been dismissed.

A few days after the dismissal the office of Congressman Elijah Cummings contacted me. Now that the case had been dismissed, they wanted my help in crafting legislation to prevent what happened to me from happening to someone else. As I looked at the draft proposal of the legislation, I wondered whether it would ever be possible to legislate our way out of the type of systemic corruption and incompetence I had witnessed.

Not long after that, my lawyer called me. Someone from the Federal Reserve Board wanted to meet with me in Washington, DC. As she relayed the request and the proposal, I thought back to all those times Silva and the SSO team had discussed the board.

The proposal sounded very much like one of those cover-your-ass, check-the-box exercises, as if they wanted to make sure they could say they talked to me and took my input into consideration in case I ever opened my mouth to criticize them in the future. I realized there was, of course, a litmus test for such types of proposals. I call it the "Transparency Test."

I told my lawyer to go back to them and tell them I would meet with them on two conditions: I would come accompanied and I would record the meeting.

I never heard back from them again.

Epilogue

Over the past few years a steady drip of New York Fed employees has continued to reach out to me, each delivering the same message: the congressional hearings changed nothing. If anything, it seems from their stories that the New York Fed is using its powers and my case to support the continued firing and silencing of bank examiners who object to the Fed way of doing things. This is not surprising, given both the culture and the critical mass of problematic employees who, by their accounts, seem to continue to work there.

As of the time of this writing, Michael Silva, his colleagues at the New York Fed, and his acquaintances at Goldman Sachs have been rewarded. Indeed, they have flourished.

Bill Dudley spent the rest of his New York Fed tenure promoting a lot of the characters in this book. Michael Koh became a senior officer, as did Ryan O'Hara and Kevin Stiroh.[1] Johnathon Kim, Mila, Riley, and Sung were also promoted to officers.[2] Lily became a senior bank examiner. Connor O'Sullivan left his role as Bill Dudley's chief of staff and returned to the New York Fed legal department, where he is now a senior officer and deputy general counsel. David Gross also became a senior officer and is the director of the law enforcement unit at the New York Fed.

In November 2017, after being denied Janet Yellen's job as president of the Federal Reserve Board, Bill Dudley announced his retirement, effective June 17, 2018.[3] "I have had the honor to work at the Fed with colleagues who are amongst the most dedicated and talented public servants anywhere," said Dudley, adding he was "extremely proud" of the work done during his tenure, "from our efforts to help the nation navigate the financial crisis ... to our work on reforming the culture of the financial services industry. I have every confidence in the institution, its leadership and staff, and I know that well after I leave, the New York Fed, as a critical part of the Federal Reserve System, will continue to contribute strongly to the nation's well-being."[4] Hours after the announcement Dudley delivered a speech warning against rolling back regulatory reforms and referred to the present regulatory regime as "much better now."[5]

John C. Williams, the president of the San Francisco Fed—the one the New York Fed management did not deem capable of supervising Wells Fargo—became the president of the New York Fed as of June 18, 2018.[6] His dubious "experience" overseeing the supervision of Wells Fargo will come in handy as he moves from supervising that too-big-to-fail bank to the considerably larger New York Fed too-big-to-fail bank portfolio. He will be reporting to Jerome Powell, Janet Yellen's replacement as chairman of the Federal Reserve Board. Earlier in his career Powell was a managing director at Bankers Trust.

Tom Baxter retired from the New York Fed in 2017 and joined Sullivan & Cromwell's financial legal services practice group.[7] Sarah Dahlgren left McKinsey early in 2018 for a new job—head of regulatory affairs at Wells Fargo.[8]

Michael Francis Silva, having secured his two New York Fed pensions, put in his resignation and joined GE's financial unit just as my lawsuit was filed. GE honored the offer, and he began working there in December of 2013. Goldman went on to buy GE's financial unit, announcing the deal in August of 2015. According to my sources, Silva was in charge of navigating the New York Fed's approval of Goldman's purchase of the GE unit. As of this writing, he is partner and chair of the financial services regulatory practice at the British-American law firm DLA Piper. His official company biography describes him as "the only Federal Reserve lawyer to have ever led an embedded on-site team of examiners for a systemically important financial institution (SIFI) [Goldman] and also serve in the private sector as SIFI c-suite executive [at GE]."[9]

Donna Bianca left the New York Fed and joined GE. She now works at DLA Piper.

The New York Fed has worked hard with the press to cleanse both its image and that of some of the characters in this book. It's even engaged in some token enforcement actions against some of the too-big-to-fail banks.

As for Goldman's employees, Jeffrey Date is still the general counsel, and Rachel Epstein continues to oversee conflicts. James Muller and Bruce Acton II are still part of the legal group, and Alexander Lambert is still part of the compliance group. Jerry retired in 2016. Esther eventually left Goldman Sachs, which she had joined in March of 2014, and is now back at the Fed, this time as senior bank examiner in the Federal Reserve Bank of Atlanta. Erin O'Brien became partner at the firm and eventually the head of Goldman's regulatory practices group. She moved from Goldman to BlackRock Inc. in the spring of 2018. Alan Cohen is now a senior adviser and part of the executive staff of SEC Chairman Jay Clayton.[10] And David Solomon is scheduled to take over as CEO of Goldman Sachs October 1, 2018.[11]

Goldman's grip on senior US government positions continues to grow. As of this writing, former Goldman Sachs employees hold three of the twelve presidencies of the Federal Reserve Banks. Ex-Goldman employees also hold senior positions at the US Treasury Department and in the president's cabinet.

As for the risk specialists, they steadily trickled out of the New York Fed over the following years. Quite a few of my former colleagues are now working at big private banks. As are some of the other regulators in this book.

I have joined the millions of individuals who, over the course of time, have sacrificed their comfortable lives when called upon to do their civic duty. It was a privilege and an honor, and I would not trade it for all the gold in the New York Fed's vault.

Still, like all valuable things, it came at a price—one I pay every day.

Although I continue to work multiple jobs, my earnings have not recovered to the level they were at during my time at the New York Fed. I am fine with that. As an avid history buff, I know I am lucky to live in a time and place where doing your civic duty does not come with a price on your head.

I was profoundly lucky to have such an incredible, loving, and resourceful support group, led by my husband, Hendrik. And the experience allowed us to discover that our network of friends, family, and Allies was strong and true. Their continued presence, friendship, trust, and support is truly humbling.

Still, I remain worried about the continued impact of this systemic corruption and haunted by the stories and messages from former regulators, all asking me the same thing: Isn't there something more you can do to help?

As time passed and I reflected on my experience, I realized the biggest contribution I could make was to tell this story—our story.

You see, this story is actually not unique. There are plenty of other former regulators who share it. Some only parts—others much more. We've done what we could, but other than share the knowledge, there isn't much we can do without your help. Even if you're not a lawyer or a regulator, there is plenty you can do with this newfound knowledge to help get things moving in the right direction—indeed, particularly if you are *not* a regulator or a lawyer.

Don't forget: the US consumer is still the most powerful economic consumer in the world. It's time for you to exercise that power.

Be conscious of *where* you put your money. When you put your money in a bank, you are lending it to them. Banks and broker dealers need your money more than you need them.

Demand transparency and accountability from your banks, your brokers, your pension funds. Peek under the hood. Research their employees. Find out who finances the products you buy. Refuse to reward bad actors with your money. Demand that your pension funds refuse to do so as well.

When the American consumer becomes an informed actor, the markets can function as they are supposed to. Good banks and businesses will thrive. Bad banks and businesses will go bankrupt.

It starts with you. Hold yourself and others accountable. Don't reward bad behavior. Speak up. Get involved.

And do not fly paint.

ACKNOWLEDGMENTS

Writing a book that seeks to illuminate the depth and complexity of the problems facing the US Federal Reserve through the prism of events I lived and witnessed at the New York Fed was, I assure you, not what I dreamed of doing when I accepted their job offer all those years ago. I pushed myself to write this book because I believe in the importance of telling this story. I could not have done it without a lot of help.

I am deeply indebted to the many individuals from various backgrounds who read the various drafts. Some have requested their names be withheld. Others, especially Ira Bitner, Valence Meijer, Srinivas Gandhi, and Karla Sanchez, have not—and so I share them with you. Thanks to Roberto Busó, Camille Lizarribar, Fernando Rovira, the Cafecito Network, my many friends, and especially the Allies—too many to name and properly thank. You know who you are, and I will shower you with my personal thanks in due course. Thank you to the many reporters who helped bring this story to light—I am humbled by your courage. And to my husband, my knight in shining armor whose ever-present love and support made this book possible. His many jokes and cheerful disposition helped keep my spirits up through the many dark hours full of disheartening episodes I relived while writing this book.

Thanks to all my lawyers who, through the years, have generously contributed their time and expertise. Thanks to Jamie Diaferia of Infinite Global, my public relations agent, for his unfailing assistance in guiding me through the complexities of dealing with the press. Thanks to Kenneth M. Weinrib of Franklin, Weinrib, Rudell & Vassallo P.C. for his invaluable assistance in guiding me through the legal complexities of writing a book such as this one. Thanks to Ellen Levine and

Alexa Stark of Trident Media Group, my agents, who expertly guided me through the complex world of book publishing. Thanks to Nation Books and Hachette, who believed in this project and agreed to take it on, and especially Alessandra Bastagli, my editor, for her valuable contributions and words of wisdom. Thanks also to Katy O'Donnell and Christine E. Marra.

Finally, thanks to the Dominican nuns at Academia San José and to Harvard College, Columbia University, University of Paris, and Cornell Law School, all of whom provided me with the opportunity to develop intellectually and learn many invaluable lessons on the roles that courage, morals, critical thinking, and choice play in helping to advance society in general and individuals in particular. Insofar as I have failed to learn or embody their lessons, the fault lies with me.

AUTHOR'S NOTE

In writing this book I tried to rely as much as possible on the extensive record, which included hundreds of hours of conversations with various participants and former regulators. Part of this record was produced by me and part by others who were present or took part in the events described in the book. I have also relied on my recollections as well as those of participants in these events. Much of the dialogue in the book comes from these sources. The dialogue is of course not an exact transcript. It does, however, stick as closely as possible to the source material without sacrificing clarity and makes every attempt possible at accuracy. In a few instances the dialogue is only as good as the memories of those involved in the events. No human being is perfect, and I am certain that, despite my best efforts and constant verification of the available record, I have made inadvertent errors, for which I apologize. Finally, it is worth noting that the events described in the book are by no means exhaustive. Many anecdotes and stories have been left out in the interest of keeping the book focused. The events selected to tell this story were chosen both for their importance in advancing the story as well as for the reliability of the available record.

Prologue.
November 21, 2014

1. See "Improving Financial Institution Supervision: Examining and Addressing Regulatory Capture," US Senate, Subcommittee on Financial Institutions and Consumer Protection, Committee on Banking, Housing, and Urban Affairs, Washington, DC, November 21, 2014, www.gpo.gov/fdsys/pkg/CHRG-113shrg93411/pdf/CHRG-113shrg93411.pdf.

2. For photos from the hearing, see "DC: Senator Sherrod Brown Holds Hearing on 'Regulatory Capture' with New York Fed's Dudley," Getty Images, www.gettyimages.com/search/events/524682437?sort=best&exclude nudity=true&phrase=&family=editorial. Also see video at "Dudley Defends New York Fed in Heated Senate Hearing," *Bloomberg*, November 21, 2014, www.bloomberg.com/news/videos/2014-11-21/dudley-defends-new-york-fed-in-heated-senate-hearing-video.

Chapter 1.
Special Team. Different Training

1. Ben Rooney, "Goldman Blasted for Conflicts of Interest," *CNN Money*, April 14, 2011, http://money.cnn.com/2011/04/13/news/economy/goldman_sachs_senate_report/index.htm.

2. Grant McCool and Basil Katz, "Ex-Goldman Director Gupta Charged in Insider Case," Reuters, October 25, 2011, www.reuters.com/article/us-gupta-charges/ex-goldman-director-gupta-charged-in-insider-case-idUSTRE79 P06520111026.

CHAPTER 3.
WE WANT THEM TO FEEL PAIN, BUT NOT TOO MUCH

1. The NYSDFS is tasked with regulating and supervising banking, financial services, and insurance providers that are chartered or licensed to operate under the laws of the State of New York. These include state licensed banks, trust companies, and holding companies. Its mission is to guard against financial crises and to protect consumers and markets from fraud. It is headed by a superintendent appointed by the governor of the State of New York and confirmed by the New York legislature. Its bank examiners are responsible for the day-to-day supervision and examination of banking and financial services providers to ensure compliance with applicable New York laws, rules, and regulations.

2. The FDIC, an independent agency of the US federal government, insures deposits in banks up to $250,000 per depositor, per insured bank. The agency is managed by a board of directors appointed by the president of the United States and confirmed by the Senate. Its bank examiners directly examine and supervise banks for compliance with operational safety and soundness as well as for compliance with consumer protection laws and the Community Reinvestment Act. The FDIC is the backup supervisor for banks chartered (i.e., licensed) by the states that choose to join the Federal Reserve System and the primary regulator for banks chartered by states that do not join the Federal Reserve System. From the public's perspective, their "claim to fame" is to step in and protect depositors when a chartered bank fails.

3. Jason Philyaw, "Litton Loan Whistle-Blower Letter Given to NY Fed," *Housingwire*, May 26, 2011, www.housingwire.com/articles/litton-loan-whistle -blower-letter-given-ny-fed.

4. A voluntary contractual agreement entered into between two parties to a litigation that is presented to and approved by a judge.

5. Lauren Tara LaCapra, "Fed Orders Goldman to Review Foreclosures," Reuters, September 1, 2011, www.reuters.com/article/us-goldman-robosign ing/fed-orders-goldman-to-review-foreclosures-idUSTRE78010B20110901.

CHAPTER 4. THE SHADOW

1. "Anti-Austerity Movement in Spain," Wikipedia, https://en.wikipedia .org/wiki/Anti-austerity_movement_in_Spain.

2. "Occupy Movement," Wikipedia, https://en.wikipedia.org/wiki/Occupy _movement.

3. Post Staff Report, "Greek Premier Papandreou Narrowly Survives Confidence Vote," *New York Post*, November 4, 2011, http://nypost.com/2011/11/04/greek-premier-papandreou-narrowly-survives-confidence-vote.

4. Susanne Craig, "For Goldman, Trading Losses on 21 Days in Third Quarter," *New York Times*, November 9, 2011, http://dealbook.nytimes.com/2011/11/09/for-goldman-21-days-of-trading-losses-in-quarter.

5. Rodrigo Campos, "Stocks, Euro Plunge as Italy Debt Crisis Deepens," Reuters, November 8, 2011, www.reuters.com/article/uk-markets-global/stocks-euro-plunge-as-italy-debt-crisis-deepens-idUKTRE7A60Z820111109.

6. "Table of Contents," CFPB Monitor, www.cfpbmonitor.com/wp-content/uploads/sites/5/2011/12/Title-X.pdf, and 12 U.S. Code, sec. 5515, "Supervision of Very Large Banks, Savings Associations and Credit Unions," www.gpo.gov/fdsys/granule/USCODE-2011-title12/USCODE-2011-title12-chap53-subchapV-partB-sec5515.

Chapter 5. The Goldman Lawyers

1. "Cash Remains King. Yesterday Was a Forerunner of Things Worse," Harry Newton's in Search of the Perfect Investment, June 30, 2010, www.technologyinvestor.com/?p=2872.

2. Goldman Sachs, "Report of the Business Standards Committee," January 2011, www.goldmansachs.com/who-we-are/business-standards/committee-report/business-standards-committee-report-pdf.pdf.

3. William D. Cohan, "Solyndra Failure Hits Goldman's Reputation: William D. Cohan," *Bloomberg*, September 26, 2011, www.bloomberg.com/view/articles/2011-09-26/solyndra-meltdown-may-hit-goldman-s-reputation-william-d-cohan.

4. "El Paso Corp.," Wikipedia, https://en.wikipedia.org/wiki/El_Paso_Corp.

5. "Proposed KMI and El Paso Merger Would Create largest U.S. Natural Gas Pipeline Company," *Today in Energy*, November 29, 2011, www.eia.gov/todayinenergy/detail.php?id=4090.

6. Michael J. de la Merced, "The Advisers Behind Kinder Morgan's Deal for El Paso," *New York Times*, October 16, 2011, https://dealbook.nytimes.com/2011/10/16/the-advisers-behind-kinder-morgans-deal-for-el-paso.

7. Jonathan Stempel, "Goldman Sued by Capmark, Conflicts Alleged," Reuters, October 24, 2011, www.reuters.com/article/us-goldman-capmark/goldman-sued-by-capmark-conflicts-alleged-idUSTRE79N7OL20111024; Ole Petter Skonnord, "Aker Energy Buys Hess Ghana Business, Expects First Oil

in 2021," Reuters, February 19, 2018, www.reuters.com/article/us-hess-dives
titure-aker/aker-energy-buys-hess-ghana-business-expects-first-oil-in-2021-id
USKCN1G30OA.

8. Stempel, "Goldman Sued by Capmark, Conflicts Alleged."

9. Per my official meeting minutes, appended to the complaint filed in
federal court.

Chapter 6. You Should Not Have Come

1. Supervision and Regulation Letter SR 08-8, Federal Reserve Board, October 16, 2008, www.federalreserve.gov/boarddocs/srletters/2008/SR0808
.htm#Footnote10.

Chapter 8. Fly Paint

1. Nathaniel Popper, "How I Made It: Michael Silva: Michael Silva Has
Been Chief of Staff at the Federal Reserve Bank of New York for Four Years,"
LA Times, June 13, 2010, https://insurancenewsnet.com/oarticle/HOW-I
-MADE-IT-Michael-Silva-Michael-Silva-has-been-chief-of-staff-at-the-Feder
-a-197748.

2. He was making a reference to what is known in the financial services industry as the Volcker Rule. Paul Volcker, an economist and former Fed chair,
had proposed a rule that, after many changes that gutted it, was included in
the Dodd-Frank Act and intended to restrict banks from conducting certain
types of financial activities with their own funds.

Chapter 15. The Fed's Way of Doing Things

1. Andrew Clark, "Goldman Sachs Charged with $1bn Fraud over Toxic
Sup-Prime Securities," *Guardian*, April 16, 2010, www.theguardian.com
/business/2010/apr/16/goldman-sachs-fraud-charges.

2. Courtney Comstock, "The Latest Goldman Scandal: Did a Goldman
Sachs Guy Pay a Kickback So the Firm Could Underwrite Government Securities?" *Business Insider*, January 24, 2011, www.businessinsider.com/neil
-morrison-goldman-sachs.

3. "Federal Reserve Board Announces a Formal Enforcement Action Against
the Goldman Sachs Group, Inc. and Goldman Sachs Bank USA," Board of Gov-

ernors of the Federal Reserve System, Press Release, September 1, 2011, www
.federalreserve.gov/newsevents/pressreleases/enforcement20110901b.htm.

4. Marjorie E. Gross, "What You Need to Know About the New York Mortgage Servicing Agreement," 2012, https://marjoriegross.com/wp-content/up
loads/2013/07/What-you-need-to-know-about-the-Mortgage-Regulation.pdf.

Chapter 16. Santander

1. Simone Foxman, "Fitch Just Downgraded a Bunch of Spanish Banks,"
Business Insider, October 11, 2011, www.businessinsider.com/fitch-just-down
graded-a-bunch-of-spanish-banks-2011-10.

2. "Santander Reports Sale of Colombian Units for $1.225 bln," *Expat-
ica*, December 7, 2011, www.expatica.com/es/news/country-news/Santander
-reports-sale-of-Colombian-units-for-1225-bln_304746.html.

Chapter 18. Plowing in the Sea

1. Bloomberg, "Goldman Sachs Settles with Mississippi Pension Plan in
Class Action over MBS Offering," *Pensions & Investments*, July 18, 2012, www
.pionline.com/article/20120718/ONLINE/120719869/goldman-sachs-settles
-with-mississippi-pension-plan-in-class-action-over-mbs-offering; "Exhibit
1," *Public Employees' Retirement System of Mississippi vs. The Goldman Sachs
Group, Inc.*, Civil Action no. 09-CV-1110, http://securities.stanford.edu/filings
-documents/1042/GMSC09_01/2012731_r01s_09CV1110.pdf.

2. "Dutch Fund Giant ABP Sues Goldman Sachs over RMBS Statements,"
Pensions & Investments, January 27, 2012, www.pionline.com/article/20120127
/ONLINE/120129879/dutch-fund-giant-abp-sues-goldman-sachs-over-rmbs
-statements.

Chapter 19. The Dog and Pony Show

1. Associated Press, "Former Fed Official Corrigan to Join Goldman, Sachs
& Co.," *Los Angeles Times*, October 20, 1993, http://articles.latimes.com/1993
-10-20/business/fi-47671_1_jerry-corrigan.

2. Associated Press, "Corrigan to Resign Top Job at N.Y. Fed Reserve
Bank," *Los Angeles Times*, January 6, 1993, http://articles.latimes.com/1993-01
-06/business/fi-1013_1_fed-chairman-alan-greenspan.

3. "Executive Summary," Business Principles and Standards Committee Report, Goldman Sachs, www.goldmansachs.com/who-we-are/business -standards/committee-report/business-standards-committee-report.html.

4. Goldman Sachs, "Report of the Business Standards Committee," January 2011, www.goldmansachs.com/who-we-are/business-standards/commit tee-report/business-standards-committee-report-pdf.pdf, 2.

5. The Financial Industry Regulatory Authority (FINRA)—which is not part of the US government—is a not-for-profit self-regulatory organization authorized by Congress and focused on regulating broker-dealer financial activities. For more, see FINRA, www.finra.org.

6. Aaron Zitner, "Minehan Acts to Avoid Any Conflict of Interest," High Beam Research, March 22, 1997, www.highbeam.com/doc/1P2-8410772 .html.

7. Peter Truell, "A Fed Official's Romance Raises Issue of Conflict," *New York Times*, April 9, 1997, www.nytimes.com/1997/04/09/business/a-fed -official-s-romance-raises-issue-of-conflict.html.

8. Ibid.

9. Zitner, "Minehan Acts to Avoid Any Conflict of Interest."

10. Jo Becker and Gretchen Morgenson, "Geithner, Member and Overseer of Finance Club," *New York Times*, April 26, 2009, www.nytimes.com/2009 /04/27/business/27geithner.html.

11. Ibid.

CHAPTER 20. SARAH DAHLGREN

1. "Chancellor Strine's Opinion in re El Paso Corporation Shareholder Litigation," Scribd, www.scribd.com/document/83262746/Chancellor-Strine -s-opinion-in-re-El-Paso-Corporation-shareholder-litigation.

2. Ibid.

3. Andrew Ross Sorkin, "As an Adviser, Goldman Guaranteed Its Payday," DealBook, *New York Times*, March 5, 2012, https://dealbook.nytimes .com/2012/03/05/advising-deal-goldman-sachs-had-all-angles-for-a-payday.

4. "Chancellor Strine's Opinion in re El Paso Corporation Shareholder Litigation."

5. Ibid.

6. Greg Smith, "Why I Am Leaving Goldman Sachs," *New York Times*, March 14, 2012, www.nytimes.com/2012/03/14/opinion/why-i-am-leaving -goldman-sachs.html?_r=0.

7. Ibid.

8. Timothy L. O'Brien, "The Deep Slush at Bankers Trust," *New York Times*, May 30, 1999, www.nytimes.com/1999/05/30/business/the-deep-slush -at-bankers-trust.html.

CHAPTER 21. THE ANNUAL RATINGS REPORT

1. Nicholas Kristof, "Financiers and Sex Trafficking," *New York Times*, April 1, 2012, www.nytimes.com/2012/04/01/opinion/sunday/kristof-financ ers-and-sex-trafficking.html?mtrref=www.google.nl&gwh=0F8B4AA96 CEC8070F9B83C826C8DCF3B&gwt=pay&assetType=opinion; and Nicholas Kristof, "Not Quite a Teen, Yet Sold for Sex," *New York Times*, April 19, 2012, www.nytimes.com/2012/04/19/opinion/kristof-not-quite-a-teen-yet-sold-for -sex.html?mtrref=www.google.nl&gwh=6EE507EDA0808BE436851FF2EF 242B19&gwt=pay&assetType=opinion.

CHAPTER 25. LET THIS CUP PASS FROM ME

1. Sudeep Reddy, "Congress Joins Libor Probes," *Wall Street Journal*, July 10, 2012, www.wsj.com/articles/SB100014240527023040220045775187 2113 2675342.

2. Cora Currier, "Libor Scandal Timeline: What Did the Fed Know and When Did It Know It?" *ProPublica*, July 25, 2012, www.propublica.org/article/ libor-scandal-timeline-what-did-the-fed-know-and-when-did-it-know-it.

CHAPTER 27. GAGGED BY THE JUDGE

1. Dina Spector, "Michael Lewis: The 'Ray Rice Video' of Wall Street Has Arrived," *Business Insider*, September 26, 2014, www.businessinsider.com/ michael-lewis-the-ray-rice-video-of-wall-street-has-arrived-2014-9.

2. Louis Bien, "A Complete Timeline of the Ray Rice Assault Case," *SB-Nation*, November 28, 2014, www.sbnation.com/nfl/2014/5/23/5744964/ray -rice-arrest-assault-statement-apology-ravens.

3. Jake Bernstein, "Secret Tapes Hint at Turmoil in New York Fed Team Monitoring JPMorgan," *ProPublica*, November 17, 2014, www.propublica.org/article /secret-tapes-hint-at-turmoil-in-new-york-fed-team-monitoring-jpmorgan.

4. Jake Bernstein, "Leak at Federal Reserve Revealed Confidential Bond-Buying Details," *ProPublica*, December 1, 2014, www.propublica.org/article/leak-at-federal-reserve-revealed-confidential-bond-buying-details.

5. McKinsey & Company, "Our People," Sarah Dahlgren profile, https://web.archive.org/web/20171115004311/https://www.mckinsey.com/our-people/sarah-dahlgren.

6. Pedro Nicolaci da Costa, "Yellen: Fed Was Advised Against Fully Complying with Subpoena on Leak Probe," *Wall Street Journal*, June 5, 2015, www.wsj.com/articles/yellen-fed-advised-against-fully-complying-with-subpoena-on-leak-probe-1433523063.

7. Bernstein, "Leak at Federal Reserve Revealed Confidential Bond-Buying Details."

8. Binyamin Applebaum, "Janet Yellen Warns Congress Against Adding to Fed's Oversight," *New York Times*, July 16, 2015, www.nytimes.com/2015/07/16/business/yellen-federal-reserve-house-testimony-oversight.html.

9. Katy Burne, "New York Financial Regulator Fines Goldman Sachs $50 Million," *Wall Street Journal*, October 28, 2015, www.wsj.com/articles/new-york-financial-regulator-fines-goldman-50-million-1446055273.

10. Jeff Cox, "Fed Fines Goldman for Profiting Off Confidential Information," *CNBC*, August 3, 2016, www.cnbc.com/2016/08/03/fed-fines-goldman-sachs-for-profiting-off-confidential-information.html.

EPILOGUE

1. Federal Reserve Bank of New York, 2017 annual report, www.newyorkfed.org/medialibrary/media/aboutthefed/annual/annual17/Bank-Leadership-4-3.pdf.

2. Federal Reserve Bank of New York, 2015 annual report, www.newyorkfed.org/medialibrary/media/aboutthefed/annual/annual15/officers.pdf.

3. Christopher Condon, "Departure of Fed's Dudley Will Open the Door for a Hawk on FOMC," *Bloomberg*, May 7, 2018, www.bloomberg.com/news/articles/2018-05-07/departure-of-fed-s-dudley-will-open-the-door-for-a-hawk-on-fomc.

4. Federal Reserve Bank of New York, "New York Fed President Dudley to Retire," press release, November 6, 2017, www.newyorkfed.org/newsevents/news/aboutthefed/2017/oa171106.

5. Bill Dudley, "Lessons from the Financial Crisis," prepared remarks delivered at the Economic Club of New York, November 6, 2017, www.newyorkfed.org/newsevents/speeches/2017/dud171106.

6. Federal Reserve Bank of New York, "John C. Williams Named President and CEO of New York Fed," press release, April 3, 2018, www.newyork fed.org/newsevents/news/aboutthefed/2018/oa180403.

7. Sullivan & Cromwell, "Lawyers," Thomas C. Baxter Jr., www.sullcrom .com/lawyers/thomas-c-baxterjr.

8. Emily Glazer and Allison Prang, "Wells Fargo Names New Regulatory Executive," *Wall Street Journal*, January 30, 2018, www.wsj.com/articles/ wells-fargo-names-new-regulatory-executive-1517332921.

9. DLA Piper, "People," Michael Francis Silva, https://www.dlapiper.com /en/us/people/s/silva-michael-f.

10. Securities and Exchange Commission, "Chairman Clayton Names Executive Staff," press release, August 31, 2017, www.sec.gov/news/press -release/2017-155.

11. Andrew Ross Sorkin and Kate Kelly, "Goldman's President, David Solomon, to Become C.E.O. on Oct.1," Dealbook, *New York Times*, July 17, 2018, https://www.nytimes.com/2018/07/17/business/dealbook/goldman-sachs -ceo-david-solomon.html.

ABOUT THE AUTHOR

© D. Miranda

Carmen Segarra is an attorney in private practice and cofounder of Apron & Hare. Before serving as a regulator for the Federal Reserve Bank of New York, she worked at MBNA (now Bank of America), Citigroup, and Société Générale. A graduate of Harvard University, Columbia University, and Cornell Law School, she currently lives in New York.